At the Roots
of a Nation

At the Roots of a Nation

The Story of Colegio San Andrés,
a Christian School in Lima, Peru

John M. MacPherson

THE KNOX PRESS (EDINBURGH)

THE KNOX PRESS (EDINBURGH)
15 North Bank Street, Edinburgh EH1 2LS

© John M. MacPherson 1993
First published 1993
ISBN 0 904422 51 8

Typeset by Action Typesetting Limited, Gloucester
Printed by Cromwell Press, Melksham, Wilts.

Contents

Map on page viii by W. Iain Mackay

Illustrations appear between pages 118 and 119

To
la familia sanandresina
scattered throughout the world
this book is affectionately dedicated

Note on terms used

The school's first name was Escuela Anglo-Peruana (Anglo-Peruvian School). When the secondary department was added in 1919, it became known as Colegio Anglo-Peruano (Anglo-Peruvian College). In 1942 the name was changed to Colegio San Andrés (St Andrew's College). Throughout the book the chronologically appropriate title is used, but overlap does sometimes occur.

Protestant churches in Peru much prefer to call themselves *Evangelical*, which they consider gives a less negative impression of what they stand for. The more common English usage of *Evangelical* to describe those who hold to the central doctrines of historic Christianity is also applicable to almost all Peruvian Protestant churches. In this book the terms *Protestant* and *Evangelical* are used interchangeably when referring to the non-Roman Catholic Christian church in Peru.

The term *catholic* in its original sense of *universal* is applicable to all true Christian churches. It is historically and theologically incorrect to limit its use to one denomination centred on Rome. However, current usage, especially in Roman Catholic countries, understands *Catholic* to mean *Roman Catholic*, and it is employed in this way throughout this book.

In 1961 the Free Church of Scotland General Assembly recognised the need for a more efficient administration of its overseas missionary programme. A Foreign Missions *Board*, independent of other committees and able to choose its own times of meeting, took the place of the Foreign Missions *Committee*. It met under its own Chairman (not a Convener as formerly), and had its own part-time Secretary, instead of sharing a Clerk with other committees. In this book the appropriate terms are used in accordance with the period being discussed.

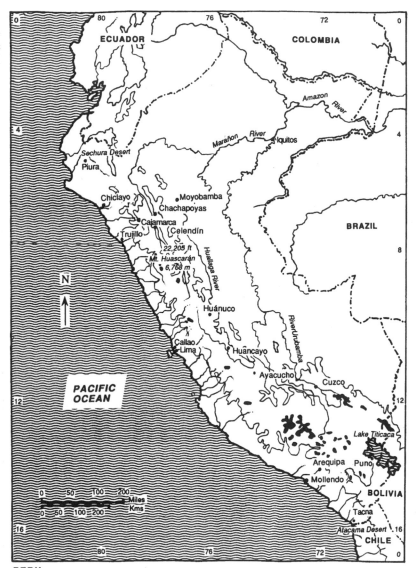

ECUADOR

COLOMBIA

Amazon River

Marañon River

Iquitos

Sechura Desert

Piura

Chiclayo

Moyobamba

Chachapoyas

Cajamarca

Celendín

Trujillo

BRAZIL

22,205 ft
Mt. Huascarán
6,768 m

Huallaga River

N

Huánuco

River Urubamba

Callao
Lima

Huancayo

Ayacucho

Cuzco

PACIFIC
OCEAN

Lake Titicaca

Arequipa   Puno

Mollendo

0   50   100   200
Miles
0   50   100   200
Kms

BOLIVIA

Tacna

Atacama Desert

CHILE

PERU

Preface

On a Sunday morning in 1929, Dr John A. Mackay, first Headmaster of Colegio San Andrés (formerly called Colegio Anglo-Peruano), the Christian school founded in Lima, Peru by the Free Church of Scotland, preached in Dudhope Street Free Church, Dundee. As so often in his long career, he called on the church of Jesus Christ to respond unreservedly to the marching orders of her great Head: "Go into all the world and preach the Gospel to every creature." In particular he pleaded for young men and women of the Free Church of Scotland to seize the spring-tide of missionary opportunity in the land of Peru, only recently embarked on the second century of its existence as an independent, sovereign state. *"Lay your lives at the roots of a nation*, and claim Peru for Jesus Christ", was his rallying-cry.

Listening to him that day was a young schoolboy, who until then had fully intended pursuing a business career, as his father had done before him. But fired by the challenge of Dr Mackay's words, he went home to inform his mother that in response to the preacher's plea he was going to be the Maths and Science teacher the school so greatly needed. Nearly twenty years were to elapse before that promise could be made good, and Sam Will joined the ranks of those who through the testimony of Colegio San Andrés laid their lives at the roots of the Peruvian nation, in the prayerful expectation that from those roots would grow a fruitful tree whose branches of righteousness would fill the land.

This book, commissioned by the Foreign Missions Board of the Free Church of Scotland, is the second of a series aimed at recording the overseas missionary activity of the Church. The first, *Near India's Heart*, by Dr Anne Urquhart, was published in 1990, also by Knox Press. The original request was to write the history of all Free Church missionary work in Peru, which covers a wide range of church planting, medical missions, education and community development, undertaken by many missionaries from Scotland, Peru and elsewhere. But to do justice to so much heroic pioneer work in a wide geographical area, the patient consolidation of it by so many different people, the emergence of the Evangelical Presbyterian Church of Peru, involvement in a variety of other ministries and a consideration of important matters of missionary policy and practice, either a very long book would have to be written or the subject would have to be treated much too superficially.

This book, therefore, has the more modest aim of recording the history of one small part of the wider missionary work of the Free Church of Scotland in Peru. Along with research carried out by various people within Peru, it may hopefully be of service in the eventual writing of the fuller history that is desired. Sincere thanks are due to the many former pupils and former teachers who shared with me their memories of Colegio San Andrés. I am also deeply indebted to my wife for her loving support and encouragement, and I thank her, my daughter, Cairine, and other friends who read the manuscript and made helpful suggestions. My thanks go too to my niece, Mairi MacPherson, for the final typing of the manuscript on to computer disc. And I cannot fail to mention a very special friend and colleague, Rev Pedro Arana, a former pupil and former teacher of Colegio San Andrés, whose devotion to Christ and practical commitment to the welfare of his old school have always been an encouragement and a call to an ever more faithful Christian service.

1

School and Nation: Roots Entwining

The surging yet orderly mass of twenty thousand people crowded into the ancient precincts of Lima's San Marcos University. Almost without exception they had been baptized into the Roman Catholic Church and retained a social connection with it, perhaps even participating in some of its festivals and religious ceremonies. But today, 23 May 1923, they were gathering in vociferous protest against the Church hierarchy which had unilaterally, though with Government connivance, decreed the consecration of Peru to a massive bronze image. The Archbishop's proclamation read:

> We announce a great event which will be the source of much joy to all our people. The Republic of Peru, Catholic by conviction, by tradition and by the constitution, will be officially consecrated to the Most Sacred Heart of Jesus next month, and the image of this most sacred heart will be enthroned in the principal plaza of the capital. Who knows but that for many people the Sacred Heart of Jesus is even the Unknown God ...Thus shall we say with Saint Paul, "That God whom you ignorantly worship, Him declare we unto you".

The campaign of opposition, political and religious, which culminated in the massive public rally was inspired and led by Víctor Raúl Haya de la Torre. A zealous campaigner for university reform and improved conditions for the working classes, Haya was also a part-time teacher in the six-year-old Colegio Anglo-Peruano. Introduced to the Bible and Protestant thinking by the School's Headmaster, Dr John A. Mackay, Haya became more and more convinced that the Roman Catholic Church as known in Peru was a retrograde institution, and an obstacle in the way of the country's true progress.

1

And so that evening his words flowed with impassioned eloquence. Agreeing to hold a general strike the day before the proposed consecration, the crowd made its way to the central Plaza de Armas. But as they passed through the narrow, crowded streets, shots rang out and mounted troops charged the unarmed demonstrators. Soon a student and a workman lay dead, and a dozen others wounded.

In spite of all the terror and confusion many thousands made their way to the central square, and there on the very steps of the Cathedral Haya continued to harangue the crowds. Over the next few days passions ran high, and only Haya's opposition to violence prevented unruly elements from burning and pillaging churches and private property. At the funeral service Haya and another teacher from the Colegio Anglo-Peruano were among the leading speakers, but since an order was out for his arrest Haya had to swim the Rimac river and take refuge in the home of friends.

That very night the Archbishop issued a decree stating that as the Church had a mission of peace and fraternity, the act of consecration would be suspended. Confident that a mighty blow had been struck for liberty and justice, the protestors called off the strike, and Lima gradually returned to normality. Although Haya de la Torre was a marked man, he eventually felt it safe to resume teaching in the Anglo-Peruano, though taking up residence in the boarding department of the School under the watchful eye of missionary teachers, Stanley Rycroft and Leslie Cutbill.

By the end of July things had quietened down sufficiently for Dr John A. Mackay to leave for Chile on a tour of evangelism sponsored by the Y.M.C.A.. But the appearance of calm was deceptive. On 1 October Haya failed to return home, and the next day the School staff learned that he had been arrested and summarily deported. Word also came through that an order had been signed for Dr Mackay's deportation, on the specious charge that in Chile − Peru's traditional enemy − he was engaged in political propaganda injurious to the best interests of Peru.

The situation of the Free Church of Scotland school was critical. One of its best Peruvian teachers had been deported; another, on the advice of the British Embassy, had to be dismissed; and the Headmaster was likely to be thrown out of the country if he dared set foot in it again. Mrs Jane Mackay, the Headmaster's wife, stepped into the breach on the teaching side, and Rycroft and Cutbill, only a year out from England, showed their resourcefulness and total loyalty to the School and its Christian mission. Rycroft went urgently in search of a young lady, Margaret Robb (who later became his wife), asked her to board a ship going south the very next day, and try to make contact with Mackay in a port along the route, he having been advised by cable of the situation. Miss Robb valiantly agreed, and on the way south sent a radiogram to Mackay on the ship she presumed he would have caught with the curt message, "Destroy hay goods". She reckoned he would understand the reference was to documents and photographs relating to Sr Haya.

They met in the port of Mollendo where Mackay destroyed some documents, and Miss Robb stitched others and some photographs into the lining of her jacket. When the boat docked in Callao, the port of Lima, the immigration authorities refused Mackay permission to land. Leslie Cutbill went in urgent search of the British Ambassador, finding him at a service in the Anglican Church. He immediately left, contacted the Government and persuaded them, with minutes to go, to let Mackay land. They kept his baggage for two weeks, but in spite of a thorough search could find no politically incriminatory material.

Back in tranquil Edinburgh the Foreign Missions Committee must have wondered what their staff in Lima were up to, when a letter arrived from the Foreign Office in Whitehall, informing them that Dr Mackay and certain members of their school staff were being charged by the Peruvian Government with being implicated in political controversies. A flurry of correspondence ensued between the Committee, the Foreign Office, the British Embassy in Lima and Dr John A. Mackay. Charges were repudiated, caution was advised, representations were made, vindication was complete. But the teacher from the Free Church School languished for eight more years in exile, before eventually returning to a distinguished, though tempestuous, political career in his native land.

3

* * *

The cablegram from Lima lay on the Committee table. It was July 1929, holiday time in Scotland, but no carnival spirit prevailed as the Foreign Missions Committee members who had managed to gather together contemplated the stark message before them:

> Government decree closure all schools not conforming completely Catholic doctrine. British Minister seen President. Sympathetic but says necessary conform law. Americans appealed Washington. We cannot conscientiously continue after this year. Renwick.

Did this spell the end of Gospel witness through the Colegio Anglo-Peruano? Could something somehow be done? And where did all this leave the Committee's hard-won victory of two months before, when in spite of strong opposition, the General Assembly had approved the Committee's request to invest £20,000 of Foreign Mission capital in a new school for Lima? A quarter of the money had already been spent buying a site, but could they let the remainder disappear into thin air?
Another cable arrived:

> Situation more hopeful. Favourable developments August but still uncertain. Meanwhile no interference experienced so far. Renwick.

Thank God for such a development, but things could still be critical. The international wires were humming as urgent cables were dispatched — to the Committee Convener, Dr Alexander Stewart, attending a Conference in Montreal; to Dr Alexander Renwick, the Headmaster in Lima assuring him of the Committee's full support; to former Headmaster, Dr John A. Mackay in Montevideo, Uruguay, soliciting his help.
From Mackay there came back a hearty message:

> Cabling American friends urging diplomatic pressure. Suggest Committee approach Foreign Office and Renwick British Minister. Courage God reigns.

And from across the Atlantic came Dr Stewart and his colleague Dr Donald Maclean, reporting on their visit to Boston

4

to confer with the internationally renowned Secretary of the Presbyterian Board of Foreign Missions, Dr Robert Speer, who assured them that the increasing spirit of toleration in public affairs would not support the Roman Catholic Church in extreme actions such as these.

Meanwhile, in Lima, how were the staff of the Anglo-Peruano and other Evangelical schools reacting? First and foremost, in earnest pleading that God would preserve his cause and allow his Word to be taught in all purity to every pupil. The decree, signed by the President, Augusto B. Leguía, threatened not only closure of recalcitrant schools but confiscation of their property, and was clearly intended to curry favour with the powerful Roman Catholic hierarchy, though ironically Leguía himself was anti-clerical and a high-ranking Mason.

Approaches were made to the British and American ambassadors and both proved cooperative. But the clearest evidence of the good hand of God on the school stemmed from the presence on the staff as History teacher of one of Peru's most distinguished historians, who was sadly to die relatively young, Dr Jorge Leguía. He was, no less, the nephew of the President, and he listened sympathetically as Dr Renwick and his Deputy Head, Dr Rycroft, explained how the Colegio Anglo-Peruano would close rather than yield up its freedom to proclaim the Word of God. "Oh," he said, "Don't you worry, I'll talk to my uncle tonight." True to his word, he tackled the President on the subject and came back to say that his uncle had only signed the decree under pressure from the Archbishop, but had no intention of putting it into effect. As a token of his good-will to his friends in the Anglo-Peruano, he sent along a full-length signed portrait of himself, which, hanging in the Director's Office, would naturally make any would-be accusers of the School think long and hard before taking action.

And so, relief all round, in Lima and in Edinburgh. God had answered the prayers of his people and preserved the testimony for his truth of the Anglo-Peruvian College. The home Committee felt able to authorise the signing of a binding contract for the construction of the eagerly awaited new school building, and work began immediately. By the time President Leguía was overthrown some months later in a revolution, captured in his flight by gunboats and left to die in a Lima jail, the crisis for Protestant schools was averted — till the next time. In the Colegio Anglo-Peruano down came Leguía's portrait, to be ignominiously stored out of sight in a cupboard. Decades later, when new political conflicts occupied men's minds and passions, it surfaced afresh, and gazes down today on all who pass the threshold of the library of Colegio San Andrés.

* * *

On 13 June 1979 the former pupils of Colegio San Andrés were meeting according to time-honoured custom on the School Anniversary to elect the new Committee of the "Old Boys' Association". But one old boy was conspicuous by his absence. Pedro Arana, a former President of the Association, was on his feet in the National Parliament taking part in a debate on the country's new Constitution.

While a pupil in San Andrés, Pedro had heard and believed the message of salvation in Jesus Christ. He went on to study chemical engineering in San Marcos University and, at a later date, theology in the Free Church College in Edinburgh. Always active in student affairs, Pedro eventually became General Secretary for Latin America of the International Fellowship of Evangelical Students, until an unexpected phone call launched him into political participation in the life of the nation. The call was from Dr José Ferreira, the only Evangelical Senator in the previous Parliament, whose son and five nephews had all studied in Colegio San Andrés. And his earnest plea to Pedro Arana was that he would stand as a candidate in the forthcoming nation-wide elections called by the military Government with the express purpose of framing a new Peruvian Constitution. Believing that Ferreira's call was also a call from God, Arana accepted, and to the astonishment of many, the unknown Presbyterian minister took his place among the hundred elected members of the year-long Constituent Assembly.

The first President of the Assembly was 83-year-old Víctor Raúl Haya de la Torre, the same man who fifty-five years before had taught in the Colegio Anglo-Peruano and led the people's protest against the idolatrous attempt to dedicate the nation to an image of the Sacred Heart of Jesus. And today,

6

13 June, a much younger disciple of John A. Mackay, a former pupil and former teacher of the School, was passionately defending in the National Congress the sovereignty of God over the affairs of the nation.

The point at issue was the proposed Preamble to the new Constitution. "We, representatives at the Constituent Assembly," it read, "calling on the protection of God, and exercising the sovereign power which the Peruvian people have given us ... declare as follows." Innocent-sounding words. But they brought down on the Assembly the wrath of the Marxist delegates, who demanded that all reference to God and his protection be eliminated from the Constitution.

And so Pedro Arana rose to his feet. Disclaiming any interest in a merely abstract or sentimental use of the name of God, he went on to refer to the Constitution's assertion that all human beings have dignity and universal human rights. And who, he demanded, gives such dignity to human beings other than "the Creator God who has revealed himself fully in the concrete, historic person of Jesus of Nazareth?" Going on to expound the clamant need for God's justice to be manifest in every sphere of Peruvian life, he ended with these ringing words:

And it is in that Christ, revelation of the God on whom we call, that we believe, and we must assert that today more than ever his protection is necessary for every one of us, those who claim to be Christians and those who do not in this country which morally and spiritually is heading for disaster through the corruption which is rampant at every level of life, through its separation from, its forgetfulness and transgression of the commandments of God, that God on whom we often profess to call and in whom we do not always believe with the commitment that we should.

As Arana sat down the public galleries burst into spontaneous applause, while some time later *El Comercio*, Peru's leading newspaper, normally no friend of the Protestant cause, commented in an article on *God and the Constitution*:

The finest speech on the religious topic was delivered by Pedro Arana Quiroz of the Aprista Party, minister of the Evangelical Presbyterian Church, and belonging therefore to another denomination. In his remarkably perceptive speech we recognise the existence of common values, essential and permanent among all Christians.

Two months earlier another significant debate had taken place in the Constituent Assembly on the question of freedom of religion. By 1979 the days of open persecution of Protestants by Roman Catholics had faded into history, apart from a few isolated pockets in remote areas. While fundamental Roman Catholic doctrine remained unchanged and essentially unbiblical, attitudes had improved enormously since the Second Vatican Council. No longer did Colegio San Andrés face the threats to its religious liberty that had brought tension-filled days to successive Headmasters and their staff from the twenties to the fifties. But the statute-book still discriminated against non-Catholics, and the time was now ripe for change. Once again Pedro Arana took the floor. He acknowledged with gratitude the victory won by pioneers for religious liberty who in 1915 had succeeded in persuading Congress to modify the article of the Constitution which stated:

The Nation professes the Catholic, Apostolic and Roman religion and the State protects it and does not permit the public practice of any other.

But even though the last phrase was eliminated, the basic rights of non-Catholics remained unaffirmed and had often been attacked. Arana, supported by a large majority of Assembly members, called for unrestricted liberty of worship for all, and assured the State of the wholehearted support of the Evangelical churches in their spiritual, moral and humanitarian activities:

This, Mr President, is where the Evangelical churches have a word of Evangelical brotherhood for all Peruvians, believers and unbelievers, Catholics and non-Catholics — the word of the Cross, the word of reconciliation, the word Jesus, the Christ, Lord and Saviour, the only authentic creator of the new man and the new human society.

8

And today, in respect of Church-State relations, the Constitution of Peru merely affirms:

> The State recognises the Catholic Church as an important element in the historical, cultural and moral development of Peru. It lends her its cooperation. The State may also establish forms of cooperation with other confessions.

There is total freedom to believe, total freedom to worship, total freedom to preach and propagate the faith. And though by no means the sole architect of this freedom, it fell to a man who first heard the Gospel in the classrooms of Colegio San Andrés to give clear expression in the highest legislative chamber of the nation to the evangelical faith for which many had suffered and even died. What greater challenge to Colegio San Andrés and to every Christian believer in Peru to proclaim to every citizen of the land the message of true freedom in Jesus Christ!

* * *

Once again the Old Boys of Colegio San Andrés were meeting on Founder's Day. On this occasion, 13 June 1991, they appointed by acclamation as their new President David Díaz, whose class were celebrating their Silver Jubilee. On leaving School in 1966, David took up a position with a leading textile firm, later on studying in England and rising to become a valued Plant Manager. He was enthusiastic about how the Association could contribute to the School's welfare, and promised active help throughout the year. True, his firm had been experiencing severe financial problems — not unusual in view of Peru's mega-inflation of 7,500% in 1990 — and also infiltration of the unions by militant left-wing elements, but David was confident he and his Committee would still manage to be of service to their old School.

The following Saturday he came with his wife and children to the annual Open Day, when the School is thrown open to parents and former pupils, and a full programme of educational, sporting and social activities is on offer. In the Headmaster's Office he showed his children the Caledonian Cup, donated many years before by the Caledonian Society of Lima, meeting-place of exiled Scots, and on which is engraved each year the name of the pupil reckoned to have shown the highest level of Cooperation and Initiative. There in the space for 1966, was the name of David Díaz.

On Monday morning, at the close of the Secondary Assembly, the Headmaster found waiting for him outside his office David Díaz's brother José, a surgeon in the Social Security hospital. He was accompanied by a colleague who wished to enrol his young son in San Andrés the following year, and knew only too well that competition is stiff for the limited number of vacancies. They chatted briefly, remembering José's prowess in English during his schooldays, and commenting too on his brother's recent election as President of the Old Boys' Association.

Little did they know that at that very moment, as David was entering his factory gates, armed terrorists were lying in wait and cold-bloodedly gunning him down. Killed instantly, he lay slumped over the driving-wheel of his car, one more cold statistic in the horrendous catalogue of victims of the extreme Marxist *Sendero Luminoso*, which for ten years had been waging a relentless war against the Peruvian State.

Colegio San Andrés was far from being alone in suffering at the hands of the *Shining Path*. Twenty thousand lives had been lost, among them many Evangelical Christians in the central sierra, Catholic activists for social justice, Government officials, local councillors and members of the police and armed forces. The fathers of two pupils in the school had been cruelly murdered, while at least one former pupil in the armed forces had perished at the hands of the Communist insurgents. The previous year the home of the Minister of Finance, also a former pupil of San Andrés, had been assaulted, with the death of a police guard. As with all public figures, his life continued in danger, but he refused to be cowed into leaving his post of duty.

And so, as Peru suffered, Colegio San Andrés, Peruvian to the core, suffered too. But not merely with the victims from its own school community. A programme of rehabilitation and, in some cases, relocation of displaced families was spearheaded by a former pupil under the aegis of the National Evangelical Council. Follow-up work with one such group in the Peace and Hope Village in the northern jungle was undertaken by another former pupil who on graduating as the top student of his year in the National Agrarian University chose to offer

10

for poorly remunerated Christian service instead of seeking the more lucrative post for which his qualifications fitted him. And in Moyobamba, capital of the San Martín department, centre of coca growing and drug trafficking, and also the main sphere of operations of yet another terrorist group, the Tupac Amaru Revolutionary Movement, two former pupils of the School joined forces with others to offer medical care to the suffering poor and economical housing to earthquake victims.

Peru still bleeds at the hands of terrorists, and sadly too, at the hands of repressive elements within the police and armed forces. And Colegio San Andrés, sharing in Peru's sorrow, proclaims the only source of true healing and lasting peace in Jesus Christ.

* * *

In 1992 Colegio San Andrés celebrated its 75th anniversary. As the foregoing incidents demonstrate, it has known moments of deep crisis, clear answers to prayer, remarkable opportunities of pastoral and evangelistic witness, close contact with the leaders of the nation, encouragements to persevere with its God-given task of Christian education for which the door remains wide open. In a striking way, the School was founded at a crucial juncture in the history of Peru, truly laid at the roots of the nation. In its early days, Dr John A. Mackay could write home to his Committee:

> Our confidence remains unshaken that the Free Church of Scotland has a great God-given mission in this land, and that Jesus Christ is calling her to make Peru hers that it may become His. But only unity, prayer and consecration on the part of all sections of the Church at home will ever plant the banner of the Cross "where Satan's seat is" in Peru.

This book seeks to chronicle the road followed by the school Dr Mackay founded, to consider to what extent the Free Church of Scotland has been able to fulfil the vision of those early days, to reflect on lessons learned along the way, and to face the challenge of the years ahead as Colegio San Andrés presses towards its centenary.

But first the scene must be set. The next chapter deals with the historical development of Peru prior to the arrival on its

11

shores of Free Church of Scotland pioneers; and also the religious history of the country which for centuries was denied the light of Gospel truth. And then comes the unfolding story of a Christian school of which a former pupil, Dr Manuel Reaño, has recently written:

> Nowadays as a physician involved in the missionary task, I meet very frequently with people related to the good old Anglo (as teachers or former students or whatever) also involved in different ways of serving the Lord, and I think it is the major accomplishment of our beloved school. I learned many other things there: discipline, order, honesty, scientific and humanistic knowledge, and a lot of things that I could have learned perhaps at other schools or even at home, but God sent me there to learn, in the words of the school motto:
>
> *Timor Domini Initium Sapientiae*
> The Fear of the Lord is the Beginning of Wisdom

2

Preparing the Soil

Think Peru, think Incas. Not surprisingly, when on every hand can be seen striking reminders of the great Inca Empire: Coricancha, the Temple of the Sun, in the Inca capital of Cuzco; Machu Picchu, the lost city of the Incas, stupendously situated yet skilfully hidden from view on a mountain peak in the Urubamba valley; remarkable irrigation terraces; the remains of an efficient nation-wide road system; and Quechua, the language of the Empire, still spoken by millions of Peruvians, Ecuadorians and Bolivians.

Yet the Incas came late, and their sway of imperial greatness was short. Over a period of perhaps two hundred years they emerged from inter-tribal struggles, finally obtaining undisputed sovereignty about the middle of the fifteenth century over a vast area, incorporating most of present-day Peru, Bolivia and Ecuador, and reaching into southern Colombia, northern Chile and northern Argentina. But for hundreds, even thousands of years before them, other native cultures flourished in Peru, whose textiles, ceramics and metallurgy still excite admiration. Incorporated by conquest into the *Tahuantinsuyo* (Inca Empire), their skills served to enrich the breathtaking heritage that Peru's ancient inhabitants have bequeathed to the nation of today.

Under the all-powerful Inca, Son of the Sun, and his immediate family, supported by the nobility, the people were kept in a subjection that was highly organised, productively self-sufficient and, within certain limits, benevolent. The ethical framework sought to exclude lying, stealing and laziness. The religious practices of the subject races — various manifestations of animism and idolatry — were tolerated by the Incas, provided pride of place was given to the worship

13

of the sun. Yet throughout what is known of Inca and some pre-Inca history, there is clear acknowledgment of a Creator-God, known as Huiracocha. Indeed, the greatest of the Inca emperors, Pachacutec, sought to promote the worship of this one, invisible God, while recognising the utility of sun-worship for his royal authority and the unity of the empire.

When Pachacutec's grandson, Huayna Capac, the last great Inca, died in 1528, he left a divided empire, with a secondary capital in Ecuador. In Quito his son, Atahualpa, proclaimed himself emperor, and in Cuzco another son, Huascar, did likewise. A bloody power struggle ensued, with Atahualpa finally defeating and imprisoning his brother.

The Conquest

Disconcerting news, however, was reaching both brothers. Strangers, white and bearded, were landing along the coast, equipped with unknown powers – firearms and horses. The Spanish adventurers, headed by Francisco Pizarro, had arrived. Driven on by their lust for gold and power, and displaying incredible personal bravery, Pizarro and his small band of men confronted the Inca Atahualpa in the Northern Andean town of Cajamarca. Enormously helped by the fatal division within the empire and the fratricidal animosities it had engendered, as also by the initial hope entertained by both brothers and their supporters that these white strangers emerging from the western sea might be none other than Huiracocha and his emissaries, Pizarro won a stunning victory, and sealed the fate of the great Inca empire.

The following decades saw bitter civil wars among the conquerors, and the eventual crushing of all Indian dissent. Spain became undisputed mistress of Peru, enslaving its native population and plundering the country to enrich the Spanish crown and its South American representatives. The Roman Catholic faith was imposed nation-wide, often as a mere veneer over animistic beliefs and practices, and usually proving a potent means of further oppression. Some Catholic missionaries lived sacrificial lives, and some experienced martyrdom in their efforts to penetrate remote jungle regions with the Church's message. As laws passed for the protection of the subject races were constantly flouted, some voices within the Church were raised in protest, the best known in Hispanic America being the Dominican friar, Bartolomé de las Casas. Sadly, the protests rarely led to direct action, and the native populations remained as exploited as ever.

In 1570 Lima was accorded the dubious honour of being chosen as the headquarters of the Holy Office of the Inquisition for Hispanic America. From then until its abolition in 1814, hundreds of suspected Jews, Mohammedans, Lutherans and other heretics, as well as those accused of blasphemy, sexual crimes or witchcraft, were tried and condemned, some to exile, floggings or loss of office, and others to death by burning.

As the seventeenth and eighteenth centuries progressed, tension increased between the privileged *peninsulares* (native Spaniards who held all the best positions) and the *criollos* (those born in Peru but racially Spanish) and *mestizos* (those of racially mixed parentage). Various unsuccessful Indian uprisings led on to the rebellion in 1780, headed by the *mestizo*, José Gabriel Condorcanqui, known as Tupac Amaru II, because of his descent from the last Inca to have resisted Spanish rule. Despite initial successes, the revolt was cruelly suppressed. But winds of liberty were blowing in North America and France , and resistance to Spanish rule was taking root in many sectors of the population.

Independence

In 1820 the Argentinian general, José de San Martín, landed in Peru, having previously freed Argentina and Chile from the Spanish yoke. On 28 July 1821 he proclaimed in Lima Peru's independence, and although much resistance was still offered by the Spanish forces, their final withdrawal was secured as a result of the Battle of Ayacucho in 1824. For the next twenty years Peru was plunged into a state of political and economic chaos, but in 1845 Ramón Castilla, a military strongman of great ability came to power. Except for a period of three years he ruled the country until 1862, creating a climate of sufficient stability for Peru to make significant advances, economically and organisationally.

However, in 1879 the disastrous War of the Pacific broke out in which Peru and Bolivia were decisively defeated by Chile, both losing territory to their southern neighbour. While the defeat still rankles in Peruvian minds, the country was forced to recognise its need to move towards more effective democratic government. Despite many periods of conservative reaction and military regimes, more liberal ideas and desires for social justice gradually entered into the mainstream of Peruvian life, a pattern that has continued till the present day.

Protestantism in Peru

For centuries Spain viewed Roman Catholicism as an essential part of her national life. Religious dissent was therefore equivalent to high treason, as many a loathsome dungeon and blazing pyre could testify. And what was true in Spain was true in all her colonies, particularly in Peru, her prized seat of royal power and guardian of religious orthodoxy.

Totally insulated against all extraneous religious influences, with the direst penalties meted out against even the slightest suspicion of dissent, it is little wonder that the records of the Tribunal of the Inquisition contain scant reference to Protestants, or "Lutherans", as they would normally be termed. A few English sailors, captured as pirates, who resolutely refused to deny their faith were probably the first to bear witness to fully biblical truth in Peru, sealing that witness with their blood. One man, Mateo Salado, described as mad because of his constant attacks on Roman Catholic practices, which he condemned as unbiblical, was burned to death; his memory is still preserved in the name of a Lima square.

The first Protestant missionary to enter Peru was a Baptist minister from Scotland, James Thomson (known in Spanish as Diego Thomson). When one considers the iron grip that the Church of Rome had exercised over South America for centuries, not only the fact of his free entry into several of the new republics but the nature of his work there are absolutely astonishing. As an advocate of the Lancaster school system which used the New Testament as its main text-book, and more advanced pupils as teachers of the younger ones while they themselves were still learning, Thomson arrived alone in Buenos Aires in 1818. Aware that the newly independent nation could not cope with the education of huge numbers of children, he offered his services. By the time he left in 1821, there were eight schools functioning in Buenos Aires, all supported by the government, in addition to several others outside the capital. Granted Argentinian citizenship by a grateful government, Thomson travelled on to Chile, invited by the government there. So successful was he again in setting up schools that he was granted Chilean citizenship "on account of his notable patriotism and the outstanding merit of his work in Chile."

In July 1822 Thomson arrived in Peru. The very same day he presented his credentials to the Liberator, San Martín, who welcomed him warmly and promised him every assistance in his work. A Dominican monastery was vacated by government order, and Thomson opened a school which soon had 200 pupils. He was eventually able to establish another smaller one in Lima, and later on another was founded in the Andean town of Huánuco. Not only so, but the government recognised the Lima school as the first "normal school" in Peru for the training of teachers, with Thomson as Principal.

If Thomson's achievements in Argentina and Chile were remarkable, his success in Peru was even more extraordinary. He was treated as a friend by San Martín, the greatest figure, along with Bolívar, in the emancipation of South America. He was looked up to as an outstanding educator and Christian gentleman by the government of Peru. He was offered every support by several Roman Catholic priests in a land where Protestantism was still strictly prohibited. Making the most of his opportunities, Thomson succeeded in selling thousands of Bibles and New Testaments, a fact even more significant when it is borne in mind that he refused to distribute free or even subsidised Scriptures, and that Peru was in a state of revolutionary turmoil, with highly unfavourable economic conditions. He even succeeded in having the New Testament translated into Quechua, though he left Peru before it could be printed.

During Thomson's two and a half years in Peru, Lima was twice retaken by the Spanish forces, and the republican government was forced to flee. Attendance was at times erratic in the school, and often Thomson's salary was not paid. Eventually he felt he could no longer carry on his work in the city, and made his way to Colombia to plant God's Word in yet another republic. However, his colleague, Francisco de Navarrete, a Roman Catholic priest whom Thomson describes as "a very worthy priest, a lover of education and of the Bible" continued the work and as late as 1847 wrote Thomson that since his departure thirty more schools had been founded. As a result of President Castilla's energetic reorganisation of the national educational system in 1850, the schools ceased their separate existence.

There is no doubting Thomson's wholehearted commitment to evangelical Protestant doctrine, as many references in his letters make clear. But he was a man of great tact, very gifted in making friends, and aware that his missionary work had to be undertaken in the situation as it was, employing methods appropriate to that situation. He used a Roman Catholic translation of the Bible, without notes, and welcomed the cooperation of the Catholic clergy and people in his schools and in Scripture distribution. He believed strongly in the transforming power of God's Word applied by God's Spirit, and seems to have hoped that the greater openness to liberal ideas of those priests who supported the independence movement would contribute towards a reformation within the Roman Church.

Commenting on the danger that many thinking people who had rejected Catholicism would also reject all religion and espouse deism, he goes on to say:

> I realise that this is the most favourable moment for sowing, as far as we can, the sacred religion of our Lord Jesus Christ. This is the time for working in this field, either by introducing the Bible or by any other prudent method.

However, the reformation that Thomson looked for did not materialise. In the decades following his departure from Peru, reactionary forces gained the upper hand both politically and religiously. Popular education and access to the

Bible were viewed with suspicion, and in spite of Navarrete's valiant labours, no missionary voice was heard in Peru for sixty years after Thomson left. John Kessler, in his *Study of the Older Protestant Churches in Peru and Chile*, indicates that Thomson, towards the end of his life, realised that the "inner, spontaneous reformation of the existing church" had not taken place. He appealed for the first time "to the Protestant church for help in setting up a missionary society for South America. This was done in 1852, but Thomson's death two years later brought the plans to nought." Nothing, however, should be allowed to detract from Thomson's heroic achievements, and only eternity will reveal how many people throughout South America were blessed as a result of his single-handed distribution of God's Word and demonstration of a Christlike life.

Further Protestant progress

Sporadic visits were paid to Peru by Bible Society representatives in the following decades, but without any evident success. In 1845 the Peruvian government gave permission for Protestant services in English, provided no Peruvians attended, and the first Anglican chaplain arrived in 1849. In 1885 the congregation moved into its own building, but were not allowed to give any indication from the outside that it was a place of worship. Since the Church of the Good Shepherd, as it was named, kept strictly to the terms of its agreement with the Peruvian government, it was not till the nineteen sixties that the Anglican Church began any deliberate evangelistic outreach among Peruvians.

It was in Callao, the port of Lima, with its more cosmopolitan population that missionary work was tentatively begun. Commercial relations with Britain were increasing, especially with the establishment of a steamship line and the development of the guano industry. The American Seaman's Friend Society sent a missionary in 1859, but his stay was short. Then in 1864 the South American Missionary Society (Anglican) sent a consular chaplain to Callao, who allowed Peruvian children to attend the school he ran, and Peruvian adults to attend the English services. The Archbishop of Lima protested against the appointment to the Minister of Justice and Worship, but in spite of this the school and church went ahead, though sadly the chaplain died in 1867.

For twenty years sporadic efforts were made by various people in Callao to minister to the English-speaking community, with limited outreach to Peruvians. So limited indeed, that when the first real missionary successor to Thomson arrived in Callao, he wrote in all sincerity:

> Very little had been done with the Bible, and the Gospel had never been preached in the language of the people.

The arrival in 1888 of this missionary opened a significant new chapter in the evangelisation of Peru. Francisco Penzotti, an Argentinian of Italian birth, came as representative of the American Bible Society to establish an agency in Callao. He had already travelled extensively as a colporteur and preacher in Bolivia, Ecuador and Chile, suffering many privations but winning many Gospel victories. In Callao he began immediate door-to-door visitation with the Scriptures, and held services in his own home. "My first congregation", he wrote, "consisted of two people apart from my own family. The next Sunday there were four, the following one ten, then it went to twenty, then thirty, after that forty, fifty, sixty, seventy, eighty, till there was no more room." He obtained permission to use the chapel which had been built for the English-speaking community, which no longer held services, and over 300 people were attending. "Of course this infuriated the sons of darkness and they threatened to blow up the chapel and ourselves with dynamite. In view of these threats the committee in charge withdrew their permission, and we had to go back to our smaller meeting-place." This was a dilapidated warehouse, where Penzotti was able to build up a regular congregation of 180, with six colporteurs whom he himself had trained.

Towards the end of 1888 Penzotti sent a Uruguayan colleague and one of his new converts on a colportage trip to the south of Peru. When they were violently attacked in the port of Mollendo, Penzotti went to join them, with the result that all three ended up in prison in Arequipa, the second city of Peru. No sooner were they released by order of the President than they were back at work, and by the end of Penzotti's first year, 7000 Bibles or portions had been sold.

In 1890 the Callao congregation was organised as an official Methodist church, but its early history was punctuated by constant attacks. Opponents organised processions which chanted: "Death to Penzotti! Down with the Protestants!" and the church building was frequently pelted with stones and mud. In order to observe Peruvian law, the services were held behind closed doors, and on one occasion a priest locked the door with a padlock while the service was in progress. It so happened that one member arrived very late, and discovered to his consternation that the church was locked on the outside. He tried a key he had in his pocket, and surprisingly it fitted. Penzotti recounts how the priest, watching from the other side of the street, "put his hands on his head and exclaimed, 'These heretics are protected by the devil!'"

Eventually Penzotti was arrested, accused of violating Article 4 of the Peruvian constitution which forbade the public practice of any religion other than the Roman Catholic one. He was thrown into a filthy jail which had served as a gunpowder deposit under the Spaniards, and would undoubtedly have died there, "for what they gave me under the name of food was anything but eatable", had not his wife stood nobly by him and brought him food every day. Penzotti tells of one single occasion when his faith faltered. After several months his son came to say that his mother was unable to send any food that day since she had no money left. Overwhelmed with grief for his family, he heard the tempter say:

> Very well then! Here you are a prisoner with no hope of freedom! Your children have no bread! Where's your God now? Are you going to keep on trusting him and die here, letting your family die too? A fine religion and a fine God you have!

But God came to his aid, and he sent word to his wife that God had not died and would help them. Shortly afterwards his son came back with some letters, including one with a sum of money from an unknown well-wisher in the United States. Handing it to the boy he said:

Take it, son, to your mother and buy bread for you and me.

In an interview with Penzotti's wife, the government Minister offered to free him on condition he left the country immediately. Both she and her husband refused, since this would have been a tacit admission that any Protestant worship was illegal in Peru. The imprisonment dragged on, but liberal voices within Peru and Christian voices from abroad were making themselves heard. A photograph of an emaciated Penzotti in prison, published in *The New York Herald*, created an international scandal, and enormous pressure was brought to bear on the Peruvian government. Eventually a local court acquitted Penzotti, mainly on the evidence of the padlock, which proved that the congregation must have been meeting behind closed doors, as the law required. However, it took further acquittals in a higher court and in the supreme court before Penzotti was finally released after eight months incarceration.

Undoubtedly a tremendous blow had been struck for religious liberty, particularly as the church services continued all the time of Penzotti's imprisonment. He himself left shortly afterwards for Argentina and then undertook further Bible Society work in Central America. His place was taken in 1891 by a North American Methodist missionary, Dr Thomas Wood, who worked tirelessly in the organisation of Methodist churches, the preparation of pastors and the founding of schools. Three of these continue to be highly regarded educational institutions in Callao, Lima and Huancayo, with Callao High School, today Colegio América, celebrating its centenary in 1991. Wood and his fellow-workers had to face regular outbursts of hostility, but they persevered, and the Protestant cause in Peru owes much to the faithful witness of those early Methodists.

Extension of Protestant witness

An independent missionary from England, Charles Bright, arrived in 1893, to be followed shortly afterwards by three young men from the interdenominational missionary training centre in London, Harley College. While Bright worked in Lima, the Harley College men went on to Cuzco, the ancient Inca capital. They tried various means to gain acceptance with the people — shops, English classes, industrial training — though never hiding their Evangelical stance. Progress was difficult, but evangelistic work was gradually undertaken over wide areas of the country. The missionaries served under what became known in 1899 as the Regions Beyond Missionary Union (RBMU), and a steady number of new recruits came out from Britain to join them. There were many examples among them of self-denying Christian service, and several missionaries died as a result of their privations.

Two Scots RBMU missionaries, A. Stuart M'Nairn and John Ritchie, who arrived in 1905 and 1906 respectively, were to play an important part in the events which led up to the beginning of the Free Church of Scotland work in Peru in 1916, as is recounted in the next chapter. M'Nairn was closely involved with the formation of the Evangelical Union of South America (EUSA) in 1911, and the handing over of the RBMU work in Peru to the new body. As the EUSA General Secretary he established friendly contact with Free Church leaders, and encouraged them to consider the claims of Peru as a sphere for missionary service. John Ritchie moved from Cuzco to Lima in 1907, where, as a printer to trade, he was to develop a highly significant Christian literature programme. Also, as EUSA Superintendent in Lima, he had overall responsibility for a small school, Escuela Diego Thomson, begun in 1913 to cater primarily for the needs of Protestant children who were suffering religious discrimination in State schools. When John A. Mackay paid his first visit to Peru in 1915, he was given hospitality in the home of Mr and Mrs Ritchie.

The battle for religious liberty

Although more and more Evangelical churches were being founded, they were mostly small, and consisted almost exclusively of people with limited educational opportunities and little social influence. Furthermore, as long as the prohibition of the public exercise of all non-Roman Catholic religion remained on the statute book, outbursts of persecution, sometimes violent, could be expected at any time.

The catalyst for change occurred in a small village on the shores of Lake Titicaca, the highest navigable lake in the world. A flourishing Seventh Day Adventist evangelistic, educational and medical work had grown up under the direction of a local Indian, Manuel Zúñiga Camacho and North American missionary, Frederick Stahl. Camacho had actually pleaded in 1907 with John Ritchie and a fellow-missionary, John Jarrett, to take over responsibility for the work he had begun, but neither was able to do so. Camacho then turned to the Adventists, who were able to respond to his plea. Stahl and his wife are commended by all who knew them as energetic, self-sacrificing and spiritually minded, less interested in promoting Adventist distinctives than in meeting the material and spiritual needs of the people among whom they worked.

In March 1913 the Bishop of Puno led a crowd of more than 200 Indians, including the governor and two justices of the peace from the neighbouring town of Chucuito, to Camacho's village of La Platería. Neither the Stahls nor Camacho were there, so the mob ransacked the Stahls' home, the schools and the medical post. When five Adventist converts refused to kneel and kiss the bishop's hand, they were tied up and ordered to be taken to prison in Puno. At that moment Camacho arrived, and was likewise seized and told by the bishop that he had orders from the country's President to wipe out all heretics. When Camacho had the temerity to reply that such an order would have gone to the prefect and not to the bishop, and also to denounce the religious festivals as drunken debauches, the bishop exploded in fury. Since no Indian present would lay a finger on their respected leader, a priest lashed out at him, followed by the Chucuito authorities. Badly beaten, Camacho and the other Indians were compelled to spend a week in prison in Puno, before a judge ordered their release and referred the matter to the supreme court in Lima.

In the capital Camacho gave a written account of the events, with his own protest against the action of the ecclesiastical authorities, to a congressman, Dr Urbina. He read out the documents in the Chamber of Deputies, which led to a considerable reaction in favour of religious liberty. Some months later, in August 1913, one of the two Puno Senators presented a motion, asking for the amendment of Article 4 of the Peruvian constitution. Henceforth it would read: "The nation professes the Catholic, Apostolic and Roman religion, and the State protects it", eliminating the further phrase: "and does not allow the public practice of any other." The motion was accepted and passed to the commission on the constitution for due consideration.

One of those who read the account of the debate in the next day's press was John Ritchie. For some time he had felt God calling him to act on behalf of religious liberty in Peru, and now he knew the vital hour had struck. Joining forces with a Methodist pastor, Ruperto Algorta, and an Adventist missionary, Maxwell, he used his printing press to rally public support, and lobbied senators and any others known to be favourable to the cause of religious liberty. The crucial debates took place in both houses of Congress in September 1913. In both cases the amendment was carried, though not without dire warnings from the opponents of religious liberty that Christ was being crucified afresh, that a poisonous dart was piercing the heart of Peru, and that the country needed again the merciful protection of the Tribunal of the Inquisition, so unjustly vilified by Protestant propagandists.

By Peruvian law the President was required to promulgate the amendment to the constitution. By November 1915 this had not been done; indeed the Council of Ministers informed the nation that it had been decided not to do so. At this point Congress stepped in, since the constitution gave the Executive a time limit for promulgating laws — when that time passed, Congress itself could act. Thus it was that on 11 November 1915 in a memorable meeting of both houses of Congress, the amendment to the constitution was promulgated as law. There was pandemonium in the public galleries, mainly from opponents of the measure, and when the law was passed by a huge majority, one hostile Deputy tore it up in full view of everyone. But from that moment on liberty of worship, even though restricted, was a reality in Peru.

Ninety three years previously James Thomson had attended a session of the Peruvian Congress when it debated the proposed article on religion of the new constitution. He was impressed

25

by the liberal, even biblical sentiments expressed by some members, including priests. But to his great disappointment the prohibition on the practice of any non-Roman Catholic religion was approved. Nevertheless he felt that when Peru gained full liberty from Spain this could change. "There is still hope that religious liberty will be included in the constitution of Peru. Meanwhile the press can forward the good cause, since there is perfect liberty to speak or print anything on the subject." Nearly a hundred years later another Scotsman, John Ritchie, was able not only to use the press as Thomson had hoped, but to see the fulfilment of Thomson's longing. And in the very weeks before the victory of 11 November 1915, another Scotsman, John A. Mackay, was also in Lima. He grasped the significance of the moment and resolved to lay his life at the roots of the nation and claim Peru for Jesus Christ.

3

Selecting the Ground

Why Peru? Why should a tiny Presbyterian denomination centred largely in the rural communities of the Scottish Highlands and Islands conceive the idea of a missionary enterprise on the far western shores of South America? If she felt the urge to plant an overseas church, why not choose some better-known territory within the bounds of the still powerful British Empire?

To find the answer, we need to trace the various currents which converged to form the stream that bore Free Church of Scotland pioneers to the city of Lima and then beyond, to the mountain fastnesses of the Andes and the upper reaches of the great Amazon river.

The first significant event took place in 1900. The overwhelming majority of the Free Church of Scotland, little more than fifty years after its formation under the inspired leadership of Dr Thomas Chalmers, joined with the United Presbyterian Church to form the United Free Church of Scotland. A seemingly insignificant minority, unhappy with the doctrinal and ecclesiastical basis of the united Church, determined to carry on the witness of the Free Church. On the overseas front the remnant Church no longer existed, since all her 166 missionaries – in Budapest, Constantinople, Syria, the New Hebrides, South Arabia, Africa and India – entered the Union. But well aware of the fact that no Church is worthy of the name which does not strive to preach the Gospel to every creature, the first General Assembly of the continuing Church included in its proceedings the appointment of a Foreign Missions Committee. It was a stupendous act of faith – by human reckoning, of folly – for there were literally no funds, no missionaries, no fields of labour and scarcely any of the leaders

27

had first-hand contact with the world beyond their own shores. But the Lord's command to go into all the world rang in their ears, as too his promise of strength made perfect in weakness.

In less than a year a Free Church doctor sailed to India to work with the Original Secession Church. In 1905 a Church delegate was sent to Africa "to visit and convey the Church's brotherly greetings to the Presbyterian churches there", and in 1908 the first Free Church overseas appointment since 1900 was made — a minister to work in South Africa.

However, there were those within the Free Church who felt that these positive developments fell short of the wholehearted missionary commitment that should characterise their denomination. They prayed for the extension of the Gospel to every nation, they supported other missionary societies and churches, and they waited. God, they felt sure, would show them the way to go.

The second event of importance occured in 1910, when Edinburgh hosted the largest Missionary Conference the world had ever seen. One thousand two hundred delegates from all over the globe debated issues affecting missions, and agreed to strive for greater unity in fulfilling the Church's missionary mandate. The Free Church of Scotland was represented by the Convener of her Foreign Missions Committee, whose subsequent report in the Church's magazine, *The Monthly Record*, was careful to highlight some of the praiseworthy features of the Conference. Yet neither the report, nor the sparse references to the event in the magazine, suggest much enthusiasm for the Conference nor high hopes for its contribution to biblically-based world evangelisation. It is undoubtedly the case, however, that the conference proved a catalyst in directing Free Church attention to South America as a field of missionary endeavour. Not through any of the stirring missionary challenges that some speakers presented. Not as a result of the volumes of valuable missionary information later published. Rather it was what was *not* said that moved some hearts within the Church to embrace a topic that was considered taboo by the Conference organisers, and was excluded from its agenda.

This is best explained by quoting from the November 1913 issue of *The Monthly Record*:

That remarkable Missionary Conference could only take action on behalf of non-Christian peoples, and the appalling fact is that its Continuation Committee declares now that South America must still remain outside its sphere of operations. A conference or committee which arrives at a decision of this nature has no claim to the title "Missionary" ... The "Christianity" of South America is emphatically only baptised paganism, and no more appalling story of corrupt morals and debased humanity can be written today than that which concerns the South American Republics, and the neglected natives of that vast continent.

This callous neglect of present duty by a so-called World Conference on missions is the strongest possible reason why lovers of Evangelical truth should make the needs of South America their peculiar charge, and by every means in their power seek to make known to the native population and the Latinised "Christians" of that dark land, the terms of Christian morality, and the true basis of political freedom. In all the Republics but one — Peru — there is now officially declared and guaranteed religious liberty; in Peru a Government has recently been returned which is favourable to granting that right.

The Editor's words were written in the context of a very favourable report of the annual London meeting of the recently formed Evangelical Union of South America. Distinguished English church leaders — chief among them Dr G. Campbell Morgan, Rev Charles Inwood and Dr J. Stuart Holden — had refused to take part in the Edinburgh Conference in protest at the exclusion of South America from its missionary purview in deference to Anglo-Catholic susceptibilities. Their action led directly to the formation of the Evangelical Union of South America, which was to play a vital role in the evangelisation of South America for almost eighty years, and has recently joined with the Regions Beyond Missionary Union to form a new agency known as Latin Link.

At the 1913 Free Church General Assembly one of the invited speakers was Mr A. Stuart M'Nairn, General Secretary of the E.U.S.A.. He delivered what the Editor described as "an impassioned address" in which he described South America as "the land of the Christless cross", and lamented the fact that into such a vast continent all the great missionary societies but one had refrained from entering, since "theoretically it was held that South America was a Christian country". His appeal on behalf of the spiritual needs of South America " was listened to with intense interest, and at the close he was heartily applauded."

In the December *Monthly Record*, the Editor returned to the same theme:

> South America and its needs were brought forcibly before the public the past month. Large meetings were held in Glasgow and Edinburgh, at which addresses were delivered by Mr Stuart M'Nairn and others bearing on the moral condition of that vast continent, and the need for evangelical work there ... The near completion of the Panama Canal connecting two great oceans may have a startling effect on the trade relationships of South America, and the Gospel messengers should not be behind hand.

In this way the entire Free Church membership throughout Scotland were being made sensitive to the needs and opportunities of South America. At the same time, the Church's leaders were engaging in informal discussion with Mr M'Nairn and others knowledgeable about South America. And an important detail − some funds were now available for missionary work, the Free Church having received a percentage, small though it was, of the Foreign Missions capital of the pre-1900 Church.

There now appeared the third vital component of the Free Church of Scotland South American missionary equation − the man of God's choice.

Ten years previously a fourteen-year-old Inverness schoolboy was spending his summer holidays in the county of Sutherland. With his mother he attended the traditional Fast Day services of the Free Presbyterian Church in the rural parish of Rogart. As God's Word was preached, John A. Mackay recognised that the inner need he felt was being met and that Jesus Christ had become the centre of his life, quickening one who until then had been dead in trespasses and sins. And even as he heard God's saving call that day in Rogart, there was also borne in on his consciousness a conviction that he too one day would become a preacher of the Gospel of God's grace.

This conviction led him eventually to offer for the ministry of the Free Presbyterian Church, the first step being University studies in Aberdeen. Through his personal reading, through attendance at a missionary study group led by the minister of Gilcomston Baptist Church, through hearing great missionary speakers, for example, Samuel Zwemer, missionary to Muslims, and Robert Speer of the American Presbyterian church, and through his friendship with Jane Wells, a young teacher who later became his wife, Mackay's horizons were widened and his call to mission confirmed. In 1910, Robert Speer, one of the main speakers at the Edinburgh Missionary Conference who had impressed Dr Alexander Stewart, the Convener of the Free Church Foreign Missions Committee, travelled north to Aberdeen to address students there. Mackay felt he had never heard a more brilliant speaker in his life, and read avidly Speer's account of a six-month visit to South America on behalf of evangelical missions. His friendship with Jane Wells created a further link with South America, since through her church, Gilcomston Baptist, she supported the Regions Beyond Missionary Union, particularly their work in Peru.

After a brilliant academic career in Aberdeen, John Mackay resigned as a candidate for the Free Presbyterian ministry, and having won a scholarship, headed to Princeton Seminary in New Jersey, U.S.A., still presided over by the renowned defender of the Reformed faith, Benjamin B. Warfield. Mackay had already discussed with Free Church friends in Scotland his interest in missionary service in South America, and they assured him that their Foreign Missions Committee would look favourably on his offering for such work. In Princeton he was a diligent and successful student, once again winning a scholarship for post-graduate studies. As he pondered where to spend that extra year, Warfield made the suggestion that he go to Spain to study the Spanish religious tradition and master the language. Mackay's year in Spain was to have a profound impact on his thinking and help fit him in an exceptional way for the tasks that lay ahead of him in Latin America.

And so the various elements merged — a Church obedient to the Master's call to mission; the Holy Spirit using different means to impress upon that Church the spiritual needs of South America; the provision of financial resources; and the raising up of a highly gifted and keenly motivated missionary candidate.

Time for decision

Far-reaching decisions were now having to be made by the Foreign Missions Committee. South America was beckoning, but South America was no fewer than ten independent republics. It might be more natural to think of Chile or Argentina, since they had a larger British presence; indeed, a younger brother of John A. Mackay, Duncan, had already emigrated to Argentina. But Peru was the name that kept pushing itself to the foreground. Already *The Monthly Record* in 1912 had inveighed loudly against the atrocities committed in the Putumayo region of the Peruvian jungle, by the rubber barons against their native workers. In informal conversations with Free Church leaders, Stuart M'Nairn of E.U.S.A. was highlighting the needs of Peru, where hostility to the Gospel had been most marked, but where new winds of liberty were beginning to blow. In these circumstances the Committee took a wise decision. They asked John A. Mackay, on completion of his Princeton studies and before sailing for Spain, to carry out a tour of investigation in South America, and report back with his observations and recommendations to the Committee. This he did, over a period of three months, visiting Argentina, Chile, Bolivia and Peru. His extensive report transmits the account of his travels and his wide-ranging observations on the spiritual needs and missionary opportunities in South America with great lucidity and remarkable perception on the part of one so young and totally unversed in the Spanish language and Latin American culture. In fact, for anyone familiar with Dr Mackay's subsequent brilliance in the field of Spanish language and literature, it comes as a shock to realise that even he had to begin as a novice, and that on the several occasions during his journey when he preached, he had to depend on the goodwill of others to interpret for him.

The report is divided into three parts. The first, a narrative of his journeyings throughout South America, contains some references to Lima which prepare the way for his eventual recommendation that it should be the base for Free Church missionary enterprise. He describes it as "the traditional centre of Spanish culture in South America". He refers to "the inefficiency of the teaching staff and the miserable educational results" of Colegio Guadalupe, the leading boys' High School in the Republic, despite acknowledging that "a more magnificent institution as to buildings and equipment I have never seen." He bemoans the fact that among "the profusion of gaudy and fantastic images" in Lima's seventy churches, "I saw nothing in painting and sculpture that suggested the truth of the Resurrection." The megacity of today with its eight million inhabitants bears little resemblance to what Mackay describes as "a city somewhat smaller than Aberdeen", but its strategic significance was what captured the attention of the observant Scot in his capacity as ambassador of the Gospel. "Lima", he wrote, "was the seat of the Viceroys, its cathedral the largest in South America, and its university founded many years before the founding of Harvard, Yale or Princeton in the United States." As such, it was of immense strategic value for missionary outreach.

After some general observations in the second part about missionary work already being carried on in South America, Mackay presents in the third part of his report his specific recommendations to the home Committee. He prefaces these with the assurance that:

> The news that Scotland was at last to enter the mission field of South America was hailed with undisguised gladness by missionaries everywhere. The feeling was that the land of John Knox had a real contribution to make to the advance of Christ's kingdom in dark South America ... We shall not therefore enter the field as unwelcome intruders. There is a great sphere in Lima, the capital of Peru, for a Free Church Educational Mission; and an equally great sphere in

the Sierra, or mountain region of Peru, for a Free Church Medical Mission.

With regard to the former, his well thought-out arguments are worth spelling out in detail:

(a) The greatest need in South America today is a number of first-class educational institutions which would be conducted along strictly Christian lines. A good school is always welcomed in South America, and parents are generally quite agreeable that the Scriptures should be taught, so long as their children receive a good preparation for life, and especially a good moral education.

(b) A first-class educational institution which works for supreme spiritual ends has the opportunity of so *moulding the youth* of a country that with God's blessing, they shall become good Christians and good citizens. As an illustration, the work of the "Instituto Inglés" in Santiago is making an indelible impression on the national life of Chile.

(c) After a few years such an institution would, if successful, *pay its own expenses*, especially after it became possible to accommodate boarders. For the last twenty years the "Instituto Inglés" has not cost the American Presbyterian Board a penny.

(d) The best centre at the present moment for a new evangelical school is Lima, Peru. Peru has no great Christian institution such as the "Instituto Inglés", which is engaged in moulding life and thought in the country. Moreover, Peru has a unique claim upon us as being the great stronghold of Rome in South America. An onward movement in Peru ought to arouse the conscience of the Free Church, and indeed the evangelical conscience of all Scotland. And as to Lima itself, it is the centre of Spanish culture in South America as well as the centre of Peruvian life and thought. It ought also to be clear from what was said in Part 1 of this report, that it would not be difficult to compete with the national schools in Peru.

(e) There is actually in Lima a small elementary school of three years' standing which might be made the basis of a larger institution. This school belongs to Mr Ritchie of the Evangelical Union, who told me that unless his Board was able to lend him support in this particular undertaking, he would be compelled to close it down. He added, however, that rather than close the school, he would prefer to hand it over to the

Free Church, if the church would be willing to accept it.
(f) The type of work here advocated will be slower in coming to maturity, and slower in bearing fruit, than other types of missionary work in South America. It will also be singularly devoid of romance. But I am convinced that our ideal of Mission work in South America should be the same as the ideal of Dr Duff in India. When criticised by fellow-workers of other Missions as to his educational institution and methods, Duff replied, "While you engage in directly separating as many precious atoms from the mass as the stubborn resistance to ordinary appliance will admit, we shall, with the blessing of God, devote our time and strength to the preparing of a mine and the laying of a train which shall one day explode and tear up the whole from its lowest depths."

From Committee room to Assembly floor

Back in Edinburgh the Foreign Missions Committee knew that the time had come for decisive action. They were not an autonomous body, having been appointed by and being answerable to the General Assembly of the Free Church of Scotland. Any proposal for initiating and financing a new missionary venture would have to be approved by the Assembly, due to meet in May 1916. They knew that their own enthusiasm for South American missions would not be shared by all the Assembly members. Some would regard the whole project as quixotic, unlikely to succeed, and a drain on valuable resources. Others would question the legitimacy of missionary work through education instead of through direct preaching of the Gospel. Yet others would point to the many congregations in Scotland, still struggling without pastoral oversight since 1900.

The Committee, however, kept unswervingly to its course. Convinced that they were following God's own leading, they prepared their recommendations to the General Assembly, showing as they did so, a remarkable trust in the judgment of their fledgling missionary candidate. They reported as follows:

The Committee carefully considered these recommendations and approved of them in general effect. With respect to the distinctive character of the Mission, they were anxious to emphasise the fact that the preaching of the Gospel must ever be kept in the forefront of its activities; but it seemed to them that alongside this essential feature of its operations, with a view to securing stability of character and permanence of results, there should also be an educational side to the work, in accordance with Mr Mackay's suggestions.

The Committee asked the Assembly to agree to their renting the E.U.S.A. school for a year, with a view ultimately to taking it over completely. Proposals for medical work were also made, the Assembly being informed that two ladies, a doctor and a nurse, were willing to set out for Peru on the termination of their important war duties. They were clearly anxious to assure the Assembly that they were not romantic visionaries, but clear-headed realists who nonetheless believed that God was calling the Church to this new venture, and that the only obstacle to success would be lack of faith in him and his unlimited resources:

> In submitting to the General Assembly these recommenda-
> tions — the far-reaching importance of which they do not
> underestimate — the Committee desire to express the con-
> viction that the proposed mission in South America is one
> which the Free Church is well able in every respect to undertake,
> and one which, with the blessing of God, is calculated to have
> effects of the most beneficial kind, not only in the communities
> in which the work is carried on, but also upon the general life
> of the Church as a whole.

Even in cold print and at a distance of some eighty years, the presentation of the Report to the Assembly by the Committee Convener makes stirring reading. Dr Alexander Stewart, a widely-known preacher and author, claimed there was "evidence of the leading of the hand of God in this matter from first to last". He admitted that setting up educational and medical missions with a view to planting churches in a largely unknown land was "a heavy undertaking". Could they fulfil it? "We are well able to go up and possess this land", he affirmed. Sufficient funds were available and God would provide more through the generosity of his people. Dr Stewart ended his speech with what a young minister described in the correspondence columns of *The Monthly Record* as " a noble and thrilling peroration". To loud applause he assured the Assembly that a wholehearted and generous commitment to the new mission in South America would have a far-reaching influence on the life of the Church at home:

> Her branches shall spread and her beauty shall be as the olive tree, and her smell as Lebanon. The heart grows rich with giving, and the Church grows rich with giving also. There will be a general uplifting and quickening and ennobling of the whole life of the Free Church.

Not everyone shared in the applause, however. One minister objected to the whole enterprise because work at home was being neglected, resources were painfully inadequate, and the Church was "not at liberty to spend any more money in sending men to a far country." Another claimed that the Church's "first duty was to their own kith and kin in Canada, and they had not performed that duty". And it seems some members abandoned the Foreign Missions debate, unable to resist the tempting odours wafting up from the downstairs hall. Such was the complaint of a correspondent in the Church's magazine, who claimed that Dr Stewart's "magnificent speech was delivered under very depressing conditions, inasmuch as the majority (perhaps) of the members of the Assembly were at the time engaged in satisfying less spiritual appetites in the nether regions of the Assembly Hall".

Eventually, all the Committee's recommendations were approved. Peru was firmly placed on the Free Church agenda, and things moved quickly. In Inverness in the month of August John A. Mackay was ordained to the Christian ministry as a missionary to South America. A few days later a small group gathered at the station to wave goodbye to the departing couple. Among them was John Mackay's seven-year-old brother, Willie, later to spend his life as a parish minister, army chaplain and hospital chaplain, preaching till the week before his death in 1993 the same Gospel his brother was setting out to proclaim in far-off Peru. In September a well-attended meeting was held in Edinburgh to bid farewell to John and Jane Mackay. This meeting was addressed by three fervently eloquent speakers, all fully persuaded of Christ's call to worldwide mission. Dr Alexander Stewart, Convener of Foreign Missions, stressed again the leading of God in the whole enterprise, and described their hope for the future in the Psalmist's words:

> Of corn an handful in the earth,
> On tops of mountains high,
> With prosperous fruit shall shake, like trees
> On Lebanon that be.

Mr Stuart M'Nairn of the Evangelical Union of South America was deeply moved to be able to welcome fellow-labourers to the South American mission field. He expressed total agreement with the aim of reaching the educated classes for Christ, but warned that the task was far from easy: "Let the Free Church remember that she is up against the biggest thing she has ever put her hands to".

John A. Mackay's own words were keenly awaited, since his studies in Spain had prevented his being present at the General Assembly. He told the audience of a Scotsman he had met while crossing the Caribbean, who assured him he was a fool to throw his life away in Peru, and that he should work on behalf of his drunken, landlord-ridden Scotland. Others, within the Free Church, expressed it less bluntly, but were nonetheless making clear their belief that the needs of the home Church were paramount. In the light of this, Mr Mackay spoke out strongly on behalf of a vibrant evangelism and a fresh proclamation of the old truths of Calvinist theology throughout Scotland. Had God so called him, he would gladly have given himself heart and soul to such a task. But in spite of the claims and charms of a home pastorate, "for me the call is stronger to leave them all and go forth and teach a rude people the first rudiments of the Gospel of Christ. The claims of the home pastorate are to me as nothing to the duty of teaching God's truth in South America."

And so the die was cast. For the first time in the history of Scotland, one of her Churches was officially sending out missionaries of the Cross to the people of South America. But as the story unfolds, containing much to admire and inspire as the Gospel advanced from Lima, "the city of the kings", to the ancient Inca fastnesses in the Andes mountains and on to the upper reaches of the vast Amazonian river-system, a fundamental question will call for an answer. Did the Free Church ever understand or accept the commitment and sacrifice necessary to engage in a task demanding for its proper fulfilment a supply of people and funds which it signally failed to provide? Were the enthusiastic advocates of this foreign enterprise ever more than a dedicated minority within the wider Church community? If such thoughts crossed the minds of John and Jane Mackay, they were too grateful to their warm-hearted supporters to express them. Peru was beckoning, even across wartime enemy-infested waters, and their Lord had said, "Go and make disciples of all nations ... and surely I will be with you always."

4

Planting the Seed

Lima is pleasant in late November. The heavy grey blanket of cloud and mist that has hung over the city for the previous months has lifted, blue skies and warm sunshine raise the spirits, as does the new foliage, still fresh and green, its sparkle not yet fallen victim to the grimy dullness of Lima's all-pervading dust. Even the polluted, over-populated mega-city of today can boast its palm-lined avenues, its multi-coloured profusion of bougainvillaea and frangipani, poinsettia and flame of the forest. But the Lima of 1916 could more justifiably lay claim to its title of "the garden city", and offer an attractive environment for living and working. By December the Mackays found a home in the pleasant suburb of Miraflores, overlooking the Pacific Ocean, but the business for which they had come did not allow much time to enjoy its attractions.

Missionary work was to be launched with a school, and schools in Peru began their new session on the first of March. First of all, arrangements had to be made with John Ritchie for the transfer of the EUSA school to Free Church control. Not that there was much to transfer, since EUSA had been unable to fund the school adequately, pupil numbers had dwindled to twenty-eight, and a new building had to be found. "The scheme was somewhat of an adventure", wrote Mackay to friends at home, but by mid-February an old building in downtown Lima boasted a freshly-painted sign, "Escuela Anglo-Peruana", and was open for business. The missionaries themselves had turned their hands to painting, window-cleaning and carpentry, but now came the acid test — would any parents put their children in this unknown, unpretentious school? The session began with forty pupils, but by the end of April numbers had more than doubled. One qualified teacher, an active member of the Peruvian Evangelical Church, remained from the previous school. Both she and her niece were to give many years of loyal service to the new institution, stretching, in the case of the latter, Srta Zoraida Baca, into the nineteen sixties. Other inexperienced staff were given on-the-job training by Mrs Mackay, an experienced and gifted teacher.

Six sparsely-furnished rooms looking out on to a roofless corridor, with another small room in use as an office, were what functioned as the Anglo-Peruvian School. In order to be taught the morning Bible lesson, the pupils had to squeeze into two adjacent rooms, while the teacher positioned himself in the outside corridor. There were pupils to teach, but not all remained, especially as the Roman Catholic Church hurled anathemas on those parents who dared to send their children to Protestant schools. Yet in these outwardly unimpressive circumstances, John Mackay could write to Free Church children in *The Instructor*:

> I wish our school, boys and girls, to grow into the finest and most efficient mission school in South America.

And to the Church at large he wrote in *The Monthly Record*:

> With her school, the Free Church holds the key to the present missionary situation in Peru.

How could he use such exalted language in the face of such mundane reality? Did later events justify his grandiose vision? First, we need to understand Mackay's aims both for the School and for evangelism on a wider scale, before going on to trace the development of the institution during the nine years of his leadership.

The EUSA school had been established with the primary aim of meeting the educational needs of Protestant children. As reported in *South America* in 1915:

> This was made imperative by the new law enacted, enforcing religious instruction in all the national schools, thus placing the children of our Church members directly under the power and influence of the priest. The parents in our congregation have now withdrawn their children from the Government schools, and enrolled them in the Protestant school.

41

From the very outset it was recognised that the school would need to be subsidised; since it was "largely for working-class children the fees charged are much too low to cover the expenditure." Mackay, however, saw things differently. His mission school would reach out to families not themselves Evangelical, but eager to find an education that was academically and morally sound. If the product was good, they would pay for it, rather than inflict on their children the poor standards of much State education or the immorality and narrow-minded clericalism of many Roman Catholic schools. Mackay firmly believed that a quality education, firmly rooted in Christian values, would attract many liberally-minded people, even though still members of the Catholic Church. It would then be possible "to influence the community through the children who pass through our hands."

Not that the children of Evangelical believers were to be neglected. An important aim was "to meet the educational needs of the Protestant cause in Peru", and that meant recognising that nearly every Protestant child came from the ranks of the poor. But neither the school fees nor the school standards were to be lowered on that account. The School itself would budget for a proportion of bursaried pupils, and the Church at home would be urged to contribute to the expenses of needy Evangelical children. This was successfully done, and has continued to be School policy till the present day, though the neediest are no longer exclusively identified with the Protestant community.

Another fundamental element in Mackay's thinking was what he called "the Carey principle". William Carey, the great pioneer of Christian missions to India, believed that where possible missionaries themselves should contribute towards their missionary work being self-financing. His own income as a Government translator and College professor was all ploughed into the missionary cause. Mackay knew full well that it would be many years before evangelistic work among the masses — work he entirely approved of and supported — could be self-supporting. But educational missions were different. He himself contributed to mission funds by translation of documents, by teaching English in the University, and especially in 1925 when he occupied the Chairs of the History of

Modern Philosophy and of Metaphysics in San Marcos University. Most missionaries would, of course, lack the skills necessary for such tasks, but Mackay still insisted that the School should pay its way. For several years a boarding department was run, which, in addition to its obvious spiritual and moral value, usually succeeded in generating income for the School. And the fees themselves were fixed at realistic levels, as is explained in the Headmaster's 1918 Report:

> I have on frequent occasions emphasised the fact that the people of Lima are accustomed to pay for the education of their children ... One of the objections made to our school was that the fees were too low for the school to be worth anything. So this year we raised our fees somewhat, while granting a rebate of from 25 to 30 per cent to the children of Evangelical parents.

As a result the first year's debt was wiped out, and the salaries of two locally contracted missionary teachers were totally covered by the School itself. Free Church support took the form of the Headmaster's salary and an equipment grant, in addition to the costs involved in sending out and providing accommodation for new missionary teachers.

Mackay's vision of winning over the nation's future decision-makers to Christian faith and values led to his application of another important principle in the Colegio Anglo-Peruano. He explains it in the same 1918 Report:

> Hitherto the policy of Protestant education in South America has had two distinctive features: first, the use of English as the chief medium of instruction, and secondly, the imposition of foreign programmes of study. The Free Church school in Lima has the distinction of being the first missionary institution in South America to break with this tradition. It has been our policy from the beginning, while giving careful and systematic instruction in English, to give the place of honour to the national tongue.

Mackay considered that in teaching English so exclusively, because of the great demand for it in commercial circles, missions were following "a temporising policy". His aim was to capture the future teachers and lawyers, doctors and engineers, for Christ. This meant fitting them for a University career, and demanded Peruvian academic qualifications and studies carried out in the national tongue. John Mackay was a great admirer of Dr Alexander Duff, the Scottish pioneer of educational missions in India; indeed he named his own son Duncan Alexander Duff. But in this matter he struck an independent course. While acknowledging that Duff's insistence on English as the main medium in his schools may have been right for India and for the Christian assault on Hindu idolatry, Mackay believed strongly that both for educational and spiritual reasons Spanish should have pride of place in South American mission schools.

The final aim expressed by Dr Mackay was "to prepare teachers and preachers for direct missionary service". In the nature of the case, this could not materialise for a good number of years, particularly with the great majority of the pupils being Roman Catholic. From that day to this, both school teaching and the Christian ministry have had a low profile and poor remuneration in Peru, and the number of students from Colegio San Andrés with a vocation for either has been very limited. With regard to pastors for the Evangelical churches, Dr Mackay took part in evening classes held in the premises of the Anglo-Peruano. His successors and other missionary teachers on the staff were to play a vital role in the founding and development of the Peruvian Bible Institute, today known as the Evangelical Seminary of Lima, a Government-accredited centre for theological studies. The School has never proved to be "a nursery for preachers and pastors", but nonetheless some who came there to faith in Christ or had their faith strengthened and challenged, went on to prepare for the Christian ministry and other forms of Christian service. As far as the teaching profession is concerned, a later chapter will discuss the key role of Colegio San Andrés in more recent times.

Fully persuaded that if these fundamental aims were kept in view, his Christian school would take root and prosper, Mackay kept up a stream of correspondence with the home Committee and the home Church. It is doubtful if either anticipated the great success of the new venture, and particularly the demands it would make for a constant supply of missionary teachers and of others with evangelistic and pastoral gifts. When the School was only two months old, Mackay wrote home:

> Let the Free Church provide men and women of outstanding Christian character and gifts who will develop the School, with funds to enable them to work, and abounding prayer to make their work successful, and a people will one day arise from among these mountains to call her blessed ... The field is ripe, and according to every indication, God's hour has now struck; may He not have to send us back into the wilderness for forty years more from the very borders of the waving harvest.

A year later his clarion call was for "true hearts in the Lowlands and Highlands of Scotland whose robust Protestantism will overcome their denominational bias, and who will follow the leadership of the Free Church in its endeavour to create an institution on the Pacific Coast of South America which will cast the sovereign rays of truth from the Isthmus to the Horn ... Somebody under God must do this thing: why not we?"

His 1920 Report, giving details of great progress on every front, pleaded:

> The School's development and very existence will be imperilled, as well as the whole future of the mission, unless teachers are found of sufficient vision and worth to throw in their lot with us here. I speak with a full sense of responsibility; the next move lies with the home Church. Nothing new can be done while what has been already done is in danger. Silver and gold will not be unwelcome, but our supreme need is men and women. Give us the human gold and we will find its metallic equivalent.

The same vision and the same plea come to the fore in his two final Reports as Headmaster. In 1924 he wrote:

> I also reiterate my faith in the Church's school in Lima. It is now in the most interesting and hopeful stage of its development. If properly staffed and supported, it is in a position such as no other missionary institution in the country is, to shake the powers of darkness.

And in his final Report, penned in March 1926, when he was no longer a missionary of the Free Church of Scotland he declared:

All I have ever said or written about the Anglo-Peruvian College I believe. I feel it has been my providential function to be an initiator and to have the joy of being able to hand over to the Mission I have served a growing work of which they need not be ashamed.

Growth and development

The statistics are impressive.

The School began in 1917 with 40 pupils, and ended with 85. The second year 137 pupils enrolled. The third year saw 260 pupils complete the session. In both 1920 and 1921 there were 337 pupils in the School, but an increasing number of applicants had to be turned away for lack of space and qualified staff. In 1922 the numbers rose to 388, and remained at approximately that level during the remainder of Dr Mackay's tenure of office.

Who were the families clamouring to place their children in the young Scotsman's Protestant school? Certainly not many Protestants, since Protestants in Peru were still as scarce as the rain on the country's desert coast. With extraordinary rapidity the School became known and admired among the middle classes of Lima, so that after only three years the Headmaster could write:

It is not too much to say that already on the eve of a fourth session our school is regarded in Lima as one of the best in the city. Some go further and say it is the best. At least such is the reputation it enjoys that we receive the boys of University Professors, Cabinet Ministers, foreign diplomats, leading doctors and lawyers.

The Argentinian Ambassador deliberately chose the Anglo-Peruano for his two sons. Indeed, as early as 1917, after appreciative articles appeared in two of Lima's leading papers, Mackay told of:

an interview with the head of a large French business concern in the city, who has decided to take his boy away from the Church school in which he has been up to the present and put him in ours, offering at the same time to pay double our fee for the education of his son.

46

The School's official licence to operate specified only boys, but for the first few years girls were also received. There were never more than thirty, and when Government-appointed teachers came to conduct the end-of-year examinations for the top Primary and all Secondary classes, the girls were excluded. Special arrangements had to be made for them to sit their examinations in State schools. These difficulties, combined with the problems of running a mixed school in cramped premises, led to the decision in 1924 to receive only boys. The few remaining girls completed their education elsewhere, except for one strong-willed Protestant girl. The daughter of a teacher in the mountains who had recently died, in 1993 she is still alive, enormously proud of being the only female former pupil among several thousand men.

This was evident when, in 1973, special celebrations were held in honour of the first group of pupils to complete, in 1923, their Secondary education in the School. In place of Dr John A. Mackay, unable for reasons of age to make the journey to Peru, the main invited guest was a later Headmaster, Dr Neil A. R. Mackay. In his report of the various activities in *From the Frontiers* magazine, he describes the concluding event — a dinner in the Bolívar Hotel, which was attended by a good number of Old Boys of all ages:

> It was greatly enlivened by the presence of an "Old Girl" — much to the astonishment of all who did not know or remember that the group of primary school children taken over by Dr Mackay in 1917 was made up of boys and girls. The latter were not allowed by official regulations to continue in a mixed group during the secondary stage, but one of them — Isabel Rodríguez, as she then was — thwarted all attempts to move her to a girls' school, and finished her school career with the 1923 group. At the dinner she gave a spirited account of those far-off events, and left the Old Boys' Association with a question as to the validity of their title.

The search for teachers

More pupils meant more teachers. As numbers on the roll increased, Mackay became more than ever convinced of the wisdom of his strategy of penetrating Peruvian society with the Gospel through education. But throughout 1917, 1918 and even 1919 his appeals to the home Committee for teachers met with no success. The problem was not lack of sympathy with his aims, but the war raging in Europe. The British Government had refused permission to a Free Church doctor and nurse to travel to South America, and teachers were likewise viewed as key personnel in the war effort.

During 1917 Mrs Jane Mackay had been, in her husband's words, "the soul of the institution". But in 1918 their first baby was on the way, so who would take her place? At this point God showed his special interest in the work as stated in the Headmaster's Annual Report:

> On the very week that my wife had finally and sorrowfully to bid farewell to the school, there came to the rescue Mr Vere Rochelle Browne, a distinguished graduate of the University of New Zealand, who landed in the port of Callao like Paul on the shores of Macedon, guided by a vision, but without definite plan or promise.

Not only so, but two months later Miss Elsie Yeats, a young graduate of Aberdeen Teacher Training College, appeared on the scene. A governess with a Peruvian family in the sierra, she found the altitude undermining her health, and made her way to Lima. Reading about the Anglo-Peruano in a city newspaper, she offered her services and proved herself invaluable in the lower grades until her marriage some two years later.

Vere Rochelle Browne deserves more than a passing mention. A massive physique, a brilliant intellect, an ebullient personality, eccentric habits and missionary zeal all combined to make him an ideal acquisition for the school at this pioneering stage. So highly did Mackay esteem him that he soon appointed him Deputy Head, and in 1922, during his own absence in Scotland, left him in complete control. A later teacher, also from New Zealand, Dr Herbert Money, writes in his Memoirs of Browne's extraordinary talents and versatility:

> While in charge of the boarding department, which was housed in an old villa on the Malecón in Miraflores, he

constructed for himself a study in one of the tall pine trees on the property. Strange things had happened in Peru before, but the Police had no previous experience of tree dwellers. They therefore mounted an extensive investigation but were relieved to find that the unusual happenings in the tree were merely due to the eccentricities of an inoffensive school teacher.

Among the inventions for which Browne distinguished himself was a mechanical alarm, which not only announced it was time to get up but also, after a short interval, reinforced the announcement by tipping the bed up and shooting the occupant out. Ingenious though it may have been, it never became popular enough to merit mass production or patenting.

Browne taught Science in the School, demonstrating his academic ability by adding a doctorate from San Marcos University to the Bachelor's and Master's degrees he already possessed. His practical abilities must have enormously impressed the boys. Not only did he make his own suits and shoes, but he also constructed with the boys a glider in the playground, an achievement considered worthy enough to merit a mention in the official *History of Peruvian Aviation.* He also organised the first-ever inter-schools athletics competition held in Peru, using for the purpose the National Stadium donated by Britain to Peru on the occasion of the 1921 Centenary celebrations of Peruvian independence.

When, like many another teacher in Peru, he found himself frustrated by the pupils' consummate skill in cheating at written examinations, he refused to own defeat. Money tells the story:

Courses such as woodwork were unheard of prior to this time, but this did not deter Browne. Having found that the supervision of written examinations was a problem that he had not had to deal with before on account of the extraordinary national capacity in the art of cheating, he conceived a way in which to enlist the pupils to defeat their own ends. They were delighted when he suggested woodwork classes and so he soon had them making individual desks (the others were double) and in a short time had produced enough to outfit a whole class. When examination time came, the boys and the desks were set out in the patio separated from one another by several feet. The boys

found their copying techniques thrown completely out of gear.
They lost this battle, but not the war.

Not only did Browne give five years invaluable service to the
School, but his sister came for about two years as matron of
the boarding department, where up to twenty-five boys from
the provinces were under constant Christian care. When circumstances combined towards the end of 1924 to make the
boarding department no longer financially viable, Miss Browne
left, "leaving behind her fragrant memories of an exception-
ally beautiful Christian personality." As for Browne himself,
he followed up previous pioneering visits to the mountains and
jungles of Peru with a decision to penetrate into unevangelised
territory. When last heard of, he was involved in missionary
witness in Africa.

In 1920 the first Free Church missionary teacher arrived.
She was Netta Kemp from Cullicudden in the Black Isle, a
young woman of great strength of character and a deep sense
of God's call to missionary service. She was later to marry a
fellow-teacher in the School, Herbert Money, who tells how
her resolution was tested when she first volunteered as a teacher
for the Anglo-Peruano: "Loyal as he was to the Church, her
father could not understand why she should think of leaving
the security of Scotland for a country so frequently rocked
by revolutions." Dr Money also quotes the testimonial she
received from the local minister who had recently arrived in
the parish and knew very little about the young woman absent
in Edinburgh:

> Miss Netta Kemp is a young lady of respectable antecedents,
> which, to my knowledge and full belief, she has done nothing
> to discredit.

No doubt the young lady was vouched for by other members
of the Missions Committee resident in Edinburgh. At any rate
she was accepted, and sailed on the Orellana to begin a missionary career stretching till 1939 with the Free Church school,
and on to eventual retirement from Peru in 1968. In addition
to the unfailing support she gave her husband, she put her
Spanish literary abilities to good use. A book on *The Historical Geography of Bible Lands* became a standard text in

many Bible Institutes, while her *Women of the Bible* continues to be in demand for popular devotional use.

It was a matter of intense disappointment to John A. Mackay that during his entire nine years in the Colegio Anglo-Peruano not one male teacher materialised from the Free Church of Scotland. However, his year's furlough in 1922 proved very fruitful, since he was able to interview and recommend for acceptance no fewer than four missionary volunteers. Miss Christina Mackay from Tain was to give well over forty years service in Peru, some of it in Cajamarca, where Rev and Mrs Calvin Mackay had succeeded in establishing an Evangelical church and school in the face of much clerical opposition. By the time she left Peru in 1964 Christina Mackay was both Head of Primary and School Administrator.

Also from the Free Church came Miss Mary Hutchison from Carrbridge. Although she only taught for five years in Peru, having to stay in Scotland to look after her ailing mother, old men who remember her from their schooldays speak admiringly of "the red-haired beauty who taught in Primary". Till her dying day she always spoke affectionately of her "little Peruvian boys".

In view of the poor response from Free Church men, the Foreign Missions Committee placed advertisements for teachers in various Christian periodicals. One in the *Christian Herald* brought replies from two young Liverpool graduates, W. Stanley Rycroft and Leslie Cutbill, who were invited to Edinburgh to be interviewed by John A. Mackay and the Committee. Mackay was impressed with both of them, and they in turn were captivated by his charm, ability and vision. As a result they sailed to Peru in September, 1922, and by the time Mackay returned for the 1923 session were already giving a good account of themselves both in the School and the boarding department. Cutbill gave valuable help in the Science department and in school sports, but early in 1925 he had to be invalided home with severe tuberculosis. Yet his two years in Lima were enough for him to catch the vision of the work and long for its fuller development. Though no longer connected with the Free Church of Scotland, he wrote in the December 1926 issue of *The Monthly Record*:

I have eagerly awaited each recent issue of *The Monthly Record* to see if there had been any response to the appeal of the Foreign Missions Committee for teachers to staff the Lima School. I view with considerable disappointment the continued lack of response to that appeal, because the work in Lima is in urgent need of both men and women teachers. Having spent more than two years as a teacher in the school, I have a very great interest in the work there, and I can confidently and wholeheartedly support the appeal of the Committee, adding that no worthier or needier sphere of service is offered by any Missionary Society.

Stanley Rycroft remained in the school till 1940, most of the time as Deputy Head and on two occasions serving as Headmaster. A competent teacher and skilled administrator, he eventually took up a post as Secretary of the Committee on Cooperation in Latin America, becoming well known as a perceptive writer on Protestant missions and general religious affairs in Latin America.

On several occasions Dr Mackay pleaded with his home Committee to intensify their search for Christian teachers, so that the School would not need to depend on locally contracted Peruvian staff, lacking in Evangelical conviction and often with no teacher training. Since so few foreign teachers were found, Mackay had to scout around for suitable Peruvians to staff his institution. And herein lies a most remarkable paradox. On the one hand, he would have preferred not to employ most of those he invited to the School, because of their ignorance of biblical Christianity. On the other hand, he was so successful in selecting liberally-minded men of great intellectual ability — mostly as part-time teachers in the fields of Literature, History and Philosophy — that to this day Colegio San Andrés enjoys the reputation of having had as teachers some of the most outstanding figures in Peruvian life.

Foremost among them was Víctor Raúl Haya de la Torre, the young lawyer and political idealist, who founded the Alianza Popular Revolucionaria Americana (APRA), and was to play a leading role in Peruvian national life for several decades. But there were others, such as Raúl Porres Barrenechea who became Peru's greatest expert on border demarcations and was eventually appointed Foreign Minister; Jorge Guillermo

Leguía, who became a distinguished historian but died before his literary productions came to full flower; Luciano Castillo, Erasmo Roca and Alberto Arca Parró, all of them lawyers who became distinguished congressmen, the latter also being responsible for carrying out the national census; Manuel Beltroy, who was to receive fame as a poet and a literary figure; Andrés Aramburú Menchaca, who replaced Beltroy as History teacher, and in 1992 was still serving as Dean of the College of Advocates. Though never on the official teaching staff, a frequent visitor and speaker in the school was Luis Alberto Sánchez, future Rector of San Marcos University, distinguished litterateur and from 1985-90 Vice President of the Republic. When Sánchez on one occasion returned from a period of political exile in Chile, he immediately sought out the Anglo-Peruano as the school where he wanted his son to complete his education.

Reasons for success

Why did an unknown Protestant school in a solidly Roman Catholic country enjoy such phenomenal success?

The teaching of English was an important factor, especially when taught by native speakers. But other schools in Lima taught English, and did so more intensively than the Anglo-Peruano.

The British connection, at that particular juncture in Peruvian history, was of great significance. Britain had more commercial interests in Peru than any other country, and was looked up to for her business ability and business integrity. "We are not the most loved, but we *are* the most respected race in Peru;" wrote Mackay, " and that very fact gives enormous prestige to any institution that is run by British."

Dissatisfaction with the low academic standards of most State education played a part. Challenged by the success of foreign-led schools, the Roman Catholic Church began to stir itself to improve standards in its own schools, but many intellectuals and professional people saw the Church as obscurantist and dominated by clerical intrigue. A serious school like the Anglo-Peruano provided a welcome alternative to both State and Church institutions.

Of great importance was the school's insistence on discipline, punctuality, honesty and respect. Probably many of the parents signally failed to exemplify some of these qualities in their own lives, but they felt they were good for their children, and would do their families and the country a lot of good. In *The Instructor* of November 1917, Dr Mackay gives a graphic instance of the School's moral standards and the impact they made. The occasion was an end-of-term exhibition of the children's work for the benefit of parents, at which some flowers were stolen:

One boy was caught red-handed – although I believe that some of his elders were greater culprits than he – and made to put back what he had stolen. The following morning, instead of beginning school by reading a passage of the Bible, I repeated slowly three times in succession the words of the Eighth Commandment, "Thou shalt not steal". Amid an intense stillness I began to teach a lesson on the nature of theft, emphasising the points that it makes no difference to the wickedness of this sin who the person might be who committed it, nor yet the value of the article stolen. Having all agreed on the principle at stake, I asked the offender of the preceding day to stand up before the school, I explained the disagreeable incident of the flowers and calling the boy beside me on the floor, I asked him to express to the whole school his regret for what he had done. He began to murmur. I took out my watch and gave him three minutes to consider. There had been various complaints of articles disappearing during the past few weeks and I was resolved to meet refusal with drastic action. The three minutes were up and the boy remained sullen and obdurate. With a few sorrowful words to the school on the impossibility of allowing to remain among them one who refused to acknowledge his fault, I expelled him.

The two weeks of the mid-year holiday passed and I was prepared to find when school reopened that the children of one whole family, one of our best, had all been withdrawn because of what I had dealt out to their brother. But I was mistaken. On the second morning I was called into the office to meet the mother of the boy expelled. The boy himself was with her, and both were in tears. Truth and righteousness had conquered. The mother pleaded for her son; the boy in tears expressed his sorrow for what had happened, and that afternoon I called the school together to reinstate him. It was a wonderful opportunity to explain the nature of repentance, and I presented to the boys their former companion, whose character, because of his repentance, they were to regard as spotless.

Seventy-five years later hundreds of parents apply each year to put their sons in Colegio San Andrés. In their interview with the Headmaster and Director they are asked, among other things, why they have chosen San Andrés. Of the various reasons given, the most common is *la buena formación moral* — good moral training. They may not understand yet that the Gospel is not synonymous with morality, but in a society riddled with bribery and corruption, they recognise in Colegio San Andrés an institution that from its earliest days has held inflexibly to its motto that only "the fear of the Lord is the beginning of wisdom".

Unquestionably, however, the weightiest factor in the School's rapid early success was the personality, ability and vision of its founder, John A. Mackay. In little over a year he had gained his doctorate from San Marcos University with a highly acclaimed thesis on the Spanish philosopher, Miguel de Unamuno. He was invited to lecture on English literature, and at a later date was appointed to the Chairs of Philosophy and Metaphysics. He was a member of the select group of intellectuals who published the literary journal, *El Mercurio Peruano*, and received countless invitations to lecture on literary, philosophical and religious subjects. His personal charm and intellectual brilliance attracted students and teachers to him, and he carefully selected the best of them to cooperate with him in the Anglo-Peruano. Dr Luis Alberto Sánchez, one of Peru's leading intellectuals and politicians, reminisced about Mackay in a San Andrés School Assembly in 1972:

Mackay left Peru really heartbroken, because he had made it his second country. He was accustomed not just to Peru, but to treating Peruvians as his friends, children and brothers. In San Marcos he was one of the most loved professors. Nobody missed his classes, and he never kept an attendance record because there was no need to. He was the teacher "par excellence" that everyone wants to keep on talking to after the class is over — the kind of thing so many teachers would like to happen after their classes.

There are not many of Mackay's Anglo-Peruano pupils still living today, but one of them, retired Methodist bishop Juan Hollemweguer who in 1993 is still pastoring a small congregation in Lima, has clear memories of his former Headmaster. He studied under Mackay in 1924 and 1925, and remembers his skill in dealing with his pupils:

> Then as now, there were boys who misbehaved, but Mackay seemed able to keep them under control without ever raising his voice. On one occasion a boy was objecting audibly to having to study Religion, and Mackay said quietly to him and the class, "No-one who is ignorant of the Holy Scriptures can ever be truly cultured." That phrase has remained with me all my life. Another time a boy sneaked a look at the teacher's desk while Mackay was discussing some points of Christian doctrine with the class. We all knew that Mackay spoke excellent Spanish, but our respect for him grew enormously when we realised that the book that lay open on his desk was the New Testament in Greek.

A school led by such a man had a head start over any other. And along with his unequalled reputation as a Hispanic scholar went his capacity for inspiring devotion and loyalty on the part of his colleagues, expatriate and Peruvian. They may well have realised that his idealism had to be matched by the practical teaching and administrative ability of his wife, of Vere Rochelle Browne and of Stanley Rycroft, but they were stirred by his vision for the School and were inspired to give of their best to make it a success. Thus we find, as early as 1920, an outside observer, Dr Webster Browning, Educational Secretary to the Committee on Cooperation in Latin America, writing in the following terms to the Foreign Missions Committee in Edinburgh:

> I consider the opportunity of your Church in Peru as absolutely unique ... knowing Latin America as I do, I can say that no other man whom I know has been able to accomplish so much in such a short time, nor does any other missionary now stand on the threshold of such a magnificent opportunity, and at the beginning of a work that promises to be so helpful ... A Christian institution, well equipped with buildings and grounds, and provided with a faculty of men and women whose final aim

56

in all their teaching is the bringing to Peru of the pure Gospel of Jesus Christ, which the Peruvians have never known, is the most immediate and urgent need.

Mackay's departure

As early as the closing of the first school session in 1917, Mackay was making his position clear to the home Church:

> I will continue to advocate the establishment of a strong educational institution in Lima, which will represent the highest ideals of Christian Education, and be a buttress to the missionary cause. At the same time, I never for a moment think our chief aim here is education. Personally I do not feel that God has called or fitted me to be a pedagogue ... I burn to be able to give myself with abandon to the active and positive work of the Gospel.

In 1918, commenting on the opportunity given him to lecture in the University on aspects of English Literature, he wrote:

> My great ambition is that at no distant date I may have the opportunity of lecturing to the same type of audience on vital religious subjects. For I desire that each new opening door may lead me to the vantage ground I seek, to declare in the ears of all the riches of love in Christ Jesus.

Along with his school work, he preached frequently, taught Bible Institute classes and wrote articles for an Evangelical magazine. But these efforts were not reaching the great majority of Peruvians, particularly the intellectual classes and future decision-makers, who would never dream of attending a Protestant service. Mackay described his feelings as "an unutterable pent-upness, and a longing to do something more."

As time went on, he was able to create more and more opportunities for what he called *conferencias sin culto*. These were "straight talks on God and the human soul" without any of the outward trappings or normally integral features of religious worship. On several occasions he went on lecture tours to other South American countries under the auspices of the YMCA, and was able to speak on Christian topics to an amazing cross-section of the population. These tours were arranged by agreement between the Free Church of Scotland and the North American YMCA, though not without justifiable misgivings on the part of some within the Free Church on account of the increasing theological liberalism of the YMCA.

Mackay, however, felt that "bringing the truth of Christ's Gospel to the restless and aspiring youth of South America" outweighed both the theological risks and the dangers inherent in a widening ecumenical participation. Within the Free Church of Scotland some would have little desire to cooperate with other denominations, but the leaders in the Foreign Missions cause had a wide vision of evangelical cooperation, embracing all who stood firmly for the fundamental doctrines of the faith. Relationships between Dr Mackay and his Committee remained positive and cordial, and his resignation at the end of 1925 was received with deep regret and thankfulness to God for what he had been able to accomplish in such a short time. In their report to the 1926 General Assembly they speak of his "incessant efforts, conspicuous abilities and wonderful devotion." They wish him "the choicest favours of Heaven for himself and his work" as Religious Work Director for Latin America under the auspices of the YMCA, though in coming years they would find themselves treading very divergent ecumenical paths.

So Mackay took his leave of the Anglo-Peruano, "with the freedom I need to do the work of a Christian evangelist." In his final Report he expressed his affection for the Free Church of Scotland and the Free Presbyterian Church of Scotland as being "the Christian denominations God employed, one to lead me to His Son, and the other to send me to my apprenticeship in the Foreign Field. If I forget thee, O Jerusalem, let my right hand forget its cunning."

What would happen now to the Free Church School in Lima? Different days lay ahead, different people at the helm, but the same God, the same Gospel, the same field of opportunity among thousands of young people, still untouched by the normal evangelism of Peru's evangelical churches.

5

Ensuring Growth

The September 1932 issue of *Leader*, the Anglo-Peruvian College magazine contains a full and lively account of what it called the Seventh Panamerican Conference, held in the school auditorium. Previous Panamerican Conferences had been attended by the heads of state or foreign ministers of various American republics, north, south and central. This, however, was organised by the Debating Club of Colegio Anglo-Peruano, with Fifth Year pupils representing Central America; Fourth year, the United States; and Third Year, South America. The British concept of debating societies to foster among the young skills in public speaking and clear thinking on important or amusing issues was unknown in Peru, but its introduction into the Anglo-Peruano was enthusiastically received.

The topic under debate was the foreign policy of the United States, guaranteed then as now to stir the passions of all hot-blooded Latin Americans. If British educational practice sowed the original idea, Latin verve and eloquence brought it to full flower. For guiding the teams, few schools could call on teachers of the calibre of Raúl Porres, later to be Peru's delegate at the League of Nations and the country's Foreign Minister, or Jorge Leguía, recognised as one of Peru's leading historians and a nephew of the President of the Republic. According to the magazine report, the dozen boys who participated showed remarkable historical knowledge and political awareness. They spoke lucidly and passionately, but, not surprisingly for Latin Americans, found time limits and debating rules irksome in the extreme. At the end of the debate the public, consisting of all Secondary pupils, voted overwhelmingly against the foreign policy of the United States.

When the jury, made up of six impartial teachers, awarded the victory by 133 points to 130 to the Fourth Year team representing the United States, the reporter laconically stated that the audience were "displeased".

Only fifteen years had passed since the Anglo-Peruvian school opened its doors to 40 Primary pupils. Six years previously it lost its visionary founder, whose talented personality was the main driving force behind the young institution's rapid and successful growth. Other schools had blossomed for a time and then faded away. Would the Anglo suffer the same fate?

The 1932 debate, held in the school's commodious new premises, gave proof not of mere survival, but of vibrant growth, a motivated student body, disciplined and imaginative teaching and the support of families of the highest intellectual and social calibre. How had Mackay's momentum been maintained since 1926?

The Free Church Committee in Edinburgh had no easy task in its search for a new Headmaster. Stanley Rycroft was capable, but still young, and in any case the Committee felt a Free Church school should be led by a Free Churchman, totally familiar with and committed to the Free Church's Reformed theology and Presbyterian practice. Furthermore his dual role as School Headmaster and Superintendent of the expanding Free Church mission in the *sierra* and *montana* meant a minister was required. Though all ministers of the Church were informed and invited to volunteer their services, none did so. The Committee, therefore, made direct approaches, and eventually set their sights on one man, Alexander M. Renwick, minister of Dumbarton Free Church of Scotland.

A Gaelic-speaking native of Wester Ross, Renwick had pastored a small congregation in Aberdeen and served with distinction as an Army chaplain in the War before accepting a call to Dumbarton. As Assistant Clerk to the General Assembly, he was well-known and much esteemed in Church circles. Out of a sense of Christian duty he agreed to uproot his family and leave his warm-hearted congregation, placing the Church greatly in his debt.

He did, however, labour under certain disadvantages which made his task as successor of John A. Mackay a formidable one. He had no experience and little knowledge of cross-cultural missionary work. His predecessor was an acknowledged authority on Hispanic culture and Latin American affairs, whereas he was unversed in both. He spoke no Spanish, and while he was to learn it reasonably well, he never attained the fluency of either Mackay or most of his younger colleagues. While he had been a diligent student, graduating in both Arts and Theology, and later working hard for his D.Litt. from San Marcos University, he was largely unfamiliar with Secondary education. His original post-Primary studies were in the local village school, which he left at an early age to begin work, later studying privately for his University entrance. During his years as Director of the Anglo-Peruano, his genial, gentlemanly manner won him great respect in Lima's academic, business and diplomatic circles, while his unswerving devotion to duty and great affection for the boys committed to his care helped to ensure the continuing success and rising reputation of the Colegio Anglo-Peruano. His talents did not lie, however, in the field of school administration, and at times his expatriate members of staff found it difficult to implement improvements in general discipline and educational practice. But Dr Renwick, who agreed in the first instance to serve for five years in Peru, yielded again and again to the insistence of the home Church that he remain at his post, giving no less than seventeen years arduous and self-denying labour to the Anglo-Peruvian College.

Alexander Renwick was not long settled in his post when he wrote the home Committee stressing two issues that had been raised by John A. Mackay. The first was the clamant need for a much larger, purpose-built school. The roll kept increasing, but many suitable applicants had to be turned away because the premises in Plaza Francia were bursting at the seams. These consisted of a large two-storey house, constructed round a central patio, but never intended as a school. Some of the rooms were rented to other tenants, and in any case the owner had made clear that when the second five-year lease expired in 1929 he would not renew it. Another large enough building could not be found in the whole of Lima.

More and more convinced of the unique value of the School to Peruvian national life and to the missionary cause, Renwick bombarded the home Committee with persuasive reasons for investing in a new building. The annual rent being paid by the home Committee would be converted into interest on a loan. The School itself would increase its income through matriculating more pupils and would gradually pay back the debt. The possibility of the School's closure was being viewed with horror by academic circles in Lima. The Roman Catholic Church would be happy to see the demise of the Anglo-Peruano, and the Evangelical cause in Peru would be struck a severe blow. Heavy indemnities would have to be paid to Peruvian teachers if they lost their jobs, while foreign teachers could justifiably accuse the Church of not honouring their contracts.

The Free Church actually had the money necessary. In Foreign Missions capital there was £32,000, of which the Anglo-Peruano was requesting £20,000. Renwick succeeded in persuading the Committee, but only the General Assembly could authorise such a large capital expenditure. The 1928 Assembly sent the matter down to individual Presbyteries, who approved the project, but only by a slender majority. A movement of opposition within the Church, not merely to spending money on a building, but more particularly to the concept of a school as a valid missionary agency, shown by the alleged lack of spiritual results in the Anglo-Peruvian College, seemed to be gathering momentum. The stage was set for a warmly-fought debate in the 1929 Assembly. In Lima the missionary staff, united behind their Headmaster, waited on tenterhooks for the cable that would signal a new beginning or an ignominious end to all their efforts.

A later chapter will consider in detail the accusations levelled against the School, and assess their validity. Proposals at the Assembly to close down the School; to reduce it to Primary only; to transfer it to some other unnamed body; to form a Committee to study the matter and report to the next Assembly were all eventually defeated. The favourable cable was dispatched, and before the Assembly had ended its sittings, it heard the reply from Lima:

Most profoundly thankful. Renwick.

The site chosen was considered to be on the outskirts of Lima proper, though within reasonable walking distance of the city centre. It cost £5,500, and for the remarkably low figure of £15,000 a solid structure able to cope with up to 450 pupils was erected. To those who know the building today, hemmed in on every side, suffering the unceasing roar of Lima traffic as it spews out its noxious fumes, and striving in cramped premises to cater for 830 pupils, the contemporary descriptions have an ironic sound − "surrounded by beautiful parks and gardens"; "one of the healthiest, most attractive parts of Lima"; "the pupils breathe in the pure air away from the city centre". Certainly the staff and pupils who moved there at the end of March, 1930 were "most profoundly thankful" for the facilities at their disposal, though it would not be long before they sang again the sad litany that Colegio San Andrés has sung from its inception to the present day − lack of adequate space to function properly.

However, March 1930 was a time for celebration. Nothing could have spoken more eloquently of the School's high standing in Peru's national life than the composition of the platform party at the opening ceremony. The chief guest of honour was Augusto B. Leguía, President of the Republic. At his side were the Prime Minister and the Minister of Education. Also prominent was the British Ambassador, Sir Charles Bentinck, while various other notable personalities from the British community and Peruvian educational and political circles mingled in the audience.

Not all present were aware that behind the choice of date, Saturday 22 March, there lay a stand for Christian principle on the part of the School's Headmaster. President Leguía was the very man who some months previously had signed the decree making Roman Catholic religious teaching compulsory in every school in the Republic. In spite of this he warmly agreed to perform the opening ceremony for a Protestant school which was regularly denounced from Catholic pulpits in the city. But his agreeing to do so presented Renwick with a problem:

> There followed for us, a most embarrassing situation. In Latin America, Sabbath observance, as we know it, is virtually unknown. Even missionaries of the best type travel on the Lord's Day, hold receptions, and do many things entirely foreign to the atmosphere of the old religious order in Scotland. This is one of the difficulties the real Free Church missionary

is up against, and in regard to Sabbath observance he finds himself in a very isolated position indeed.

Renwick's dilemma stemmed from the President's choosing Sunday 23 March for his visit to the School, indicating that his public engagements made any other day well-nigh impossible:

> Would it seem churlish to suggest to the President the undesirability of coming that day? On the other hand, what was our duty to the King of kings?

Using the good offices of the British Ambassador, Renwick requested a change of date, and was greatly relieved when the President agreed to it, commenting to a friend that "Sabbath observance was a very respectable article of faith when sincere." The missionaries' stand for the permanent validity of the Fourth Commandment had been vindicated.

With the new building and the enhanced prestige of the institution, demand for places increased rapidly. Soon the two small patios proved hopelessly inadequate for the boys' recreational needs, and Renwick launched an appeal to buy adjoining land for a small playground. He didn't dare approach the Foreign Missions Committee for money, but received their permission to seek donations in Scotland, Peru or wherever else he might hope to find them. The Committee members, in fact, showed their confidence in him and the work of the School by dipping into their own pockets and heading the donation list with the not inconsiderable sum of £306.3s.6d. Eventually the most generous donor proved to be a leading Edinburgh elder and businessman, Walter Sinclair, and to this day the school playground bears the name, "Campo Sinclair". Throughout the thirties additional classrooms were built on the first floor, paid for by the School's own income, and when Renwick left at the end of 1942 the school roll had risen to 653.

Staffing problems

The second matter that Renwick constantly brought to the home Committee's attention was the need for committed

Christian teachers. His initial survey, written only four days after his arrival in Lima in March 1926, contained the words:

> I have been greatly impressed to find the eagerness with which more British teachers are looked for. I want to emphasise as strongly as I can that the effectiveness of the School will be enormously increased when we get more teachers from home.

In nearly every annual Report Renwick explained to the home Church the situation with regard to Peruvian teachers, especially in Secondary. With few exceptions they were part-time, gifted academically, but limiting their participation in school life to teaching their subjects in the classroom. They might be lawyers, doctors, engineers, even Members of Parliament, who enjoyed a few hours teaching every week and were glad to increase their income. Renwick tells of one teacher appointed in 1932 Secretary to the Rector of the University who preferred at personal sacrifice to continue teaching in the School, because "it gives a man moral standing in the community to be on the staff of the Anglo-Peruano." Another, a University Professor, was promoted to the position of Judge, "but still continues his class in the School just for the love of it." Such men, however gifted, were of no help in the general running of the School, the maintenance of discipline outside their classrooms or extra-mural activities. And although most were merely nominal Catholics and some were very sympathetic to the Protestant position, they were unable to promote actively the Evangelical faith that lay at the heart of the School's whole existence. Full-time qualified teachers, converted to faith in Christ, were actively sought, but in those early days of the Evangelical Church in Peru, they were rare indeed.

Hence Renwick's pleas, echoing Mackay, and reiterated by Rycroft on the two occasions he served as Acting Head. In 1927 Renwick wrote:

> Our great want during the year has been more British teachers. Appeal after appeal has been made during the year, but with most disappointing results.

In 1930 he stated:

The Church has made great sacrifices for the Colegio Anglo-Peruano. Are these sacrifices to be nullified through lack of men and women of the right kind to permeate the institution with our ideals? ... I honestly believe the greatest danger facing the school in the coming years will not be Romish aggression so much as the failure to secure suitable Free Church men and women worthily to maintain what we stand for.

Sometimes Peruvian Government restrictions on the number of foreign teachers allowed in schools muted the appeals for teachers from home, but as often as not the restrictions were eased after a year or two. The most piteous pleas came at a time when the home Church could do little to help, during the Second World War. In 1941 Dr Renwick wrote: "During 1941 Mr Neil A.R. Mackay was the only missionary teacher along with me on the staff." He describes as "a stunning blow" the fact that war regulations had prevented one new teacher from joining the staff, and were rendering difficult the return of another after furlough.

Some missionary staff did, however, arrive during Renwick's headmastership. In 1926 John A. Mackay made contact with Miss Flora MacLullich, a native of Argyll, who was working in Buenos Aires as a private teacher. He recommended her to Mr Renwick, and she arrived in March 1927 to begin several years of full-time teaching in the Anglo. Her marriage to Mr Tom Graham, a well-known member of the local British community, interrupted her teaching career, but years later she returned to give valuable part-time help in the English and Religious Education departments. Two other young ladies were sent out as Free Church missionaries — Miss Isabella More, a Maths graduate from Burghead, who gave five greatly appreciated years to the School, but was unable to return to Peru for family reasons; and Miss Joanna Miller from Lybster in Caithness, whose teaching was characterised by great affection for her Primary pupils, and who eventually during her second term of service, resigned from the School, dedicating herself to helping pupils in a private capacity.

The Free Church of Scotland continued unable, however, to provide male teachers, obviously so essential in a boys' school. But once again New Zealand came to the rescue in the person of Herbert Money, a highly talented member of the Baptist

66

Church and well qualified in the field of education. Arriving in 1927, he spent two five-year periods in the Anglo-Peruano, and still alive in 1993, never tires of saying that he could not have found a better place to serve his missionary apprenticeship. On leaving the School, he went on to play a key role in the development of the Peruvian Evangelical Church, the Peruvian Bible Institute and, as its first General Secretary, the National Evangelical Council of Peru.

The Headmaster's Reports to the Missions Committee, constant references to his activities in the school magazine, and the recollections of former pupils, all demonstrate that Herbert Money played a crucial role in the period of consolidation following on John A. Mackay's pioneering efforts. A towering personality, nicknamed *Siete Pisos* by the boys (the tallest building then in Lima was seven storeys high, and Money was the tallest teacher in the School), he threw himself wholeheartedly into the life of the institution. Particularly popular were the many outings he organised, not only on Saturdays and public holidays (of which there were many in honour of the Catholic Church's myriad saints, but in grave detriment to the national economy), but also during the school holidays to the remote mountains and jungles. For most Lima youngsters, Peru meant Lima, and Money opened their eyes to the great beauty and enormous potential of Lima's vast hinterland. The highly significant work he and his wife carried on in the Sunday School of the Anglo-Peruano will be referred to in a later chapter.

The failure to secure Free Churchmen from Scotland was not due to inertia on the part of the Committee. In 1930 they published "a stirring appeal to the young men and women of the Free Church who are in the teaching profession ... There can be no doubt that in the Free Church herself there is ample material on which to draw for all the demands of the enterprise, if only the call of the Lord of the harvest made itself felt in the hearts of her educated youth." In spite of this, the Convener had to confess to the 1933 General Assembly that "they had failed to find a single man to go out particularly to the Lima College where the need was greatest ... It seemed to him that that was a standing reproach to the Free Church."

Some of the Committee members had an intelligent, practical and prayerful interest in Foreign Missions. But they were battling against an ecclesiastical system which was hopelessly inadequate for supervising and promoting missionary work that had branched out to three continents — Asia, Africa and America — in addition to a Jewish Missions enterprise and Free Church congregations in Canada. They normally met about five times a year, and even then for only part of a day, since the same people functioned as members of other Committees appointed by the General Assembly. Many of the Committee members began their stint profoundly ignorant of the realities of cross-cultural mission, but however strenuous their efforts to familiarise themselves with the work, they usually served for only three or four years, when others, equally ignorant, took their place. Apart from a minutes secretary, there was no one to maintain regular correspondence with the missionaries, other than the Convener. Some Conveners, in the midst of busy pastorates, made heroic efforts in this regard, but it is little wonder that missionaries on the field felt constant frustration at the long delays involved in answering correspondence and dealing with vital issues.

With respect to the recruitment of Free Church missionaries, the Committee relied mainly on advertisements in *The Monthly Record* with its limited circulation, and the personal attempts of a small number of concerned ministers to interest teachers of their acquaintance. The idea of a Missions Secretary, one of whose tasks would be to inform and enthuse home congregations, and make personal contact with potential missionaries, was initially not thought of; from the forties to the nineties it was regularly proposed but equally regularly rejected "because it would cost too much".

During the twenties and thirties occasional advertisements were placed in interdenominational and educational journals. These led to two missionary teachers being sent to the Free Church primary school in Cajamarca, but most applicants for the Anglo-Peruano proved unsuitable. For example, one teacher from Belfast showed by his answers that he was "unsound on the question of the plenary inspiration of the Scripture". Another, from the island of Mull, withdrew his application on the grounds that he only wanted to be a teacher,

68

not a missionary. A Free Church teacher from Lochgilphead applied, but later withdrew, indicating that on reflection he felt unable to adhere to the doctrinal position required by the Free Church, namely a sincere acceptance of the doctrine contained in the Westminster Shorter Catechism and a belief in the full inspiration of the Bible.

A similar situation arose with a young Free Church teacher from the island of Arran, who had originally intended studying for the ministry, but then felt a vocation for teaching. He applied to the Committee, was accepted, and the Report to the 1932 General Assembly informed of his impending departure. However, just before the Assembly he contacted the Committee, saying that he had scruples with respect to some articles of Reformed theology. According to his minister, he was "honest and sincere, and his doubts mainly philosophical". A lengthy and very sympathetic interview with a specially appointed sub-committee, which included an offer that he study for a year in the Free Church College in Edinburgh, failed to satisfy either himself or the Committee as to the soundness of his doctrinal views. "The Committee were regretfully compelled to accept his decision, recognising that in his present state of mind it would be impossible for them to accept him as a missionary teacher of the Free Church."

Yet another case led to a division of opinion in the Committee, and a lengthy debate in the 1934 General Assembly. Since a fundamental principle with respect to Christian missionary schools was involved, the incident is deeply interesting and highly relevant. In response to the Committee's advertisements, an Honours graduate from Glasgow University with a teaching qualification and some teaching experience offered to go to Lima. He was personally known to Dr Renwick, who was ready to have him on the school staff. The Committee were greatly impressed with his character and his understanding of the Free Church's Evangelical convictions.

The sticking-point was this: he was not a communicant member of the Church. Now it was well-known that within the Free Church many people had, and still have, so exalted a view of the qualifications necessary for church membership that some sincere Christian people spent their entire lives as loyal adherents without ever coming to the Lord's Table. Both

69

in the Committee and at the Assembly some members claimed that, recognising this, the applicant should be received and go out as a teacher on probation, a course he was willing to adopt.

This, however, did not satisfy some Committee members, whose views were expressed in the following terms by the Convener:

> The applicant is not able to say, and frankly declines to say, that he is a personal believer in the Lord Jesus Christ. He accepts the whole doctrine of the Free Church, he is willing to subscribe to all her standards, but he is not prepared to say that he has had a personal experience of the grace of God. So he was asked in the Committee a straight question — whether in addition to seeking to find in the Lima College a sphere for his professional aspirations he was also to any extent conscious of a missionary urge. He honestly said that he was going out simply as a teacher. So what the minority in the Committee feel is this — our College in Lima is first of all a missionary college: can we therefore expect the blessing of God to rest on that institution if, with our eyes open, we deliberately send out as a member of its staff a man who is not able to say that he is a believer in the Lord Jesus Christ in the distinctive sense of that word?

Because of their divided views, the Committee brought the matter to the Assembly. Some speakers pointed out that if the person concerned made his own way to Lima and offered his services to the Headmaster, he could without difficulty be accepted on local contract. All Assembly members knew that most of the Peruvian teachers were nominal Catholics, to all appearances unconverted. Would a well-taught Protestant, in total sympathy with the Free Church, not be far better? However, the Edinburgh elder who moved the amendment disapproving of the appointment, was unwilling to accept such arguments. While commending the applicant's academic qualifications, moral standing and teaching experience, and also his "perfect frankness and honesty" in his interview with the Committee, he said there was a profound objection to his being sent to the Church's missionary school:

> He was asked if he felt any urge towards missionary work in the cause of Christ, and the answer he gave was, No. Asked

why he was offering himself he said it was to earn his live-lihood. Is that the kind of man we want to select as a missionary to aid in bringing the Peruvians to Christ? If the Church is going to send out missionaries, it should send out men who are not merely teachers but men who have the missionary spirit in their hearts.

The Assembly's decision to reject the applicant, who went on to a distinguished career as a teacher and author in Scotland, was no easy one. Both he and his family were highly regarded in the Church; the Headmaster was pleading for teachers and was very willing to receive him, having known him from childhood; he was ideally suited academically, and was the first male teacher from Scotland in the seventeen years of the School's existence. But it was undoubtedly the right decision. If an Anglo-Peruano pupil, awakened to spiritual concern through what he heard in the School, were to ask a missionary teacher, "Sir, what must I do to be saved?" should he not expect to receive a clear answer, born of personal experience of faith in Christ? Would the finest teaching of English ever compensate for darkness in the soul? At its 1934 General Assembly the Free Church of Scotland proclaimed loud and clear that every teacher it would ever send to any of its missionary schools must first and foremost know God's grace in his or her own soul. That has limited the options for Colegio San Andrés, but has preserved it as a clear witness for Gospel truth.

Significantly the next issue of *The Monthly Record* was able to report, after commenting on the loss of a prospective teacher: "Yet such is the Divine resourcefulness that, when the Committee met on the day after the rising of the Assembly, they had before them offers from two men teachers who, after interview, were found to be suitable in many respects." One of these, Neil A.R. Mackay, was to sail with his wife to Lima in 1935 and will figure prominently in a later chapter.

The search for teachers went on, though during the late thirties the expanding Free Church missionary work was not matched by a large enough increase in income. The Committee overspent its budget for several years, and, urged as it was by the General Assembly to trim its expenses, had to postpone acceptance of some suitable applicants for both

India and Peru. At least one of these was a teacher for Lima, who after a long period of waiting, withdrew her application. But early in 1939 a welcome offer was received from Mr Sam Will, a native of Dundee, at that time teaching Science in Lairg Secondary School in Sutherland. The Committee were satisfied with his suitability, the Headmaster was delighted at the prospect of his arrival, but then Adolf Hitler intervened. In August 1939 Mr Will informed the Committee that he expected to be called up for military service. Since nothing happened for several months he did a brief theological course at the Free Church College, while the Committee made every effort to have him exempted from war service. They enlisted the support of the British Ambassador in Lima on the grounds that an active British presence would help counteract Axis influence there. They received the backing of the International Missionary Council, whose world-famous Secretary, Dr John R. Mott, presented the case to the British Ambassador in Washington. They suceeded in winning over the Foreign Secretary who communicated his willingness to recommend "to the War Office for Mr Will's release upon the receipt of a categorical assurance that there is to their knowledge no-one unfit for military service or over military age available in this country with sufficient qualifications to substitute Mr Will." This categorical assurance was given, but in a war situation the Foreign Office could not prevail against the War Office. They suggested the Ministry of Labour and National Service might have more success. They too expressed their willingness to forego Mr Will's services, but war was war. Churchill needed every available man to smash Hitler and his allies, so late in 1942 Sam Will gave up his temporary teaching post and marched away to battle. Five more years were to elapse before he finally set foot on Peruvian soil.

Glimpses into School Life

In 1926 Stanley Rycroft founded *Leader*, the school magazine, a concept well-known in his native England, but a "first" for Peruvian schools. Leafing through the early issues provides some fascinating insights into the general spirit and varied activities of the Anglo-Peruano.

In 1927 the School won first place in the national inter-schools shooting competition, this being the first time that a private school had ever won the trophy. In 1928 an Anglo-Peruano pupil won the individual championship, and his photograph still adorns the school walls.

In 1930 sixteen Anglo pupils sat University entrance exams. Although sixty per cent of all applicants failed the examination, fifteen of the Anglo boys were successful. In the vastly changed circumstances of today, when applicants number hundreds of thousands and Lima boasts dozens of universities, it is still one of the characteristics of Colegio San Andrés that its pupils are well represented on the list of accepted students.

That human nature doesn't change is obvious from *Leader*'s 1932 campaign "to uproot certain vices and habits from the School." The references are to dirty, untidy classrooms, to graffiti on the blackboards, to the vandalising of desks, blackboards and toilets, and to rude and anti-hygienic behaviour. The last reference is not spelt out, but doubtless refers to spitting, rarely viewed in Peru as a practice worthy of censure.

That same year *Leader* reported in detail on a visit over several days of a Mexican educator, Dr Gonzalo Baez-Camargo, who was returning home from an International Sunday School Convention in Brazil (and who was to forge another link with the School years later as the translator into Spanish of Dr John A. Mackay's most celebrated book, *The Other Spanish Christ*). He gave a series of talks to Secondary pupils, both in the morning assembly and to smaller groups, on sexual matters, dealing sympathetically with sexual temptations and placing the whole subject in a firmly Christian framework.

In 1933 there is a lengthy tribute to the retiring British Ambassador, Sir Charles Bentinck, who had proved himself a loyal supporter of the School in times of crisis. A former pupil whose name was the first to be engraved on the "Bentinck Shield" in 1929, and who was already making a name for himself in the field of journalism, tells of the standing his achievement gave him in University and in his chosen profession. "They would say I was the man who had won the Bentinck Prize in the Anglo, and that made me feel I had grown several centimetres intellectually." He doesn't say whether he had carefully read his prize — a leather-bound edition of the *Poetical Works of Sir Walter Scott.*

The 1935 issue tells of the introduction of the House system, another initiative of Stanley Rycroft. After hearing of the virtues of the system in promoting healthy competition in sporting and academic activities, the boys professed themselves enthusiastically in favour of its adoption, and were asked to choose names for the four houses. No-one now remembers why the particular names were selected, but the Scottish influence was obvious — Douglas, Macgregor, Mackay and Stuart. Even the casual visitor to the School today cannot fail to notice the four large clan crests in mosaic along the walls of the main corridor, a striking project of the Art Department.

Whether the Headmaster decided to cash in on the evident pro-Scottish sentiment among the boys, *Leader* doesn't say. But it does go on to report that a large stock of MacKenzie tartan ties had arrived from Edinburgh and were being enthusiastically bought by most pupils and teachers as part of the Anglo uniform. The enthusiasm, however, seems to have been short-lived, for no former pupil of the period appears to remember anything about wearing tartan ties. And does every Scot feel comfortable wearing a tartan tie?

Dr Alexander Renwick's achievements merit several references. In 1931 there is an account of his academic defence of his doctoral thesis on *The Influence of Altitude on Peruvian Beliefs*. According to Peruvian University tradition, the examiners could also engage the candidate in discussion on other academic topics, and the report indicates that he was asked to deal with the role played by Masonic lodges in the Emancipation of South America. He is said to have displayed "vast historical knowledge" of the subject, but that was doubtless not one of the academic achievements that was used to commend him to the General Assembly when in 1943 it appointed him to the Chair of Church History and Principles in the Free Church College in Edinburgh. *Leader* also reviews on two occasions Renwick's book, *Wanderings in the Peruvian Andes*, published in 1939, though no Spanish edition ever appeared. What both reviewers comment favourably on is the deep affection for Peru and her people that shines through its pages. They express their displeasure at the negative image that Peru often received in the foreign press, and warmly welcome Renwick's book as a valuable counter-balance to the adverse criticism of others.

Homage to a National Hero

In 1929 an interesting article appeared in *Leader*, written by Stanley Rycroft, the Deputy Head. Every Peruvian child knows the story of Jorge Chávez, the Peruvian aviator who in 1910 was the first person to fly across the Alps. Sadly his plane crashed on landing and he died a few days later. Rycroft tells of how one month earlier as a child of eleven he had attended an air display in Blackpool, when a Frenchman by the name of Chavez had beaten the existing altitude record. Little did he think that a few years later he himself would be a war pilot, eventually shot down and injured. Even less did it occur to him that one day he would be a missionary teacher in the daring pilot's homeland − not France where "Monsieur Chavez" was born and bred, but Peru, the land of his parents which he proudly acknowledged as his own.

But there was something else that Rycroft didn't know when he wrote his article. One of his Fourth Year Secondary pupils was Alfredo Salazar, an excellent student, keen on sport and a regular attender at the Colegio Sunday School. The following year his name was to figure as the best Secondary pupil on the Bentinck Shield at the end of the first session in the new school building. On leaving school he began engineering studies, but on the outbreak of a border conflict with Ecuador, volunteered to join the Peruvian Air Force. Stirred by flying, he decided to make it his career, and rose rapidly to become, at the age of 24, an Aviation instructor.

In September 1937 the city of Lima was due to inaugurate a monument in memory of Jorge Chávez, with air squadrons from various foreign countries invited to take part. The previous day, 14 September, Salazar with a trainee pilot was conducting a practice flight over the suburb of Miraflores. Inexplicably the engine burst into flames. Both pilots were equipped with parachutes, and Salazar ordered Fajardo to jump clear. He himself could see the densely populated suburb below him, and refused to abandon his plane. The last sight

Fajardo had of him — as he has recounted on several occasions in Colegio San Andrés — was battling heroically with the controls, flames lapping his hands and face, in an endeavour to steer the plane out to sea. On waste land not far from the shore he eventually crashed, the only loss of life being his own.

It was highly appropriate that the former pilot, Stanley Rycroft, as Acting Headmaster, should lead the School delegation at the funeral. Salazar was given posthumously the official title of *Héroe Nacional*, and every year on 14 September the pupils and staff of Colegio San Andrés commemorate his action, both in the school and at the condor-shaped Salazar monument in the Miraflores suburb on whose behalf he offered the supreme sacrifice. On such occasions it is not difficult to remind those present that while "greater love has no-one than this, that one lay down his life for his friends", there is One who "demonstrates his own love for us in this: while we were still sinners Christ died for us."

After seventeen years the second Headmaster took his leave at the end of 1942. As a contribution to the war effort, he agreed to a request that he assume the directorship of the British Council in Chile. To the Free Church home Committee he wrote:

> Seventeen years ago you laid upon my shoulders as heavy a task as has ever been laid upon any minister of the Church. I have now discharged my trust ... and I can see no reason why Colegio San Andrés should not go on growing and prospering.

Dark war clouds hung over Britain, casting their shadow over many other nations. In three years the School had lost its Director and Sub-Director, both of them men of great experience in the work. No reinforcements could be expected from Europe, so what future lay ahead for Colegio San Andrés? Could Renwick's optimism possibly be justified?

6

Needing Support

Sirens sounded and bombs rained down from the skies near Spain. Two of the three British boats being escorted in convoy by destoyers and airships went up in flames, successfully hit by the deadly marksmanship of high-level German bombers. The third boat picked up most of the survivors, and the journey continued. Not for long, however, since the next evening the Nazi planes returned to the attack. Bombs landed all around the ship, one scoring a direct hit and setting the vessel on fire. Just when crew and passengers alike were convinced they would end up at the bottom of the sea, the enemy planes flew off, their bomb supply exhausted. One of the destroyers took the passengers and survivors from the previous night on board, and with its pumps managed to extinguish the flames.

A far cry from the Anglo-Peruvian College in Lima. So it would seem except that Christina Mackay, who had already braved the terrors of the Atlantic on returning from Peru in 1941, was a passenger on the third boat. Engaged in war work in Britain, she had responded to the heartfelt pleas of her Lima colleagues, and launched out into the dangerous deep.

Steaming eastward, the convoy reached Casablanca, where Christina Mackay was the guest of the American forces for the weeks it took for the wounded ship to be repaired. Then it was back to dodging U-boats and bombers till thankfully docking in Buenos Aires. A tiring, dusty three days on a train to La Paz with its enervating altitude, a safer boat trip across Lake Titicaca, another train half-way down the Andes to Arequipa, and missionary friends from the Colegio Internacional provided just the rest needed till a plane seat was available for Lima. As Dr and Mrs Neil Mackay and other friends waited at the airport, they must have wondered if the doughty traveller would really arrive, but exactly four months from the day she left England, she set foot again on Peruvian soil at her final destination.

On her return to Lima, Christina Mackay found the school operating under a new name and with a new Headmaster. The change of name, by Government order, had been reluctantly accepted by staff, pupils and parents. Former pupils felt particularly aggrieved, and years later when the Government prohibition on names with a foreign connection no longer applied, the Old Boys' Association requested the School to consider reverting to the old title. By then, however, the new name, Colegio San Andrés, had become well-known, and it was agreed to continue with the practice of referring to the school as Colegio San Andrés (formerly Anglo-Peruano). Dr Renwick's predilection for Celtic historical roots probably led to the choice of St Andrew's College as the new name, even though the concept of Presbyterian Scotland having a patron saint sits uneasily with the theology taught in the Free Church College. As it happened, the Ministry of Education officials who appeared at the School in the last few weeks of 1941 demanded immediate compliance with this and some other Government regulations, leaving the Headmaster little time to reflect calmly or consult widely.

Much more significant was the change of Headmaster. At the height of the War it would have been a herculean task for the Foreign Missions Committee to find a suitable person in Scotland. Fortunately they didn't need to, since the ideal candidate lay to hand in Lima itself. Neil A. R. Mackay had been on the staff since 1935, and because of the War was to remain there for ten and a half years before visiting the homeland. An Arts and Commerce graduate from Edinburgh University, with a further First Class Honours degree from London, Neil Mackay's tenure as Director added lustre to the institution on a par with that it had received from John A. Mackay. A tribute written on his death in 1987 by the Editor of *The Monthly Record* describes him as "a genuine polymath who would have qualified as a specialist in a wide range of disciplines: metaphysics, psychology, educational theory, Scots law, Gaelic, History, Hispanic Studies, Latin American Studies." For a time in Lima he occupied the Chair of English Literature in San Marcos University; on the other hand, a former San

Andrés teacher remembers with great appreciation the practical classes he gave teachers in the school laboratory on how to improve the teaching of Science to their Primary pupils. Following the remarkable pattern set by John A. Mackay, Browne, Renwick, Rycroft and Money, Neil Mackay also gained a doctorate from San Marcos University "with the unanimous high approbation of the Faculty", his subject being the philosophy of A. N. Whitehead. Though he himself would have discounted the comparison, his fluent mastery of Spanish equalled John A. Mackay's, and his subsequent career shows how, like his predecessor, he moved with ease in the company of leading Latin American intellectuals, for example, Jorge Luis Borges, the visionary Argentinian poet.

In Lima Mackay became a recognised authority on educational theory and practice. In his annual Report for 1944 he analyses the Peruvian system of education, pointing out some of its worst defects, and almost in passing goes on to say:

> I had the opportunity during the last year of broadcasting several talks on the suggested reforms in British education, and as a result, I have had many discussions with different people on the possibility of applying such ideas to Peru ... The Ministry of Education has called a conference of headmasters of State schools to discuss possible reforms in Secondary Education, and their interest in what is being done elsewhere is shown by the fact that the Director of General Education has asked me to draw up, for use at the Conference, a summary of the Norwood Report and other relevant documents.

In a discussion on Peruvian school textbooks and the poor quality of most of them — he describes the average compiler of Secondary programmes of study on which the text-books were based as being "more interested in exhibiting his own knowledge than in devising a course which would interest a schoolboy" — Mackay mentions the prospective arrival of a representative of the Oxford University Press who was visiting Latin American countries in order to choose a publishing centre. No other Headmaster in Lima at the time would have been able both to grasp the issues involved and to succeed in having an immediate interview with the Minister of Education when he "urged him to do all in his power to persuade the

Oxford Press to select Lima for their venture. He immediately grasped the significance of the proposal, and he certainly gave powerful support in the attempt to convince the delegate who, I may add, went away quite impressed."

As one reads Neil Mackay's painstaking Reports for 1943 and 1944 with their wide-ranging and acute observations on educational practice, missionary policy and spiritual aspirations, one cannot be other than deeply disappointed that "the second of a series" proved to be the last. He left Peru in the middle of the 1945 school session, and was only able to provide the Committee with a "fragment of a report" for that year. In 1946 he resigned his post for personal reasons, and began a distinguished career with the British Council in Bogotá, London, Edinburgh and Buenos Aires.

Also new to the School when Christina Mackay returned was Murdo Nicolson, a Free Church minister from Raasay, Skye, who had spent several years as a missionary in Cajamarca. He had gained a considerable reputation there on account of the speed with which he mastered Spanish and preached it with great eloquence. His metrical versions of Psalms in Spanish proved acceptable in Presbyterian congregations, though their being wedded to traditional Scottish tunes meant their eventual replacement by others sung in Latin American rhythm. His other venture into print, *El Divino Pastor* (The Heavenly Shepherd) was a series of ten studies on the twenty-third Psalm, described in the following terms by Dr Wálter Montaño, a converted priest and prolific writer on religious subjects:

> Murdo Nicolson, the young Scot who has accommodated himself so well to the land of the Incas, who has dedicated himself with such sincerity to the evangelisation of our brothers in race and speech, who has achieved such ease and fluency in the language of Cervantes, who has entered with such understanding into the customs and life of our people, gives us this magnificent work ... The publication of this work meets a need and is typical of the positive contribution made by an able, intelligent and spiritually minded missionary.

No wonder that Dr. Renwick, while regretting the health problem of one of the Nicolson children, occasioned by the high altitude of the Andes, which necessitated a removal to the coast, welcomed such a competent addition to his staff in 1942! Nicolson took over responsibility for Religious Education and the Sunday services now held regularly in the School, and cooperated fully in the morning assemblies and Sunday School. When his son's health compelled the family to travel to Canada in 1944, Neil Mackay felt the loss keenly, and paid unstinting tribute to Nicolson's hard work and "unfailing good humour".

When Murdo Nicolson left, Neil Mackay and Christina Mackay were the only missionary teachers in the School. Mackay's reports commend his Peruvian colleagues, especially some of the Primary teachers who, being full-time and also active Evangelicals, were able to exercise a vitally formative influence on the children under their care. There was Sra Fonseca, already on the staff of the Diego Thomson School in 1916, and who acted as titular head of the Anglo-Peruano until John A. Mackay could get the necessary licence. Along with her were her niece, Srta Zoraida Baca, and two former pupils of the Free Church school in Cajamarca, Srta Mélida Velásquez and Sra Esperanza Zúñiga (née Rojas). Esperanza Rojas had lived in Scotland for a time with Rev and Mrs Calvin Mackay, and was now married to Sr Ignacio Zúñiga, a leading member of the Peruvian Evangelical Church. She was to go on and complete an astounding record of just under fifty years teaching in Colegio San Andrés. When her final illness in 1987 required her admission to the large Social Security Hospital in Lima, her husband was amazed at the stream of doctors who came to visit and attend to her, all of them former pupils of hers in Colegio San Andrés.

In the Secondary department Mackay battled with the same problem that plagued his predecessors and successors — part-time teaching by men whose intellectual abilities were beyond dispute, but whose contribution to school life outside the narrow confines of their own subjects in their own classrooms was minimal. In 1945 Mackay wrote:

> Anyone who knows anything about real education will accept as a basic principle that it extends far beyond the bounds of routine lessons and that its purpose is, even in the secular realm, to provide "the nurture and the environment" which will enable the child to grow aright and to grow eventually to full stature, to bring to full flowering the varying potentialities,

81

physical, spiritual and intellectual of which he is capable as an individual and member of society. Surely then this is the stage at which education and "missionary work" meet and mingle. If part of the former's task — its most important part — is the formation of character and the building up of an integrated outlook on life, where can we begin except with the Word of God and the integration of life in our Lord and Saviour?

For such a task part-time lecturers were totally inadequate. One full-time Peruvian Evangelical teacher had been giving invaluable support since 1940 in the Secondary department, though even he had to rush away each day as soon as classes ended to begin teaching in a State night school. It was — and is — a sad commentary on the low status given to teaching as a profession in Peru that no family man could hope to make ends meet unless he worked excessively long hours or his wife brought in an additional salary. The teacher in question was Aladino Escalante, converted to faith in Christ through the pioneer missionary work in isolated Andean villages of Rev Calvin Mackay. After completing his Secondary education in the Anglo-Peruano, Escalante studied Arts in Edinburgh University, Divinity in the Free Church College, and Spanish Literature in Madrid. On his return to Peru he worked first as supervisor of State schools in his native department of Cajamarca, and then made his way to Lima where he resumed his lifelong connection with Colegio San Andrés. Aladino Escalante loved Scotland and all things Scottish. His flawless English was spoken with a Scottish accent, and in his cultured home he and his wife, Cristina, lavished generous hospitality on successive generations of Free Church of Scotland missionaries until his sudden death in 1977. Ordained an elder of the San Andrés Presbyterian congregation, he never swerved from his commitment to Christ, taking up the task begun by Murdo Nicolson of rendering Spanish psalms into metrical form. He ensured himself an indelible place in the history of the School by composing the School Song:

> *Adelante, estudiantes del Anglo!*
> *A buscar la verdad presurosos*
> (Forward, Anglo students, eager in your search for truth!)

There were, however, no others like Escalante for Mackay to call on. As he put it in his 1944 Report: "There are Protestants and there are teachers in Peru, but with very few exceptions the Protestants are not teachers, and the teachers are not Protestants." He therefore decided on a policy of selecting former pupils who, even though not themselves Evangelicals, were sympathetic to the Evangelical position and also appreciated the valuable role of clubs, excursions and other extra-curricular activities in schoolboys' lives. Two of them, who attended an informal Bible Study group led by Dr Mackay, were José Paz and Wálter Peñaloza. They willingly accepted the tasks of reforming the teaching of Spanish in the school and serving as Housemasters, and Mackay was delighted with their work and their enthusiasm. But perhaps he chose too well, for not long after that Dr Paz was selected as Deputy Head of Markham College, the new British boys' school, and Dr Peñaloza went on to be Principal of a leading College of Education and subsequently Peruvian Ambassador to West Germany.

And so were heard the all-too-familiar pleas to the Home Committee. At the end of 1943 he wrote:

Let me stress our lack of missionary teachers ... We are now reduced to a minimum which could almost be described as dangerous, because if anything happened to any one of us, the strain on the others would be too great to be borne for long. I know that the times are not propitious for seeking recruits, but I would beg the Church to keep the Mission Field and its opportunities before the young men and women who are desirous of doing something in the Lord's cause. And let them not think that it is a thing of little account to which they are called. Here in Lima we require not only a sense of missionary call, which is, of course, indispensable, but also the best brains and the finest preparation that Scotland can give.

Later in the same Report he went on to say:

The fewer the missionary teachers available, the more they will be bound down to routine effort, and the less time they will have for the intimate, individual contact which is the key to successful expansion in the field of spiritual influence. We know that we are not alone, that there is One with us Who, if we be but faithful to Him, will be our Captain and our Comforter, and Who will ensure the victory of His Word. But it

is only human to look to sea, to scan the far horizon for the
ships who bear the eager ones and the strong who will turn our
long, defensive vigil into a glorious inrush into the kingdom of
the shadows where so many lie awaiting the Deliverer. But ...
the ships do not come.

And in his final brief Report, written in Scotland towards
the end of 1945, he felt constrained to return to the same
theme:

> While it is possible, by means of great exertions on the part of
> the very few missionaries in the Colegio, to keep it going as
> an institution, it cannot be expected to be a missionary effort
> commensurate with the opportunities provided until the staff is
> increased considerably.
> I cannot refrain from one closing reflection. The Free Church
> has a boys' school in Lima, and it must readily occur to anyone,
> even to the most uninterested person, that male teachers would
> be required for such an undertaking. The Colegio is now
> entering on its thirtieth year, and *in all those years not a single
> male certificated teacher has gone out from the Free Church.* It
> is difficult not to think this situation must be unique in the his-
> tory of denominational missions. In fact, when one considers
> it in conjunction with the poor response to repeated appeals for
> workers for other missionary fields, one wonders whether our
> Church is really cognisant of the situation. Increased givings,
> though comforting as an index of the people's interest, are not
> enough; prayer and action are also required if the Church is not
> to be held to account for the failure to take the Gospel message
> to hundreds of souls committed to her care.

Ethnic diversity

Since Peruvian independence, Lima has been a very cosmopolitan city. Today economic misery, unemployment on a huge
scale and terrorist violence are driving hundreds of thousands of
Peruvians to seek a better future in other countries, but it wasn't
always so. During the latter half of the nineteenth century and
the early decades of the twentieth, European, especially British,
and North American commercial interests brought many for-
eigners to Peru, some of whom decided to make the country
their home. Increasing numbers of Chinese and Japanese, many

of them very poor, escaped the overpopulation of their native countries to carve out a new life for themselves in a land of space and opportunity.

From its inception the Anglo-Peruano reflected the rich racial diversity to be found in Lima. Although from the outset the School made clear that it would not cater specifically for British children, the quality of its education, the lack of any alternative and its willingness to try and provide some special help for native English speakers, meant there was always a small number of British pupils, especially in Primary. In the early forties the proposal was seriously entertained that the Anglo would erect an additional building and run a parallel programme for native English speakers, and a small plot of land was actually bought beside the School. It was never really a practical proposition, however, especially in view of the fewness of the British teachers, and the British community, with ample funds at its disposal, went on to found Markham College. San Andrés gave the venture every encouragement, providing the Deputy Head in the person of Dr José Paz.

In his 1937 Report, Dr Renwick refers to "the general Italian renaissance under Mussolini" as a result of which "a magnificent new school, far bigger than ours" had been built. Up till then about 40 Secondary children from Italian homes studied in the Anglo-Peruano, adding to the School's racial variety. They were gradually withdrawn, though others were always glad to take their place.

Two ethnic groups stand out numerically and intellectually in the School's history. The rise of Naziism in Europe signalled a large influx of dispossessed Jews, and in his 1935 Report Renwick states: "Many lovers of Israel in our Church will be interested to know that in the past session we had no less than 50 Jewish children." In his 1938 Report he says: "I have always considered it a privilege to be able to do something for these children, descendants of God's ancient people. In these days when their people are persecuted in so many places, they seem deeply touched by the friendliness we show them." This very desire to help, however, created its own problems, and Renwick tells how he was unable to accept all Jews who sought admission, so as to avoid racial imbalance and possible tension within the school.

85

As with all other pupils, the School's Christian stance was clearly explained to the parents, and no exemption was granted from morning assemblies or religious education classes. This was readily accepted by the parents, who sensed the love shown towards them and their people, and also appreciated some concessions that were made, such as allowing their children to be absent for the main Jewish festivals. The School, in fact, provided facilities for the Jewish community to organise Hebrew classes for their boys in the Anglo. The School's willingness and the parents' enthusiasm were not matched, however, by an equal enthusiasm on the part of the boys. Poring over Hebrew roots couldn't compete with kicking a football or trips to the beach, and the classes soon fizzled out.

The 1943 statistics are an eloquent commentary on the bitter tragedy of Hitler's "final solution" to the Jewish problem. Out of 712 pupils, over 100 were Jewish, and Neil Mackay, like Renwick before him, was torn by the desire to help the Jewish community and the sober recognition that due to the huge influx of refugees "signs of anti-semitic feeling are not lacking." He reports:

> One boy changed over to our school during the year because of subtle but annoying persecution to which he was subjected in a priests' school. I have always to be on the look-out for racial, national or religious ill-feeling in such a mixed crowd of boys, but closest enquiries among pupils and parents have shown that anything said is confined to good-humoured banter. However, one must always be on the alert, for we cannot allow any form of persecution or spiteful treatment to make an appearance in the School.

It is not surprising that many Jewish pupils rewarded the School's concern for them by turning out to be brilliant students, and to this day prosperous and influential Jews in Peru and in other countries to which they may have emigrated retain great respect for Colegio San Andrés. One example was seen in 1989 when the President of Peru conferred the Order of Merit for distinguished service on Dr Benjamín Alhalel, whose studies in the field of haematology had won international acclaim. The Jewish community now has its own school, Colegio León Pinelo, in the founding and

86

Mission staff 1923 with Dr. John A. Mackay and family in the centre.

President Oscar Benavides handing over Inter-Schools shooting trophy to Dr. A. M. Renwick, 1936.

British Ambassador, Sir Charles Bentinck, speaking at inauguration of new Anglo-Peruvian College, 1930. President Augusto B. Leguía in centre, Dr. Stanley Rycroft on extreme left and Dr. Alexander Renwick second from left.

Anglo-Peruvian Sunday School, 1937.
Stanley Rycroft, Neil Mackay and Herbert Money on right of picture.

Inter-schools athletics championship in National Stadium, 1935.

Spectators at athletics championship: Stanley Rycroft and Alexander Renwick flank two Roman Catholic headmasters.

Neil Mackay with a group of senior boys, 1944.

William Mackay being congratulated by History teacher and researcher César Gutiérrez.

Elizabeth Mackenzie, San Andrés teacher since 1963.

Aladino Escalante (left) and Luis Torrejón, parents and teachers of Colegio San Andrés and founding members of the Evangelical Presbyterian Church.

Pedro Arana, Chairman of Colegio Advisory Board.

Sra Esperanza Zúñiga with Third Grade class.

Dr. José Vidal, Director till 1991.

Jorge Terrazas at Moray House graduation, 1987.

Future champions in National Stadium, 1975.

School (both buildings on left) hemmed in by traffic and street vendors.

Marcos Florit kicks off at outset 1992 Inter-House competition.

John MacPherson with former pupils Nelson Ayllón (left), minister of Cuzco Presbyterian Church and Finance Minister César Vásquez (centre).

running of which old boys of San Andrés have played a significant part.

Very few Jews who heard the Gospel in Colegio San Andrés have professed faith in Jesus as Messiah, but the seed of God's Word does not always bear immediate fruit. One Jewish former pupil, now resident in the United States, has recently been preaching in Lima under the auspices of the Christian and Missionary Alliance, but for the majority it is a case of respect without commitment. At a dinner in 1988, the "boys" of the 1948 class gathered to celebrate their fortieth anniversary, several Jews being among the company. In conversation with the Headmaster, John MacPherson, one of those who claimed to have been an atheist since his boyhood, told of an encounter with the then Headmaster, James Mackintosh. The Religion course in the final year included a section on Apologetics, and the termly examination asked the boys to assess the various "proofs" for the existence of God. This Jewish pupil not only criticised adversely the theistic proofs, but gave sturdy reasons for his own atheism. A day or two later he was called into the Headmaster's Office, fully expecting to be punished for his audacity and be given the lowest possible mark for his exam. Mackintosh told him that as a Christian he disagreed profoundly with most of what he had written, but to his surprise congratulated him for his careful study of the subject and well-thought-out arguments, and gave him a good pass mark. Though still professing in his late fifties to be an atheist, the successful Lima businessman spoke admiringly of the tolerance that had been shown him and the sincerity of the Christian principles maintained in Colegio San Andrés.

The other noteworthy ethnic group is the Oriental one, mainly Chinese but with considerable numbers also of Japanese. In 1943 " a group of Chinese boys have sought the help of their allies", transforming what were isolated individuals in the School into another racial bloc. Mackay reports that a handful of Chinese families professed Confucianism as their religion, but the vast majority were quite ready, for business and social reasons, to adopt the national religion, and become Roman Catholics, usually of a very nominal kind. The hostilities raging between China and Japan, and indeed between Britain and Japan, were not allowed to create racial disharmony in Colegio San Andrés, particularly since nearly all the pupils were born in Peru and had Peruvian nationality. As the number of Jews decreased, so the numbers of Chinese and Japanese rose steadily in the fifties and sixties, compelling the Headmaster to exercise caution once again in the admission policy lest the School be accused of undue favouritism or racial imbalance. Certainly not only the matriculation lists but the prize lists were full of Changs, Choys, Chus, Wongs and Maus, while the Land of the Rising Sun furnished its quota of Satos, Hashimotos, Namasakis, Kanashiros and so on. A leading Lima Chinese businessman has jokingly commented that in his schooldays in the early sixties, the School was popularly known as Colegio Chang Andlés! It was in that same period that the School once again showed its concern for refugees by allowing three young men who had escaped from Communist China and spoke no Spanish to matriculate in the final year and gain accelerated Peruvian qualifications. Since all three were excellent basketball players, San Andrés that year enjoyed unexpected success in the inter-schools basketball competition, only losing narrowly to the inevitable champions from Colegio Roosevelt, the American School of Lima.

Emergency assistance

During 1943 valuable assistance was given as Head of Primary by Mr Val Clear, a North American doing post graduate research in Lima. His wife gave secretarial help with English correspondence, and also taught English in Primary. Also of great support was Dr Manuel Garrido Aldama, a converted Spanish priest well-known as a preacher and broadcaster. It seemed as if the school would be tided over the war crisis, but in 1944 everything changed. Murdo Nicolson left for Canada, the Clears returned to the United States, and Manuel Aldama had to withdraw because of illness. Only Neil Mackay and Christina Mackay remained as missionary teachers, the former having been nine years on the job without a break. The home Committee were very aware of the problem, reporting to the 1945 Assembly that they had "had to seek the services of a minister immediately to take over Mr Nicolson's work in Lima and act as Director of the College when Dr Mackay left on furlough." No easy task! However they went on to inform the Assembly that "only one minister in the Church had all the necessary qualifications, and that man, Rev J. Calvin Mackay, wonderfully restored to health, cast aside all personal and selfish interests and, without hesitation, stepped into the breach."

Calvin Mackay's was an honoured name in the annals of Peruvian evangelisation. He had already spent time teaching in the School before pressing on, with his like-minded wife, Rachel, to Cajamarca, the northern Andean town which had in 1532 sealed the fate of the great Inca Empire. In the face of much clerical opposition, he succeeded in planting churches in the important towns of Cajamarca and Celendín and many surrounding villages. He became known as *el caballero cristiano* (the Christian gentleman), usually disarming by his courtesy even his most active opponents. On one occasion he reached Chachapoyas, capital of the department of Amazonas, and arranged to hold a service for interested people in the house where he had taken lodging. When news of this reached the ears of the Roman Catholic hierarchy, they stirred up some of the leading women to protest. Outside the house they demanded that the "heretic" leave immediately. Calvin Mackay, who always dressed impeccably, went out to see them, raised his hat in greeting, and assured them politely that he had no designs on their religion, but merely wished to speak about the plain message of the Gospel. He won their grudging acquiescence, though it was only several years later that an Evangelical congregation was established in Chachapoyas.

Throughout that whole area of northern Peru, evangelical believers became known as "the Mackays", primarily on account of Calvin Mackay's labours, but hardly surprisingly buttressed by there being various other Free Church missionaries who have either resided in or visited Cajamarca — John A. Mackay, Christina Mackay, Calvin Mackay's sister Catherine, Dr Kenneth Mackay from Moyobamba, Neil Mackay and Christine Mackay who served as a nurse in Cajamarca and Celendín. And none of them was related to any of the others.

In 1934 Calvin Mackay was thrown from a horse when visiting Moyobamba, and had to be invalided home. Recovery was slow, but eventually he was able to take on the pastorate of the small congregation of Ardgay, Ross-shire. While there in 1944 he heard the Church's call, and agreed to a temporary return to Lima. He and his wife arrived there in March 1945, which gave him a valuable settling-in time before Neil Mackay left in July. Not that the time was trouble-free. In May the Calvin Mackays were involved in a railway accident, which led to Mrs Mackay being hospitalised for ten weeks, and Mr Tom Graham having a leg amputated. Calvin Mackay himself was released from hospital after three weeks, and resumed his duties with a vigour similar to what he had displayed as a much younger man before his earlier accident.

In his first Annual Report he indicates that a room in the school had been attractively transformed to serve as a place of worship on Sundays and revert to being a classroom during the week. This was an attempt by Neil Mackay to follow up the spiritual contacts made by the School, and also to provide a place of worship in Lima for members of the Free Church congregations who emigrated from the provinces to Lima. Calvin Mackay echoed the wistful longings of most of his predecessors and other missionary teachers when he wrote:

> While the School is in crying need of more teachers from home, perhaps the outstanding requirement is an ordained minister to take charge of congregational work, as well as the religious instruction in the School, and to cooperate in many other ways for the advancement of the Lord's Kingdom.

Another eighteen years were to elapse before that dream would be fulfilled.

The resignation of Dr Neil Mackay must have been a great disappointment to Rev Calvin Mackay, and led him to wonder how long his spell as Acting Head would last. But he soldiered on, encouraged by the cooperation during 1946 of Rev Robert Marshburn, a graduate of Princeton Seminary and a former student there of Dr John A. Mackay. This was not the first time that help had reached the School from the United States. Back in 1924 the Methodist Episcopal Mission had closed its boys' school in Lima and transferred all its pupils to the Anglo-Peruano. Along with the boys there came a teacher, Dr Frank Stanger, seconded by the Methodist Mission and paid his salary by the School. During one of Mackay's absences as a YMCA lecturer, Stanger was Acting Head and his contribution was greatly valued by Mackay. When he left after two years, the Methodist Mission nominated Rev C. W. Brewster to take his place. With his usual eye for historical roots, Dr Renwick informed the home Board in his 1926 Report that this gentleman was a direct descendant in the tenth generation of Brewster, who was assistant pastor to the Pilgrim Fathers. Unfortunately his health failed and he had to be withdrawn after a few months, the arrangement with the Methodist Mission thereafter lapsing. Val Clear of the Church of Christ has already been mentioned, while in later years valuable part-time help was given by retired School Principal William Sommerville, a member of the Christian Brethren. In spite of conversations at different times with various Presbyterian churches in the United States, who have shown great interest in the possibility of short-term teaching help for Colegio San Andrés, no cooperation agreement has yet materialised.

A changing Peru

In an article in *The Monthly Record* in 1946 Mrs Rachel Mackay commented on the changing order as they saw it in Peru — "ladies driving the motor car, riding pillion and cycling; fathers taking up toddlers and carrying them around in their arms; men and women going hatless." In 1920, when they first taught in the school, one teacher who rarely wore a hat was considered so unusual that he was nicknamed *el sin sombrero* (the hatless one). But it was the political changes which resulted from the 1945 elections that seemed to give hope of democratic advance and new opportunities for Evangelicalism. A contributor to *The Monthly Record* wrote about the "amazing change that has taken place in the political life of the country", as a result of which it was no longer being "ruled by authoritarian governments closely in league with the Roman hierarchy." Haya de la Torre, former teacher of the Anglo, had been elected a Senator and was "by far the most influential leader in the country". The President of the Chamber of Deputies was another former teacher of the School, Dr Fernando León de Vivero, while the President of the Senate was Dr José Gálvez, scion of a famous Peruvian family, and "a staunch friend of our school, which he often visited and addressed the pupils in his own inimitable way." The anonymous writer (obviously Alexander Renwick) was unaware that his enthusiasm for the new political scenario in Peru and his confidence that "better days await the Evangelicals of Peru as a result of this overturn" would be sadly tempered by a conservative backlash, leading to a revolution in three years time. But at least Calvin Mackay was provided with a less stressful environment in which to hold the fort until fresh reinforcements arrived from the homeland.

In November 1946 the Foreign Missions Committee received a letter from Dr John A. Mackay, who had just revisited Lima. He expressed his continued support for the work of the School, indicating that Calvin Mackay was "standing by nobly" in the current emergency, but that it was essential that a permanent appointment of a new Director be made without delay. In April 1947 the new school year began, and Calvin Mackay felt so overburdened that he cabled the home Committee, asking urgently for missionary teachers.

Emergency stations yet again, but this time help was on the horizon.

7

Bearing Fruit

In July 1947 Captain Samuel Will, recently demobbed from the British Army, put in his first appearance at Colegio San Andrés. He made an immediate impact, as is seen by the Acting Headmaster's referring in his final Report to "the good effects produced in school routine by the presence in our midst of an ex-army officer and instructor, even before Mr Will was able to make extensive use of Spanish." He certainly shook up the boys since, dissatisfied with the way many of them kept on talking as the Headmaster entered the auditorium for morning assembly, he roared out one of the few words he had so far learnt in Spanish, "Silencio!" It had the desired effect.

Eight years had elapsed since Sam Will first offered for missionary service in Lima, and for the next sixteen years he was to stamp his dynamic personality on the life of the school. Though qualified in Chemistry and Maths, his teaching concentrated mainly on the latter, along with occasional help in the English department. He was soon appointed Supervisor of Secondary Studies, which brought him into fruitful contact with all Secondary teachers and pupils. His wife, Margaret, did important work in Secondary administration. But it is especially for his extra-mural activities that his contemporaries remember him — leader of the Boy Scout troop, pioneer of Scripture Union camps and promoter of a social conscience through his Christian and humanitarian involvement in Lima's sprawling shanty-towns. Some of these activities will come under consideration later in the story.

But it was not Sam Will's arrival that enabled Calvin Mackay to leave Peru with a clear conscience, take up an appointment as first chaplain to the Inverness Hospitals, and continue as a gracious and persuasive ambassador for missions until his death in 1986 at the age of 95. From the moment of Neil Mackay's resignation in May 1946, the Foreign Missions Committee had made strenuous search for a suitable replacement. Their first choice, Rev James Turnbull, a Baptist minister and qualified teacher who had given several years missionary service with the Free Church in Cajamarca in both the educational and evangelistic sphere, gave careful consideration to the request but eventually declined. They then turned to the minister of the Free Church of Scotland in Vancouver, who in addition to his pastoral experience overseas had served as chaplain with the Canadian forces during the war. This was James Mackintosh, a native of Glenurquhart in Inverness-shire, who accepted the Committee's invitation, but felt it imperative that he should first obtain an official teaching qualification. It was therefore a full year later, in October 1947, that he reached Lima, having been commended to the General Assembly of that year as one whose "varied experience, personal ability, academic attainments and Christian zeal give promise that, by the good hand of God upon him, he will prove an efficient headmaster and a zealous missionary." That hope was amply fulfilled. Mrs Hughie Mackintosh also gave valuable help as school librarian.

As Deputy Head Mackintosh had Oswaldo Regal, an affable, cooperative man, qualified both as a teacher and a lawyer. He was later to become a Member of Parliament, combining his duties in School and Parliament, except for one year when he served as one of three Regional Directors of Education, and had to make his headquarters in Pucallpa in Peru's central jungle territory. It was during his tenure of office there in 1964 that an incident took place typical of the influence that Colegio San Andrés exerted, often indirectly, on the cause of religious liberty. A representative of the Swiss Indian Mission visited James Mackintosh in Lima, distressed that one of their jungle schools was threatened with closure by local education officials as a result of Roman Catholic hostility. Although Oswaldo Regal was a nominal Catholic, his contact with Colegio San Andrés had led him to a very sympathetic attitude to Protestant principles, and when Mackintosh contacted him, he took immediate action. His subordinates were ordered to respect the Constitution guaranteeing religious liberty, and Swiss missionaries and Peruvian parents were left

94

thanking God for the standing and testimony of Colegio San Andrés.

Changing social status

As the School progressed into the fifties and sixties, a definite shift was taking place in the social origin of many of the pupils. In 1943 Neil Mackay could write to the British Ambassador enlisting his aid in securing scholarship help for two pupils keen to study medicine in Edinburgh, and assuring him that the parents were able to pay all travel and living expenses. In 1944 he replied confidentially to the Catholic University in Washington about an Anglo pupil that "as a student his performance was decidedly mediocre, but that may have been due, to some extent at least, to the carelessness about the future which so often shows itself in sons of wealthy families." And with regard to any need for scholarship help he assured the University that "his family is one of the wealthiest in Peru, and can easily pay for his education."

But now new schools were being built with excellent facilities and ample playing fields, some of them sponsored by the various foreign communities in Lima, many others under the control of the Roman Catholic Church, and still others being business ventures of private groups or individuals who saw education as a worthwhile investment in a country with such a rapidly expanding population. Recognising the booming postwar demand for English as the international "lingua franca", many of these schools contracted British or North American teachers on high expatriate salaries. So it was not surprising that families from higher income brackets who might formerly have chosen the Anglo-Peruano for their sons' education, opted for schools with more attractive facilities that San Andrés was unable to match.

Along with this went the growth in the Protestant community. Some of the earlier converts may have been barely literate, but their conviction that the Bible is God's Word stirred in them the desire to learn to read, and especially that their children would receive the education that had been denied their parents. Since State schools often discriminated against Evangelical children, parents were willing to make great sacrifices in order to place them in Evangelical schools like San Andrés. They did, however, look for scholarship help, and San Andrés endeavoured to provide them with a reduction of at least a third of the fees. But it was one thing in the nineteen forties to offer 40 Protestant children reduced fees: it was quite another to cater equally for up to 100 in the nineteen sixties. And not only had the economic factor to be considered — if the school was to be in John A. Mackay's words, "a spearhead for the Gospel" it would need to curb the matriculation of Protestants, often incurring in the process the incomprehension and even displeasure of fellow-believers.

Another significant factor in the changing social class of San Andrés families is explained by James Mackintosh in his 1959 Report:

> Our fees are fixed by the Ministry of Education, and here we suffer for our past benevolence! At one time, before I came to Lima, the private schools all raised their fees to meet a new standard of living occasioned by the Second World War. Our school, out of consideration for the parents, did not raise. Since then all rises have been closely controlled. Last year our school was placed with some other schools in the First Category of Secondary Private Schools in Lima. The fees chargeable by such schools were also published. When we applied for permission to raise our fees to the minimum of the scale that corresponded to us we were refused permission to do so, because it would imply too large a percentage rise on the sum we charged previously. So we do the work of a first class school, pay our teachers the first class rate, but charge only second class fees. This puts us on a very tight budget.

To this day similar problems exist.

And so instead of generals came middle-ranking Army officers; instead of wealthy landowners, successful shop-keepers; instead of Cabinet ministers or senior Civil Servants, doctors and lawyers, engineers and accountants. There were exceptions, of course, but the middle-class pattern that has continued into the nineties was being established. A steady stream of former pupils would be found matriculating their sons in San Andrés, but even some in that loyal constituency were gradually looking elsewhere for their children's education, in spite of much higher fees. For some, upwardly mobile socially, snobbery played a part, but others have indicated that more intensive English teaching, better educational facilities, greater space for sport and recreation or nearer access to residential suburbs were the determining factors. For example, one former pupil who visited the school in 1991 reminisced about the Saturday morning football training sessions, which had to be held in a borrowed pitch in one of the less attractive districts of Lima. While grateful to the teachers who did their best with the limited resources they had, to train the school football teams, he determined that if one day he had sons and if he could afford it, he would send them to a school with at least a football pitch to its credit.

Spiritual emphasis

During the early part of James Mackintosh's headmastership the Roman Catholic Church made its two final unsuccessful attacks on religious liberty in Protestant schools. A source of much anxiety, but also a stimulus to much prayer, they will be considered more fully in a later chapter dealing with developments in Roman Catholicism during the school's three quarters of a century existence.

Irrespective of whether Roman Catholic hostility demanded special caution or not, the Protestant staff aimed always to be courteous and avoid all unnecessary offence to the religious traditions of most of the parents and pupils. At the same time effective ways were always being sought to bring the challenge of the Gospel more directly to the pupils, and it is particularly from the nineteen fifties onwards that opportunities for this increased. One favourable factor was the slight increase in missionary staff, all of them eager to be involved in spiritual outreach. First to come in 1949 was Isabelle McDonald from Edinburgh. As soon as she had enough mastery of Spanish and felt she was coping with regular teaching, she began a Boys' Club after school hours with an average attendance of fifteen. Both there and in her Sunday School class, she discovered boys receptive to the Gospel message, one of them, Pedro Arana, going on to a place of spiritual leadership in

Peru. Although Isabelle McDonald spent only four years as a teacher in the school, due to her marriage to Mr Alfred Bell of the E.U.S.A., her prayerful and practical contribution to the spiritual welfare of the Primary pupils was of immense value.

Next to come, in 1952, was another New Zealander, Donald Mitchell, no less gifted and enthusiastic than his two fellow-countrymen who had already served on the staff. Introducing himself to *From the Frontiers* readers, he told them:

> We of Otago, in the South Island, remember with pride our Free Church heritage and the Scottish settlers of 1848 whose faith and industry underlie the present prosperity of the province.

In the teaching of English and the organisation of inter-school sports, Mitchell was to make a very positive impact during his eight years in the school, but his greatest concern was to utilise the marvellous opportunities the school presented to press the claims of Jesus Christ on young lives. In an interview in the 1952 *Leader*, he was asked what plans he had for San Andrés. Cautious as a newcomer about making statements of intent, he nonetheless affirmed clearly for all parents and pupils to hear:

> Since I believe that no education is complete unless it is permeated by God's love as it has been revealed in Jesus Christ, I shall spend a large part of my time in activities which promote this knowledge.

An example of this was a week-end camp in November 1952 for "a good group of younger boys who were showing a lively interest in the Sunday school." With great parental appreciation, the boys were taken out to the country, where "clearly and simply they were taught the Scriptural teaching concerning sin, repentance and faith." Donald Mitchell's belief that "the Holy Spirit was doing His own effective work" was shared by James Mackintosh who reported that "the boys were earnest and reverent and signs were not wanting that the Lord heard prayer when two young lads came asking to be instructed in the way of salvation." On the physical side attempts to encourage a range of activities were only successful when the activity concerned was football. "Once they were persuaded to do a little climbing but they made it clear that this was a concession to us rather than because of any love they had for it."

From an activity like this it was a natural progression to organise a longer camp on the beach during the lengthy summer vacation. And here a momentous decision was made. With the support of other Christian friends, notably John Kessler, a Dutch E.U.S.A. missionary, the first evangelistic camp held under canvas in Peru took place at Huacho, about 90 miles north of Lima. Although the campers were all San Andrés pupils and the "commandant" and several of the "officers" were San Andrés teachers, the camp was held under the auspices of the international and interdenominational movement, Scripture Union. The *Unión Bíblica* was known in some Peruvian Evangelical circles for its daily Bible reading notes, but its camps, well-known in many other countries, were a novelty in Peru. The venture was a success, and in the following years boys from other schools attended, girls' camps had to be added, permanent camp sites were obtained and Scripture Union branched out into a wide variety of activities directed by several full-time staff.

In Colegio San Andrés the Christian staff decided that the best way to channel the spiritual interest shown by some boys as a result of camp and Sunday school would be through introducing Scripture Union as a regular feature of school life. James Mackintosh described this development in his 1953 Report:

> Many will be interested to learn that a definite advance has been made in the spiritual testimony of the school as a place where the Word of God is studied. Along the lines of the Scripture Union work done at home we organised voluntary groups of boys who professed interest to come together and read the Bible and study its message reverently. In Secondary school the work was headed by Mr Mitchell, usually assisted by Mr Will. The boys met weekly and frequently called in a speaker to address them. These were open gatherings and all interested could attend. Some of the more interested boys went to Mr Mitchell's office every day for Bible reading and prayer. The main points of growth, however, were in Primary school where Miss Mackay's group grew so much in numbers and in enthusiasm that the help of another missionary had to be called for, and these two very interested and hopeful groups continued daily study until the end of the school year.

The pages of *From the Frontiers* and of *Leader* over the next few years give frequent accounts of *Unión Bíblica* activities, both inside and outside school. The names of new missionary teachers appear, all of them, in addition to their regular teaching, giving active support to S.U.. Joan French from Birmingham was there from 1955 to 1957; Margaret Mackinnon from Glasgow arrived in 1959 and stayed until 1966; and Petrena McRostie, whose mother had served for many years before her marriage as a E.U.S.A. missionary, joined the staff in 1956 (though on local contract, not as a Free Church missionary). Of special note in the case of Margaret Mackinnon was the fact that her widowed mother, by then in her late fifties, accompanied her. Though her active participation in church life was limited by language, she provided a hospitable home for other missionaries to visit and also gave the Headmaster much appreciated help with his English correspondence.

Another positive factor in developing spiritual interest was the greater ease in obtaining Latin American speakers for morning assemblies and special religious emphasis weeks. While the Evangelical Church in Peru was in its relative infancy, few of its pastors or other leaders would have had the intellectual capacity to address an Anglo-Peruano audience. But by now the Church was registering a slow but steady growth, and better trained pastors were beginning to make their appearance. There is a report of a special meeting in 1953 to which parents were invited when Rev Federico Múñoz, minister of the largest Evangelical congregation in Lima and himself a former pupil of the school, "gave a memorable message. To some of the parents, new to evangelical teaching, it was a revelation that the Bible spoke so intimately to their personal needs. They expressed much interest and we expect to see more of them in the future."

Another welcome speaker was Rev Félix Calle, first Scripture Union staff-worker in Peru, who was to become a sought-after member of the Boards of various Christian organisations looking for a level-headed leader, able to relate well with people inside and outside the Church. His own sons both studied in San Andrés. Samuel Escobar and Pedro Arana, while still students, knew how to communicate well with Secondary pupils, and would both return on many occasions, as internationally-known Evangelical leaders, to preach the Gospel in the school.

Along with the growing strength of the Evangelical cause in Peru went the great expansion of international air travel, which brought greater numbers of Evangelical leaders to the country. One such was Dr René Padilla, staff worker of the International Fellowship of Evangelical Students, who was to become well-known as a theological writer and conference speaker. Normal practice at the school assembly is for the speaker, after his talk, to pray, for which the boys all stand. Padilla, however, on his first visit to the school, began with "Let us pray", at which 350 boys, as sharply conditioned as Pavlov's dogs, sprang to immediate attention. Taken aback for a moment by such a disciplined audience, Padilla recovered his composure and delivered one of his usual clear and thoughtful addresses.

The Headmaster's 1961 Report tells of a series of meetings held for the Secondary pupils, when the preacher was a Central American evangelist, Rev Israel García:

> His message was clear and arresting. After his final talk I asked the boys who were interested in the message and wished to speak to him personally to go to the school chapel. There was no form of pressure or enticement used. About 100 boys went of their own free will and there he told them what discipleship involved and through the Scriptures sought to lead them to place their confidence in the Lord.

No doubt for many the interest was ephemeral, but one who was converted that week to Christ was the Head Prefect, Fernando Lay Sun, later to become a gifted youth evangelist with the Christian and Missionary Alliance. Later in the year he and another final year pupil, Luis Campos, now a cardiologist in Houston, Texas, "addressed assemblies, which they did in a way that challenged the rest of the boys and left the message of the Gospel clearly in their minds."

Another visitor during James Mackintosh's headmastership was Dr John White, now a famous writer on Christian issues, and at that time General Secretary for Latin America of the International Fellowship of Evangelical Students. In 1964 "he gave a series of excellent talks that made a profound impression among the lads. An opportunity was given to consult Dr White privately in the chapel after the talks had finished, and we had intended giving a relatively short time to this, but so many

101

professed their anxiety -and Dr White was convinced of their sincerity — that consultations continued for four mornings and might have gone on for even longer but for the fact that the worthy doctor was about to leave the country."

A third factor of great significance was the arrival in 1963 of a new missionary as minister of the San Andrés congregation, now housed in a new building with independent access from the street behind the school. Fergus Macdonald, from Evanton, Ross-shire, had been very active in youth work, and had two years of valuable experience in a church extension charge in Drumchapel, Glasgow. Through teaching a few hours each week in the school and also through his wife, Dolina's teaching there each morning for a couple of years, he made many profitable contacts which he put to good use. Under his able leadership and with the ordination as elders of Pedro Arana and Luis Torrejón, a former pastor from Moyobamba and now a teacher in Lima with two sons still in San Andrés, the congregation began to grow. Formerly it had been merely an adjunct to the school, cared for by missionaries with little time at their disposal, but now it had its independent existence within the Evangelical Presbyterian Church of Peru.

To begin with, Macdonald found it frustrating that due to the non-existence for several decades of a fully functioning congregation in connection with the school, "in nearly every reasonably sized evangelical congregation in Lima former Free Church people are to be found, often forming the backbone of the group." While most of these would have come from the provinces, they included former pupils of the school, sometimes with other members of their families. "Had it been possible", Macdonald went on to say in his 1963 Report, "for us to have established a congregation in Lima at the inception of the work, that congregation might well have grown to be today the largest and most active evangelical church in the city."

But minister, elders and members, including several San Andrés teachers, were enthusiastic about the new opportunities offered, and in his 1964 Report, Macdonald was able to provide some encouraging statistics:

The morning service was much better attended (average attendance up from 57 to 79). Not only were there more people attending, but we were conscious of good listening ... At the July communion we received five young people into the membership of the Church ... A youth class before the morning service averaged from 15 to 25 and was almost wholly composed of Secondary school and University students.

Fruitful ways in which school and congregation combined to reach out not only to boys but to their families will be considered in a later chapter.

Day-to-day school life

Both the school magazine, *Leader* and the recollections of former pupils combine to paint a fuller picture than can be gained from official reports.

Prominence was given in the 1950 magazine to a "Rectification" in which the editors apologise to the referee of a football match played between Markham and San Andrés, for the reporter's use of "some discourteous and unjust phrases with regard to the refereeing", and ask him to regard them as "the fruit of natural juvenile vehemence." We are not given the language used nor told if the change of heart came from the prickings of conscience or threats of legal action!

The 1959 issue reports on the resuscitation of the debating club and gives an account of several serious topics discussed. One, however, was clearly chosen to goad into action a popular teacher, Eduardo Moll. A former pupil, Moll taught Chemistry, but was best known as a modern artist with a widening reputation. The motion put to the house was that "abstract art is a mass of scribbles stemming from an immature mind." The reporter states that "as we expected, the motion didn't appeal to Mr Moll, and he came to the debate armed to the teeth and ready to sweep away all opposition." After a lively debate, "some of us left persuaded that a cockroach is as beautiful as a flower, but others weren't so sure."

The 1961 magazine contains the reminiscences of a Lima doctor who had finished his school studies twenty five years before, in 1936. Among the school friends he referred to were two brothers, Alvarez Calderón, who swam for Peru in the

Berlin Olympics of that year. Although neither of them passed the qualifying stages, a former pupil from the 1933 class, Wálter Ledgard, clocked up excellent times and was due to participate in the semi-final of the 400 metres freestyle race. There then occurred a scandalous incident that deprived Ledgard and Peru of a probable medal. The Peruvian football team had the audacity to defeat the team from Hitler's native land, and the even greater audacity to do so with a team composed mainly of mestizos and blacks. Incensed at the humiliation inflicted on his pure Aryans from Austria, Hitler had it announced that the pitch was 50 centimetres short of regulation size, and the match was declared null and void. As Ledgard points out, the highly efficient Germans would be the least likely of all nations to make a mistake in pitch measurements, but all Peru's protests were in vain. Their claim that if one match played on that pitch was invalid, then logically all others played on the same pitch should also be cancelled, was rejected, and so, on a point of honour, the whole Peruvian delegation withdrew from the Olympic Games. The Anglo-Peruano's place in Peruvian sporting history continued when the leader of the Olympic delegation later matriculated his son in the school, and again in 1938 when Peru, on the only occasion in its history, came first in the South American swimming championships. Three members of the winning 4 x 200 metres relay team were former pupils of the Anglo-Peruano — two Ledgard brothers and one Alvarez Calderón.

The article continues with the writer recollecting some of his teachers, among them an auxiliary responsible for discipline in Secondary, nicknamed *Foca Negra* (black sea-lion). His method included many unofficial slaps, and one of his victims had an advertisement inserted in the leading Lima newspaper, *El Comercio*, offering for sale a black sea-lion's skin in good condition. Years later *Foca Negra* fell into the hands of the medical former pupil in hospital, but "I reminded him who I was, and we chatted as good friends."

Not all the memories were pleasant or light-hearted. In 1953 James Mackintosh led an excursion for senior boys to the ancient Inca city of Cuzco. On a visit to Machu Picchu, the lost city of the Incas, there occurred one of those accidents dreaded by all teachers and youth leaders. On the climb to the top, one of the pupils, Luis Miranda, got into difficulties, tumbled down a hundred feet and was taken up dead. The great sorrow was mitigated by the confirmation that heart failure was the cause of death and by the boy's family acknowledging that the school bore no blame for the tragedy. Later that year a completely new Inter-College sports championship was inaugurated in Luis Miranda's memory, with an interesting variety of sports: athletics, badminton, table tennis, basketball, softball, chess and football. Four invited schools took part the first year, San Andrés being the winners, and over the years other schools joined in. Under a different name and with various changes introduced, the competition continues to the present day.

In his Report for 1955 Mr Will referred to the school's record in pre-military training (a compulsory activity in Peruvian schools):

> The School distinguished itself in the Independence Day march past, when the President took the salute. San Andrés gained the first place for marching, turn-out, discipline and pre-military training, for the fourth year in succession among the non-Catholic schools. They thus earned the distinction of being awarded the Sol Radiante (Shining Sun), and this for the first time in the history of the school. The emblem was handed over in an impressive ceremony by General Pereyra.

According to *Leader*, San Andrés's march past the presidential tribune had been enthusiastically cheered by the massed crowd of spectators present.

A political upheaval in 1962 made an unusual impression on Colegio San Andrés. As a result of a military coup, the nation's President, Manuel Prado, was deposed a few days before he was due to demit office. For most of its one-year existence, the three-man military junta was presided over by General Nicolás Lindley, former pupil of the Anglo-Peruano. The previous year he had been the speaker at the School Anniversary, when he had dwelt at considerable length on the principles of the Moral Rearmament movement which he personally espoused. His serious talk lacked the lighter touches that gain the attention of schoolboys, and the glares of teachers were unable to prevent the boys raising a cheer when their distinguished visitor reached, "Finally . . ." in his address. Lindley was highly respected in

105

military and political circles, and even people who disapproved strongly of all coups d'état as undemocratic, gave him credit for being a good President and for keeping his promise to hold elections within a year. In an interview with *Leader* he told of how the school's insistence on good discipline and on doing one's duty had always impressed him. He made particular reference to John A. Mackay's instilling in the pupils the desire to do what is right without relying on rigid controls to force such behaviour.

Renewed appeals for staff

The increase in missionary numbers was only relative. Three in 1948 was an improvement on two in 1945, but hardly an adequate spiritual force for working among nearly 700 boys. Most of the new teachers stayed relatively short times, and in any case the missionary furlough arrangements still followed by most British missions meant that after five years on the field a whole year was spent in the homeland. As a result, of a team of five missionary teachers, an average of only four would actually be working in the school at any given time.

So we find James Mackintosh in 1949 reiterating the heart-felt pleas of his predecessors, in referring to "the loss the work sustains through the paralysing shortage of missionaries." He explains, as they did, the system that prevailed of employing part-time teachers in Secondary who could be of little use in the general running or spiritual outreach of the school:

> While I feel that we have some very fine Peruvian gentlemen on the staff, and some of them are deeply interested in the school as an educational institution, few of them have any real sympathy with our spiritual aims. They have been selected mainly because of their liberal views in religion, and it was necessary to select them so, but the time has passed when we should continue with them. We need convinced believers teaching every subject, for there is a Christian way of teaching Mathematics and History, as well as the course of Religious Instruction. We are losing ground as a missionary school as long as any teaching is left to indifferent men. Is there nobody among all the teachers of the Free Church of Scotland, among our friends in the Inter-Varsity Fellowship or our Irish friends who is prepared to come?

In his 1953 Report he wrote:

We keep paring down the size of the school to keep it within reasonable proportion to the number of missionaries on the staff, but there seems to be more to do than we can manage.

The following year his Report ended:

It has to be confessed that opportunities for fruitful service have gone by default. Now that the spiritual response in the school is better, the need for more workers is greater than ever. "The harvest truly is plenteous".

The Report for 1955 was presented by the Acting Head, Mr Sam Will, who struck exactly the same note:

Conversions, baptisms and a growing evangelistic fervour amongst the boys of the Free Church School, the promise of a developing congregation and a seriousness of purpose and a respect for the things of Christ among all the boys of the school, visions of future blessing in our midst all lead us to cry for men who will dedicate themselves to this great work. Will the Church at home fail to grasp the opportunity?

In June of that year *From the Frontiers* magazine published "An Open Letter to Free Church Teachers". It began:

This letter is written by one who comes neither from your country nor from your communion, but who sees in the Free Church College in Lima a tremendous missionary opportunity – an opportunity which for lack of Christian teachers is almost passing by default.

New Zealander, Donald Mitchell, went on to say:

Do you know that for six years there has not been one new teacher from Scotland to join the staff of Colegio San Andrés? Four young women are coming out this year to join the British Girls' School – that is the number of missionary teachers that have come from Scotland to this school in the last twenty-five years.

It was a magnificent vision that led to the founding of this place and it was dedicated labour that made it the foremost school in Peru, but under the conditions that exist, how can it continue to be the best school? If the shortage of Christian teachers persists, it will only be second-rate in its standards and a place of unexploited opportunities. Should that happen, it would be because there has been no continuing vision of the possibilities, nor continuing sense of responsibility on the part of those who, like yourself, are trained for this work.

Sam Will's position as the solitary male certificated teacher to have gone to the school from Scotland since its inception in 1917 continued till the end of 1959. Appeals for help were beginning to meet with a more positive response, and the first to arrive was John MacPherson, a former teacher in Dingwall Academy, with considerable experience in youth work in connection with Scripture Union and Inter Varsity Fellowship. However, just as John MacPherson arrived, Donald Mitchell left to pursue doctoral studies at Princeton Seminary, eventually becoming President of King College in Tennessee.

1961 saw the arrival of William and Ena Mackay, graduates of St Andrews and Edinburgh Universities respectively. At the request of the Foreign Missions Committee, Mr Mackay had also studied theology for two years at the Free Church College, and travelled to Lima as both a teacher and an ordained minister of the Free Church of Scotland. Mrs Mackay's part time work as school librarian and English teacher was to prove of great value.

In 1964 Malcolm Coombe, a Maths and Science teacher from Dulwich College, London, responded to the appeals for help. His four years in the school were of particular value in leading some Peruvian teachers away from their excessive dependence on theoretical Science teaching and in modernising the equipment needed for the teaching of Physics. His active involvement in Scripture Union camps and clubs meant a continued connection with some of the San Andrés staff and pupils during the further six years he spent in Peru as a teacher in Markham College.

In 1963 Miss Elizabeth Mackenzie from Fearn, Ross-shire joined the staff, and her many-sided contribution to the cause of Christian education will feature in a later chapter. Shortly after her arrival Miss Christina Mackay retired, her final year having been spent entirely in administration. It was an encouragement to James Mackintosh, drawing near the end of his own long overseas service, to receive as a replacement for Christina Mackay a secretarially trained missionary from the Irish Evangelical Church, Miss Florence Donaldson. Since 1951 she had assisted in evangelistic and pastoral work in Moyobamba and Chachapoyas, and was now to begin an efficient 24 year career as School Adminstrator, that was to endear her to a whole generation of staff and pupils.

Another leave-taking

During his years in Lima James Mackintosh had to endure periodic separations from his wife and children and also the death of their youngest child. In spite of the personal hardship involved, he stayed at his post until he could be sure of sufficient younger men arriving who could ensure the future welfare, especially spiritual, of the institution. As the years passed, his services were increasingly sought after outside the school, and he came to hold a place of recognised leadership in the wider Evangelical world. When the Peruvian Bible Institute was upgraded to become the Lima Evangelical Seminary, Mackintosh was appointed first Chairman of the Board. When Herbert Money, General Secretary of the National Evangelical Council of Peru, went on furlough, Mackintosh added most of Money's duties to his own. He was continually invited to speak at meetings and conferences of the growing Evangelical student movement, and when the Evangelical Presbyterian Church of Peru began its independent existence in 1963 Mackintosh was unanimously chosen as Moderator of its first General Assembly.

His services to education did not go unnoticed further afield, and an *Instructor* article describes for Free Church children the 1961 end-of-year ceremony in Colegio San Andrés:

And now our guest of honour stands up to speak – Sir Berkley Gage, Her Majesty's Ambassador in Peru. He always honours us with his presence on prize-giving day, but this year he has come with a special mission, and one that thrilled us all, as it did the whole missionary community in Lima. In a few simple words the Ambassador told of the founding and work of the school, and of the magnificent contribution of the present Headmaster, Rev James Mackintosh. He then called on Mr Mackintosh to come forward, and pinned on his breast the decoration that the Queen had been pleased to grant him, Member of the British Empire. You can just imagine the enthusiastic applause of parents, pupils, staff and friends, an applause that the Ambassador had ultimately to quell by raising his hand.

The niceties of the British honours system were not fully understood by the parent who at church the following Sunday cordially greeted the new M.B.E. with, "Good morning, Sir James!"

In the same Honours List, former Headmaster, Neil Mackay, received the O.B.E., but the recognition of former school staff was not limited to the British Government. On his final visit to Peru in 1964 Dr John A. Mackay was awarded the Peruvian Government's highest award for educational services to the nation, the *Palmas Magisteriales*, while in 1967 the same honour was bestowed on Dr Herbert Money on the eve of his retirement, the actual medal being handed over by a former pupil who was at the time Minister of Agriculture.

The end of 1965 saw James Mackintosh laying down the reins of office. On the material side he was leaving behind him a four-storey block of flats for missionary teachers, a new gymnasium, a school chapel and two new classrooms. As a further legacy to his successor he left a motivated staff with more Evangelical teachers than in the past, a disciplined student body and a greater freedom for Christian witness than had ever been known before. William Mackay, the new Headmaster, would need such a solid foundation to build on, for a few years later new political pressures would start sending shock waves into the whole world of Peruvian education, threatening the very existence of private schools. James Mackintosh, meanwhile, went on to preside as Moderator over the 1966 General Assembly of the Free Church of Scotland, and later that year to take up his new appointment as Professor of Systematic Theology in the Free Church College.

8

Resisting the Storm

In a Missions History Survey in 1986, former and serving Free Church missionaries were asked in a detailed questionnaire to describe any experiences that they had found surprising, difficult, comforting, frightening or encouraging. As frightening, William Mackay referred to "the first moments of an earth tremor when school was in session. One never knew if they would build up to an earthquake and a disaster." Nor was he the only person in San Andrés to feel the same, since his administrator, Florence Donaldson, also highlighted "earthquakes in 1970 and 1974" as her most frightening experiences. And forty-six years after the event, Neil Mackay still recalled as very frightening "a massive earthquake which killed about a thousand people in Lima."

In his very first year as Headmaster in 1966, William Mackay experienced an earthquake while school was in progress. In an article in *The Instructor*, John MacPherson recounts for the magazine's young readers what it felt like to live through such an experience:

"What on earth are these fellows downstairs doing to make the place shake so much?" I asked a group of Primary boys who had stayed behind after school to practise for the forthcoming concert. But before they could reply, plaster began to fall around us, the whole room started to tremble, and in the neighbouring block of offices windows caved in one by one. This was no horse-play; it was an earthquake!

Fortunately it didn't take long to marshal the small group together and hurry along the corridor, which seemed to moan and quiver as if swept by a gusty gale. We were not down the steps into the playground before it was all over, and we found ourselves with groups of Secondary boys and teachers whose classes were still in progress, and who were excitedly pointing out cracks and broken windows in the buildings round about. Just 55 seconds it had lasted, but 55 seconds is a long time when the ground shakes and walls tremble, and you wonder if everything is going to topple down on your head.

The solid foundations of Colegio San Andrés meant that it came through the test well, but MacPherson went on to describe the fate of a modern Roman Catholic school, known as "Queen of the Angels":

Two years only it had been in use, but now it presented a pitiable sight. Huge cracks split the façade from top to bottom, while large concrete pillars stood mockingly askew. The earthquake had done its work, but even preliminary investigation had revealed two unforgivable errors: the school was built largely upon sand, and faulty material had been used in the construction.

Reading the account of a much larger earthquake which shook Lima in 1940, one can understand how deeply frightening it was and how grateful the school staff were for God's protecting hand upon them. Dr Renwick's account describes it as:

the worst that has occurred in Lima since 1746, when the nearby port of Callao was destroyed by a tidal wave. We were at work in school when it occurred; it was a beautiful day and everything seemed at its best, when in an instant the whole community was hurled into indescribable confusion. The shock lasted quite a long time. Fortunately, our boys filed out into the open air in remarkably good order and with no sign of panic. I am more thankful that I can express that no accident of any kind happened in the school.

He goes on to describe the chaos and confusion that gripped the city, and refers poignantly to a good friend of his own whose house was destroyed, killing his wife and daughter. It's not surprising that earthquake drills are a regular feature of life in Colegio San Andrés.

Peru's most serious earthquake also took place while William Mackay was Headmaster, in May 1970, but since it was a Sunday afternoon, responsibility for pupils' safety was not added to the tension. It will never be known exactly how many died in remote mountain villages, but it is reckoned that over a wide area of northern Peru some 50,000 people were left dead and 300,000 homeless. Not long after the event a report appeared in an Argentinian publication, *Primicia Evangélica*, which linked Colegio San Andrés with the earthquake, not as a victim but in demonstration of the spirit of Christian service the school constantly sought to inculcate. The report's author was a journalist and student worker, Samuel Escobar:

> On Saturday 30 May, Humberto Bullón was taking part with a dozen students in a peaceful Bible Study in the University Christian Union. The topic was from John 13: Jesus washes the disciples' feet. On Wednesday 3 June, four days later, Humberto in the cold heights of the Peruvian mountains was washing the feet of an Indian peasant so that the doctor could take action against the gangrene. The gap between theory and practice had been bridged. "I have given you an example," said Jesus. One disciple was obeying, deeply moved, twenty centuries later.
>
> Humberto Bullón is barely into his twenties. He is a student in La Molina Agricultural University, near Lima. I knew him a few years ago when he was a pupil of mine in Colegio San Andrés.

The article paints harrowing scenes of great suffering and tells of exhausting treks with injured victims. As Bullón said, when asked what opportunities there were for Christian witness: "It was time for working, not for holding services." But while the main witness was "action on behalf of suffering Peruvians", Bullón tells of how:

> In the evenings we lit a bonfire to cheer up both ourselves and the local people. On these occasions, we found it very moving to be able to say a few words for our Lord, words that came from the heart and which were likewise listened to by eager hearts.

Year of jubilee

William Mackay was the fourth Headmaster from the same clan. Though unrelated to any of his predecessors, he was a nephew of Dr Kenneth Mackay who for eleven years had provided medical services in Christ's name to the north-eastern jungle town of Moyobamba and a wide surrounding area. A History and Geography graduate of St Andrews University, William Mackay had four years teaching experience in San Andrés, and had familiarised himself with every aspect of the school's discipline and administration. In these particular areas he was to excel, giving careful attention to every detail and ensuring that no problem ever remained unattended to.

In his first year he had a great advantage, denied to most of his predecessors — a better supply of missionary teachers. As Administrator there was Florence Donaldson; in Secondary there were Malcolm Coombe and, for some R.E. classes, Fergus Macdonald; and in Primary, John MacPherson, Margaret Mackinnon, Elizabeth Mackenzie and a new recruit from the Presbyterian Church of Eastern Australia. This was Hugh Varnes, who threw himself with great enthusiasm into his task, especially concerned to involve as many of the boys as possible in extra-mural activities. His contributions to school concerts are still remembered, one former pupil who has conducted several leading Lima choirs, including those of the Republican Guard and the National Police, commenting significantly on Mr Varnes' enthusiasm for forming Primary choirs. He may not have been a great musical expert, was the comment, but he made us want to sing.

But the missionary bonanza was not to last. Margaret Mackinnon left at the end of 1966 on account of her mother's need of medical treatment. Fergus Macdonald returned to Scotland in 1966, and became responsible for a church extension work in Cumbernauld, near Glasgow. Malcolm Coombe completed his four-year contract in 1968 and went on to teach in Markham College, while Hugh Varnes left at the same time to initiate a Christian Bookshop and English Academy in connection with the Presbyterian Church in Cajamarca. Some help did come in 1970, when George Thomson arrived from Moyobamba as minister of the San Andrés congregation. Although he took no direct part in the work of the school, his assiduous pastoral oversight was invaluable in maintaining contact with families whose interest was aroused through it.

William Mackay was scarcely into the Headmaster's chair when he had to begin planning for the School's fiftieth anniversary in 1967. For a school with such a strong sense of tradition, most of whose former pupils felt keenly that they belonged to *la familia sanandresina*, this demanded a well-organised series of public events centring on the anniversary date, 13 June. Mackay's first move was to invite the school's founder, John A. Mackay, to be the guest of honour at the jubilee celebrations. Dr Mackay felt, however, that even such an inveterate traveller as he had always been had to recognise the limitations of old age, and he regretfully declined. The anniversary issue of *Leader* begins with an editorial from his pen, in which he comments on the sad paradox that in a world more united than ever through the advances of technology, mankind was more tragically divided than ever. As so often before, he urged the youth of Peru to fix their gaze on "Jesus Christ, the God-man, Saviour and Lord of life, the eternal Man who makes us new men."

Mackay then turned to another namesake and former Headmaster, Neil A.R. Mackay, at that time Director of the British Council in Argentina, who agreed to come, accompanied by his wife. The Foreign Missions Board also agreed to be represented, appointing as their delegate the Board Secretary, Rev Clement Graham (later to become Principal of the Free Church College).

Leader describes in full detail the varied programme of activities which took place: a Sports Day in the National Stadium; a Primary Games Day in the grounds of the Lima Cricket Club; a Gala Concert in the Municipal Theatre with the participation of the State Chorus and a leading orchestra conducted by Luis Meza, a former pupil; an academic function when Dr Carlos Cueto Fernandini, a former Minister of Education who had been a teacher in the school for several years, spoke on "Present-day problems in National Education", and Dr Neil Mackay spoke on "The Disintegration of Modern Culture"; various dinners and lunches for staff, senior pupils and "old boys"; and at the opening and closing of the week of celebrations, services with packed congregations in the school chapel. The assiduous reporter, who has bequeathed to future generations a very full literary and photographic record of the entire week's proceedings, quotes the Spanish words sung at the beginning of the first chapel service, saying that they remained engraved in his memory for ever:

115

All people that on earth do dwell,
Sing to the Lord with cheerful voice;
Him serve with mirth, his praise forth tell,
Come ye before him and rejoice.

Coinciding with the anniversary year came the last year as
San Andrés teacher and versatile Christian worker in Peru of
Dr Herbert Money. Apart from a brief period between 1940
and 1942, Herbert Money had spent 40 years teaching in the
school, though latterly on a very limited scale due to his other
commitments. Asked by a *Leader* interviewer what subjects he
had taught in San Andrés, he replied that he had been a teacher
of Geography, Music, Art, Handwork, History, Psychology,
Logic, Philosophy, Religion and English. When the reporter
asked him if any of his former pupils stood out in his memory,
he reeled off a list of men in the highest positions in Peruvian
life, including a former Cabinet Minister, whose nickname in
school had been "Sleepy Donkey" – according to Money, a sure
sign that he would one day be a great politician. He told, too,
of another distinguished citizen who as a pupil had agreed to
make up a relay team in an Inter-House swimming competition, even though he had only recently learned to swim. He
made a great effort, but half way across the pool his strength
gave out, he threw his arms in the air and shouted out "I'm
drowning!" For the rest of his school career he was known as
Me ahogo (I'm drowning), and when his younger brother
came to school, he was immediately dubbed, *Me ahoguito*
(Little I'm drowning). His final words to all his pupils, past and
present, were to urge them to take to heart the school motto:
"The fear of the Lord is the beginning of wisdom". The first
half century of the school's existence could hardly have ended
more appropriately than with the enthusiastic farewell given to
Herbert Money and his wife, Netta, who as the first missionary
teacher ever to arrive from Scotland was an inspiration to all
who followed after her.

Revolution

On 3 October 1968 President Fernando Belaúnde was un-
ceremoniously removed from office by a military junta under

116

the command of General Juan Velasco. An interesting sidelight
to the events of that day was provided by William Mackay in
his address to the 1970 Free Church General Assembly:

> When, less than two years ago there was a military takeover of
> the country, the outgoing President spent his last night in office
> with two former pupils of the school, visiting one of them (a
> member of the San Andrés congregation) to offer sympathy on
> the death of his father, receiving the other, a former Minister
> of State, in the Presidential Palace.

No doubt to demonstrate that Colegio San Andrés could
never be accused of any party political bias, Mackay went
on to say:

> In the new Presidential Cabinet there were two former pupils
> occupying strategic posts, and one of them took the oath from
> the incoming President.

Revolutions were nothing new in Peru. For leading political
opponents they usually meant spells of imprisonment or exile,
but for the mass of the population it tended to be a case of
life as normal, since the military, jealous of their special privi-
leges, had a vested interest in maintaining the status quo. But
as time passed, it became obvious that this revolution was different. Velasco prided himself on being a man of the people,
and made "reform" the watchword of his administration. Bastions of entrenched privilege − except the armed forces − were
to have their powers stripped away, and a wholesale programme
of reforms was undertaken. The oil industry was to be nation-
alised, lands were to be redistributed and cultivated by and on
behalf of the people, education at all levels was to be totally
reorganised. Many of the reforms contained commendable features, particularly the insistence on the need for agrarian reform
(though disastrous in its subsequent execution), but it became
increasingly clear that Marxist thinking lay behind most of them.
The Free Church General Assembly was told in 1971 that:

> A military government markedly swinging to the left has
> announced "reforms" in education. What this may mean is
> not yet known exactly. Mr Mackay is watching the situation
> carefully as he wisely plans for the future.

Not only was William Mackay carefully watching the situation: he was also bearing in mind his pastoral responsibilities towards former pupils in special need. The Minister of Finance in the deposed Government was Sandro Mariátegui, son of one of Peru's foremost political commentators and philosophical thinkers, José Carlos Mariátegui, founder of the Peruvian Socialist Party and a close friend of John A. Mackay. In order to justify their action, the coup leaders had to accuse the previous government of dishonest dealings, and Sandro Mariátegui was among several Cabinet Ministers arrested. After several months in prison, he took ill and was removed to hospital under permanent guard. While there an unexpected visitor was announced − Mackay, the Headmaster of Colegio San Andrés. My old school, thought Mariátegui, but is this John A. Mackay, my father's friend, or maybe Neil Mackay, my own old teacher? When yet another Mackay came in, he was delighted to meet him and greatly appreciated his personal concern. Eventually the military government were compelled to release him, innocent of all charges laid against him, and in President Belaúnde's second government in the early nineteen eighties he was to serve as Prime Minister.

Despite occasional protestations to the contrary, private schools, especially those with foreign connections, were viewed with increasing disfavour by the revolutionary government. So many new regulations came pouring out that in addressing the Free Church General Assembly in 1973, Florence Donaldson said that the most common question between the Headmaster and herself had become: "Have you read today's newspaper? How is this going to affect us?"

Distinctive school uniforms were abolished in favour of grey for all, which meant the disappearance of San Andrés's traditional blue blazer. The sale of most text-books and stationery by schools was forbidden, on the grounds that it led to profiteering. School magazines could no longer be charged to the matriculation fee, which was the usual way of financing their production. This in fact led to the demise for several years of *Leader*, bitterly regretted by all former pupils of that period. The workload on the administrative staff increased greatly as new regulations appeared, affecting rates and taxes on property, health and welfare taxes, pension benefits, compulsory scholarships and ever tighter controls on fees.

When the new Education Reform Law was promulgated it effectively pinpointed some glaring deficiencies in traditional Peruvian education, such as an excessive dependence on rote-learning, rigid programmes of study that took no account of individual pupils' needs, and an almost total absence of provision for up-to-date technical or commercial education. But the ideological presuppositions of the law led the framers into such a root-and-branch condemnation of all that had ever been done before in the field of Peruvian education that their proposals for wholesale change were doomed from the outset as totally unrealistic, educationally and financially. An editorial in *El Portavoz Evangélico*, magazine of the Evangelical Presbyterian Church of Peru, ironically compared the reform law's diagnosis of the ills of Peruvian education with Jerome K Jerome's discovery, on reading a medical encyclopedia, that he was suffering from every known ailment except housemaid's knee.

The law announced that the whole school structure was to be changed. Instead of six years Primary followed by five years Secondary education, there would be nine years basic education, after which all pupils would pass on to "middle schools" where they would learn a great variety of technical and practical skills, so badly needed by the country. Schools, such as San Andrés, involved in basic education, would not be allowed to operate middle schools and would therefore lose their pupils two years earlier. In this connection Florence Donaldson told the 1973 General Assembly:

> It is often the case that it is in our present senior secondary boys that the effects of the teaching given throughout the school are seen, and it is discouraging to think that we are to lose this opportunity to influence them. However, we know that the Holy Spirit can continue working as He has worked in hearts after leaving school.

Obviously such changes could not be introduced overnight, and schools continued to function as before. But life was tense, not only in schools but in society at large, as the press was muzzled and dissenting voices were silenced by summary deportations. Mackay, looking back on those days

119

in his address to the 1978 General Assembly spoke of the attempt:

> to crush the influence of private education and also to eliminate any ideals other than those of the revolutionary government. San Andrés came under pressure because its position was that of a school whose ideal was to be found in the Christ of the Scriptures and not with the Guevaras and Castros of this world. But one learned in the school the multiple ways in which God's grace abounded.

The gradual realisation by the government that it could not finance even the current limited educational provision, let alone embark on ambitious schemes of constructing, equipping and staffing thousands of new educational institutions, seemed between 1972 and 1975 to increase their hostility towards private schools. Attempts were made on nationalistic grounds to cut drastically the time given to the teaching of foreign languages, especially English, though here they ran into the insuperable barrier of parental opposition. Some in the government would dearly have loved to nationalise all private schools, in the naive belief that such rich pickings — for only nominal compensation would have been given — would solve all the country's educational problems. In the event saner counsels prevailed, but not before such anomalies were seen as a well-known Cabinet Minister, highly vocal in his attacks on "foreignising" and "profit-making" schools, handing out the prizes at an expensive school run by German nuns, and attended by his daughter.

Mackay told of how:

> pressure to conform grew in intensity — we were ordered to use special-issue government text-books and no others, government inspectors entered the school without so much as asking leave to enter, teachers and pupils were invited to denounce any aspect of life that might seem contrary to government policy.

Teachers, especially in Primary, were swamped by new regulations — homework was forbidden; no pupil could be failed in any subject but would need to be brought up to scratch in holiday time and reassessed by the teachers who were really the ones to blame for any failures; examinations were to be replaced by "continuous assessment", which demanded constant tests and mounds of bureaucratic reports, leading one San Andrés teacher to retort, when asked how his teaching was going, that he was so busy continuously assessing his pupils that he had no time left to teach them.

At difficult times like these it was encouraging to receive visits from distinguished Peruvians, such as Jorge Basadre, the most prominent Peruvian historian, who wrote in the Log Book of:

> Colegio San Andrés, the glorious Anglo-Peruano, where I had and have great friends among its ex-teachers, teachers and former pupils.

Another welcome visitor was Dr José Luis Bustamante, President of Peru from 1945-48 and then President of the International Court of Justice in The Hague, who wrote:

> On the 59th anniversary of the founding of this school, I wish to place on record my great appreciation of the work of the founder, and my sincerest wish that it continue its noble tradition of efficiency in teaching, pure moral behaviour and exemplary social conduct which have given the institution its well-earned prestige.

One important feature of the Reform Law concerned the post of school head or "Director". From 1975 on, all Directors had to be Peruvian, and San Andrés complied by appointing Dr José Vidal, who since 1968 had been Sub-Director. José Vidal was a man of wide teaching experience, who had turned down various career opportunities in the Ministry of Education because of his affection for San Andrés. When he began there in 1956, teaching just a few periods each week, his personal creed was a blend of agnosticism and nominal Catholicism. But attendance at the morning assemblies created an interest in the Bible, and he attached himself to the local Presbyterian congregation. A firm disciplinarian, he exemplified the punctuality and orderliness that he demanded of the staff, and was to remain with the school for thirty-six years, retiring finally in 1991.

Dr Vidal's punctuality, rare in a Latin American, was legendary. On one occasion he had made arrangements with an officer and two cadets from the Naval Academy for them to address the boys on Navy Day. They were told that the morning assembly began punctually at 8.00 am and that they should arrive not later than five minutes to eight. At 8.00 am they had not arrived and Dr Vidal proceeded to conduct the assembly with Bible reading, prayer and some general announcements. At seven minutes past eight the naval officers arrived, expecting the boys to be patiently waiting for their important visitors. But when José Vidal was told of their arrival as he was just about to dismiss the assembly, he refused to admit them: "They're military men, let them learn to be punctual!" With a very bad grace the officers left the school, but the following year those appointed by the Naval Academy were there at a quarter to eight. They had been warned!

The law which led to Vidal's appointment permitted the sponsoring bodies of private schools to have a representative participating actively in the running of the school. This allowed William Mackay to continue his leadership role with a new title — "General Co-ordinator", later changed to "General Superintendent". In actual fact, the lines of authority continued as before, an arrangement that suited both Mackay and Vidal, and ensured the steady progress of the school in spite of the political uncertainties.

Since James Mackintosh's time, Colegio San Andrés had formed part of a small association of private schools sponsored by non-profit-making "cultural associations". Two were Methodist schools, and most of the others were linked, directly or indirectly, with various foreign communities in Lima. William Mackay was secretary of the association, which kept him in close touch with events in the political and educational spheres. While fighting for educational freedom, the association made every effort to be constructive in its criticism of the reform proposals, and kept itself strictly non-political. This policy was eventually to bear fruit, for by 1975 the military government was losing popularity on account of its inability to make good its many promises. Velasco was deposed, and another general, Francisco Morales Bermúdez, took over as President. Many Marxist policies were shelved, and other views were once again listened to with respect. In his 1978 address to the Free Church General Assembly, William Mackay told how this led to a remarkable turn-around in the educational sphere:

In December 1975 a new Minister of Education invited a dozen headmasters to talk privately with him on a Saturday morning. He, without any other educational adviser, heard our criticism, listened sympathetically and proceeded to take significant action. Last year another new Minister invited us back. He gave a group of representatives of private schools the Regulations for Private Education and asked that a new set of regulations be prepared according to our vision of the needs of private education in Peru. Within about two months the work had been completed and responsible and positive legislation had been presented to the Minister who, after due consultation with his own advisers, and at Cabinet level, had it promulgated. In this legislation private schools, far from being limited in scope are encouraged to expand, and the Christian testimony of the school is specifically recognised as a worthwhile contribution to the Peruvian educational system. It makes one think of Moses, protected in the palace in which his death warrant had been signed. So was the school protected. It was the Lord's doing, and it was wonderful to be a spectator of it all.

The proposal to reduce schools to a nine year curriculum was never implemented, and the right of sponsoring bodies, such as churches, to own and operate schools, was specifically acknowledged.

Business as usual

Whatever the political turbulence outside, the school continued to concentrate on its academic and spiritual task. The 1970 issue of *Leader* reported that of the 39 boys who had completed their Secondary education in 1969, 35 had gained entry into universities or advanced colleges. The significance of such an achievement is seen in the success of the Head Prefect, César Pastor, who not only took first place in the San Marcos entrance examination, but did so in competition with over 16,000 candidates.

The 1971 edition of *Leader* was largely devoted to the hundred and fiftieth anniversary of Peruvian Independence. A young History teacher, César Gutiérrez, already making a name for himself as an archivist in the Riva-Agüero Institute and later as a Professor in the Catholic University, enthused the boys to tackle original research. A very worthwhile exhibition was put together in the school library, while distinguished historians, one of them a former pupil and two of them former teachers of the school, spoke at special assemblies and contributed original articles for the magazine, several concentrating on the British contribution to Peruvian independence.

On the staffing side, the proportion of Peruvians who were Evangelical Christians continued to rise slowly, though no improvement appeared in the lamentable practice of part-time Secondary teaching. This meant that even active Evangelicals were unable to be of much help outside their classrooms, and that full-time missionary staff were as needful as ever. And sadly, such staff were not forthcoming. At the end of 1973 John MacPherson left the school after fourteen years in order to complete theological studies leading to ordination. Although he returned to Peru a year later and maintained his connection with the school, his involvement in other activities meant he could give only minimal help until his departure in 1977. When William Mackay addressed the 1975 General Assembly he struck the same note so often heard before:

> In the school the staffing situation is critical. Since the beginning of 1966 four male missionary staff have left the full-time employment of the school, one has come forward. Two lady teachers have left the school — no-one has come forward.

The one new teacher referred to by Mackay was Dr Alan Fraser, whose father, Rev James Fraser, was Chairman of the Foreign Missions Board, and his father-in-law, Rev Clement Graham, was Board Secretary. From 1974 onwards his expertise in Chemistry and Mathematics were put to good use in the Science department, while his interest in photography and computers was to have a marked effect in the years that followed.

Both Mackay and Fraser reported home on the success attained by the former pupil who in 1977 gained first place in the entrance examinations of the world-renowned Massachussets Institute of Technology. What interested them most was the fact that before leaving for the United States he had begun to ask serious spiritual questions and was regularly attending the San Andrés church. Through his influence his family began to attend the services, and some of them professed faith in Christ. His father, a doctor with left-wing views, was to become an elder in the Presbyterian church, and his sister, who trained as a sociologist, later spent several sacrificial years working in the jungle on behalf of the dispossessed victims of terrorism.

At the end of 1977 William Mackay handed over the post of Headmaster to Alan Fraser. While Mackay's twelve years as Headmaster had not seen dramatic changes within the school, he had succeeded in keeping it on a steady course during turbulent times, he had gained for it a respect in political and educational circles, and he had ensured that it remained faithful to the biblical principles and spiritual vision of its founders. The much more favourable regulations for private schools, promulgated in October 1978, clearly bore the stamp of the careful study and practical recommendations of the group in which Mackay played a key role. These allowed private schools the freedom to teach according to valid principles (including religious principles), gave the proprietors the responsiblity for applying these principles in the school (instead of the State imposing its ideological beliefs on every school), allowed schools greater liberty in the choice of text-books and preparation of syllabuses, and explicitly gave religious associations the right to name one of their own members as Director. Such a climate was to prove very favourable for Alan Fraser in his first years as Headmaster, a welcome respite before the onset of the disastrous economic conditions and fratricidal violence that were to engulf Peru in the eighties and nineties.

William Mackay's missionary colleagues from the various areas in Peru where the Free Church worked gave succinct testimony to the particular strengths he had displayed during his years in Peru when they commended "his understanding of Reformed thinking, his keen interest in and knowledge of contemporary affairs and his administrative gifts." After a spell in Scotland, he was to find further scope for the exercise of these gifts as Principal of the prestigious Presbyterian Ladies' College in Melbourne, Australia.

Looking back over sixteen years in Colegio San Andrés, Mackay would undoubtedly highlight "a story that, humanly speaking, tells of tragedy, but also speaks of human courage and the riches of Christ's grace." A pupil in his fifth and final year of Secondary in 1966 had had his right arm amputated two years previously. As soon as possible he was back at school, learning to write with his left hand, and doing well in his studies. His sister, however, informed the Headmaster that the cancer had spread and that the boy knew what illness he had:

Not long after, in the English class, he was given an exercise to write — a short story beginning with the words: "It was a dark and gloomy street ..." Here is what he wrote:

"It was a dark and gloomy street — all that time I only saw a mysterious man who looked at me surprised. When he passed after a few seconds, I could swear that he was laughing at me like a mad person. My heart began to beat in such a way that I thought it could be heard ten yards away. My blood turned more and more cold. I couldn't turn my face and my feet led me to the end of the street. I was terrified, but I could do nothing: my feet seemed to be out of my control. In my mind there was only one thought — Stop! Stop! Stop! or a hundred steps more it would be too late. I was in the street where the houses were abandoned: my future was decided.

I tried to remember a prayer. I was desperate and suddenly one of these incredible things full of mystery happened — I remember "The Lord is my Shepherd ..." A huge wave of courage invaded my body. I really felt that I wasn't alone. Someone was giving comfort to me. Only then I stopped and turned back: the terror has passed now and, come what might, I would wait with calm.

A few minutes later I heard some heavy steps coming from the darkness. I knew Who it was, and for what reason He was coming. It was exactly a year since I saw Him the last time, and I said to Him that I would be here now. Soon I would forget what life is."

In August 1967 he died. After his funeral his sister came to visit me and told me that during the last months of his illness he had remained at home studying, but in his days of greatest pain, he went to his room and stayed there the whole day reading the Bible he had been given at the close of his school career. The day of his death he found great comfort in so doing.

He spoke to none of the teachers in the school about his problem. He sought no human help in his spiritual and bodily anguish — he had found a greater Comforter.

William Mackay closed his account of Pablo's story told to the 1970 General Assembly, with words that give eternal significance to the daily and yearly routine of teaching which could so easily become a monotonous burden, even for the most dedicated teacher:

> For as the rain cometh down, and the snow from heaven, and returneth not thither, but watereth the earth, and maketh it bring forth and bud, that it may give seed to the sower and bread to the eater: so shall my word be that goeth forth out of my mouth; it shall not return to me void, but it shall accomplish that which I please, and it shall prosper in the thing whereto I sent it.

A seventeen year old student dies in hope. Fifty years of strenuous effort are not in vain.

9

Branching Out

Eight-year-old Roberto tripped as he ran along the corridor. The little jar of water he was holding broke and left him with a nasty gash on his wrist. Fortunately the school's accident insurance policy covered such emergencies, and he was taken to a nearby clinic. As he walked out of the school door, holding his father's hand, he smiled cheerily at the Headmaster. The doctors decided they should operate to reconnect the severed tendons. Under anaesthetic, of course, but nothing very serious. No need for the parents to be worried.

But that night Roberto suffered a fatal attack, and a day that had begun like any other, ended in tragedy for his family and for Colegio San Andrés. The clinic disclaimed all responsibility, and the family, among the less well-off in the school, were left alone with their memories and their tears.

Yet not alone. Christian teachers rallied round in support of the bereaved family, and Alan Fraser and his wife, Anne, found themselves able to minister pastorally to a family with nowhere else to turn. Their nominal church connection brought them no comfort, but the practical love and the introduction to the Scriptures received in the Fraser home and from Elizabeth Mackenzie drew them towards the living God and into the fellowship of the San Andrés Presbyterian Church. The years ahead were not easy as they struggled with redundancy, unemployment and family separation when the husband went in desperation to find work abroad. Before he left, God had given them another son, whom they later matriculated in San Andrés, and brought regularly to Sunday School, desirous that he should be raised in the faith that had come to mean so much to them in all their trials.

One such traumatic experience was a heavy burden for Alan Fraser, still in the early years of his headmastership. But it was not the only one. A painter, rushing one Friday afternoon to finish his work on one of the school walls, was careless about his safety precautions, slipped and fell to his death. Though the school bore no blame, the material needs of a poor family left without a breadwinner in a society where welfare benefits were unknown, and also the spiritual needs of a young widow and her orphaned children, made deep inroads into the time and the material and emotional resources of Headmaster and school. Without the sure knowledge that in all such events God acts with sovereign wisdom and unfailing love, the many pressures of the Headmaster's job could well have proved a burden too heavy to bear.

School, however, had to proceed, and areas for improvement had constantly to be explored. Fraser was as convinced as his predecessors that the employment of so many part-time teachers in Secondary was a hindrance to academic excellence and spiritual usefulness, and determined to do something about it. He introduced various promoted posts in order to improve the remuneration of senior staff and encourage them to work full-time in the school. He established a policy whereby the school did its utmost to pay for any advanced professional courses that staff were willing to take. He utilised every available corner of space, including what had formerly been flats for missionary teachers, to provide better specialist facilities, especially in practical courses such as art, music, computer studies, the sciences and English language. In addition to introducing computer studies into the curriculum, he embarked on a programme of progressively computerising the administrative and financial side of the school's activity, though constantly held back by financial restraints.

Improvements in staffing

With an eye to the future, Fraser also stressed a point that had been made on several occasions by William Mackay – post-graduate training abroad for carefully selected teachers, who would strengthen the school educationally and spiritually. The favoured location for such studies (though not necessarily the only one) would be Scotland, since this would provide a valuable cross-fertilisation of ideas with the Foreign Missions'

Board, with Christians in the teaching profession, with the many interested and praying friends in Free Church congregations and with the Reformed theology that has always underlain the work and witness of Colegio San Andrés. In its Report to the 1986 General Assembly, the Missions Board stated:

> Such post-graduate training and closer contact with the Free Church of Scotland had been recommended over the years by successive headmasters, and the Board is in full agreement with the proposals in principle. The main difficulty is the financial one, and the Board is exploring various sources of funding.

One year later the Board had to confess that they were "unable to find external sources which could finance this venture". They had, however, taken an important decision. Funds that had been budgeted to cover the cost of sending a Free Church teacher to Peru had remained untouched, because no such person had materialised. The Board judged that the money would be well-spent — indeed, more economically spent in spite of the high fees charged for foreign students in British educational institutions — bringing a suitable candidate over to Scotland for further training. They therefore reported that "Mr Jorge Terrazas has been brought to Scotland — it is hoped the first of several — for studies in Moray House College of Education in the field of Maths and Computing." They went on to express the opinion:

> What is needed is a Scholarship Fund, in the setting up of which both the prayers and recommendations of members of the Assembly will be much welcomed. An important benefit of such a scheme, apart from the academic side, is the participation of the teachers concerned in Free Church life in Scotland.

Jorge Terrazas, a Bolivian by birth and Peruvian through marriage, was a member of the Christian and Missionary Alliance. His first contact with the school, in his student days, was through his cousins who were pupils there. What he learned through them of the school's principles and practice convinced him, before any direct contact was established, that San Andrés was the kind of school he would one day like to teach in.

130

When this became a reality in 1981, he gave himself wholeheartedly to his own subject of mathematics and to promoting the Christian witness of the school. His year in Scotland, during session 1986-87, accompanied by his wife Maritza, and infant daughter, gave him valuable experience in Edinburgh schools, and created strong bonds of fellowship with Christians throughout the country. When in 1991 Dr José Vidal retired as Director, Jorge Terrazas was the obvious choice to succeed him, although he specified, in accepting the appointment, that he could only tackle it if assured of the prayer support of Christian people throughout the Free Church of Scotland.

Missionary participation in the school, though far below the desired level, was maintained. When Alan Fraser assumed the headmastership, the English department was under the charge of Mr Clive Bailey, an English graduate of Aberdeen University. Although he spent only three years in the school, his quick mastery of Spanish and outgoing personality created a good rapport with Secondary pupils. He continued the San Andrés tradition of active involvement in Scripture Union camps, and forged useful links between young people in the school and in the local Presbyterian congregations.

When he left, his place was taken by Miss Janis Brand, another Aberdeen graduate, who hailed from Edinburgh. Her coming signified an interesting link with the early years of the school, since she was a grand-niece of Miss Christina Mackay, who first joined the staff in 1923, and who in her old age was delighted to know of the continuing family connection with Peru. A fluent linguist, Janis Brand was soon immersed in the life of the school, the church and the Scripture Union. In her occasional reports to the home Church, she spoke in down-to-earth terms of "the good, the bad and the ugly", deflating romantic notions of missionary life, while emphasising the supreme honour of serving Christ wherever he might call.

In 1986, after nearly six years teaching in San Andrés, she confessed:

I came here a most unwilling recruit and found it exactly the place for me. I have learnt so much here and gained so much from my time, especially spiritually.

In 1988, in her final address to the General Assembly, she presented an angle of school life, sometimes glossed over by other eager apologists:

Someone once told me he was fed up hearing about all the successes of the school and nothing about failures. Of course, we prefer to tell about our successes, but I would like to tell you about one of my pupils who could be regarded as one of my failures. His name is Richel. He was twelve years old with red hair (very unusual in Peru). He looked rather scruffy and uncared for, and I knew there were problems at home. He used to come without a pen, usually forgetting his notebook. His conduct mark was always in the red, sometimes into minuses. He failed consistently in nearly every test he was given in all his subjects. He said he was an atheist. This was not, he told me, because his parents were atheists (they were Roman Catholics) but because he had thought the matter through.

One day I saw him turning round during an exam, something absolutely forbidden because cheating is part and parcel of everyday life in Peru. He came to me again and again, assuring me he had not tried to cheat, but had only been asking for a rubber. As this is a common excuse, I did not believe him. It's the kind of situation where you feel you need either the wisdom of Solomon or second sight. I prayed about it. Had I made a mistake, or was he lying again? In the end I told him that just as Jesus had forgiven me my sins I would forgive him for talking during an exam.

After that in the R.E. class he started asking questions not just to interrupt as he had done before, but thought-out questions. His tests started with an asterisk telling me he did not believe what he was going to write but was only doing it for the test. Then at the end of the test he would write more questions like: How do we know that the Bible is true and not just Western propaganda? How can we trust the Bible's account of the resurrection? He used to stay behind at break to ask more questions. He asked about prayer, and how to become a Christian, though he was not making a personal commitment. We discussed Christ's death, and how everyone is a sinner who has to appear before a righteous God, we went over again what he had learned in class, that Jesus is the bridge between sinful

132

man and a holy God. So why do I say that this was not a success story?

At the end of the year I know he passed Physical Education and Religion, and I think he passed Art, but he failed in his eight other subjects. Because of lack of space in our classes, of the fifteen boys who failed first year and had to repeat we could only select eight boys. Richel's discipline mark was so bad it was thought that not only was he wasting his parents' money but he was a disruptive influence harmful to the education of his classmates. So this year he is studying elsewhere. Perhaps even his being put out of San Andrés will be helpful to him, as has happened to others who have realised the worth of the training they received there when they compare it with their new school. Certainly in his years in Primary and Secondary Richel has heard God's Word, and His Word never returns without accomplishing His purposes.

In the light of such an account, Janis Brand went on to speak of:

children who learn Marxist thought before they are out of Primary and money-grabbing dog-eat-dog from society in general. That's why I think Colegio San Andrés is important and that's why I believe we need more Christian teachers there ... especially men. It's a boys' school. Do we want them to think religion is only for women?

As she ended her address, she felt compelled to speak directly to all listening or who would later read her words:

I'm not telling you that God is calling you to go overseas. I'm asking you if you are where you are because God has called you there. We must be open to the possibility of God calling us overseas. We must lay on the line our careers; you lose a lot of possibilities of promotion if you go abroad, but is that more important than doing God's will? We must lay on the line our comfort; it *is* hot and humid there in the summer, there *are* mosquitoes, the buses are horrible as you are packed in like sardines and stand a good chance of having your bag slit or your pocket picked. Travelling is dangerous; the roads are bad and the buses often break down. There are blackouts and occasionally curfews. But is comfort more important than doing God's will? We must lay our families on the line. We miss them, we miss our culture. We find we are never completely part of that

133

culture, and when we return to Scotland, we are not really part of that culture either. But God never leaves us, and He is there to strengthen and comfort us whether he calls us to go abroad or remain at home.

Though Janis Brand was the only new missionary teacher sent out by the Free Church of Scotland during Alan Fraser's years as Headmaster, welcome part-time help was provided in 1981 by his brother, Andrew, who had come to Lima from Cajamarca. And then most timely assistance came from a new source. In 1977 the Reformed Missions League of the Netherlands (R.M.L.) had entered into a cooperation agreement with the Evangelical Presbyterian Church of Peru. As a result several Dutch pastoral missionaries arrived in Peru, and the RML Board also responded positively to a request from the Free Church Foreign Missions Board that they recruit teachers, especially Science teachers, in Holland. In 1982 Piet Jonkers, a Physics teacher, and Joop Wolters, a Biology teacher, joined the staff. This proved a huge relief to Alan Fraser, as he describes in his 1985 Report:

> In the Natural Sciences with the invaluable help of the two Dutch teachers, Mr Jonkers and Mr Wolters, we are producing a new course inspired by the Scottish Integrated Science materials. This is now producing some order and improvement in what could only be described a few years ago as a disaster area. The chaos in the Sciences at Secondary level over the past ten years is mainly due to Ministry imposed curriculum changes without the quality of staff to absorb such devastating changes with minimal damage.

After three years Jonkers returned to Holland, but Wolters stayed on for eight years in the school, and after that put his experience at the disposal of the Presbyterian Church as education and training officer. In San Andrés he was a hugely popular member of staff, involved not only in Science teaching but increasingly in the areas of counselling and teacher training. Both Jonkers and Wolters and their wives were also very active in the life of local Presbyterian congregations, contributing towards the long-cherished desire of the Free Church Missions Board that the school would be of service to the young church in Peru.

New Paths for Evangelical Education

In September 1982, 354 boys sat the entrance exams for First Grade in Colegio San Andrés. Only 70 were accepted. Between then and the beginning of the school year in March, many more sought admission unsuccessfully. Of the 70 selected, 17 came from Evangelical homes, but many other Evangelical children were not received. Faced with such a demand, Fraser felt like his predecessor, Neil Mackay, who in 1943 had likened himself to Canute stemming the waves of insistent and even irate parents.

In the nineteen fifties James Mackintosh had continually urged Evangelical leaders to give serious attention to the provision of new schools to meet the needs of their own Evangelical children. Slowly such schools were beginning to be founded, including one that took the name, Colegio John A. Mackay. In many cases they looked to Colegio San Andrés for guidance and encouragement, and in providing this, two Free Church missionaries, Alan Fraser and Elizabeth Mackenzie, were to play an important role.

They did this, firstly, by becoming actively involved in a body called *Centro Evangélico de Apoyo Pedagógico* (C.E.A.P. = Evangelical Centre for Pedagogical Aid). In his 1987 address to the Free Church General Assembly Alan Fraser traced the origin and aims of CEAP:

> This organisation was set up almost a decade ago by a Swiss missionary with the help of German, Swiss and Peruvian colleagues. It sought to provide a back-up service for Evangelical schools in annual conferences and visitation of these schools. It went on to produce a small magazine for Evangelical teachers and has now opened a teacher training college with full government recognition and been instrumental in greatly encouraging others in their attempts to open more Evangelical schools.

Sensing the strategic importance of such a body, both Colegio San Andrés and the Free Church mission gave it full support. Office space was provided in a former missionary flat beside the school. San Andrés teachers spoke at conferences and conducted seminars, particularly Alan Fraser and the two Dutch teachers who dealt with topics related to Science and the Bible, and gave guidance on how to teach practical Science with limited resources. The gifted head of the School's Art department, Mariano Lint, was much in demand for his talks on motivating children to be artistically creative, while Elizabeth Mackenzie lectured on Primary methods and Religious Education teaching.

Grasping the right given by the Government to use non-Catholic R.E. materials in schools, CEAP in conjunction with the National Evangelical Council launched an ambitious programme entitled, *Libros Evangélicos para Educación Religiosa* (Evangelical Books for Religious Education). Known as LEER (by a neat coincidence the initial letters combine to form the Spanish word for "to read"), the project received generous funding from Switzerland and the valuable input of Swiss missionaries and some of their Peruvian colleagues. Much of the Primary material was either written or revised by Elizabeth Mackenzie, with Alan Fraser performing the same role for the Secondary texts. In 1987 Fraser was able to inform the General Assembly:

> The demand for the materials has been most encouraging, with the first text-books produced going through several editions already. Enquiries have come from outside Peru, and indeed from Roman Catholic nuns who were looking for well-produced books for Bible teaching.

A far cry from the not very distant days when Roman Catholic insistence on ecclesiastically approved text-books and teachers threatened the school's very existence!

But an even more significant development was to follow. In an article in *From the Frontiers* in 1983, Alan Fraser spoke of a headmaster being "like a football manager who thinks in terms of training and talent." He referred to "several young teachers in the school who have a promising future in the teaching profession" and for whom he desired further training. "For the majority training abroad will not be possible and so we must think in terms of in-service training and, dare we think it, an evangelical teachers' training college in Lima."

Just two years later, in February 1985, he reported:

> A few of us met in the chapel of the San Andrés congregation to pray about the possibility of setting up a Teachers Training

Institute to supply our schools with well-trained teachers having Evangelical convictions, to send out into all parts of the country such Christian teachers who would give support to local congregations and be a powerful instrument for evangelistic impact on the country, and to take the first step towards the founding of a truly Christian university.

It was necessary to get official recognition of the Institute within a period of five months, as the change of government due later in the year would have made it impossible to launch the Institute then. To put together the necessary documents in such a short time span, and go through all the red tape necessary for any such project would normally have been considered impossible, and the open opposition of the Government to the granting of permission for any new teacher training colleges made the project seem unthinkable. But all things are possible for our God, and through the help of key figures in the Ministry of Education, everything was ready for the President's signature only two days before he demitted office.

The fledgling institution had no buildings, no staff, no students, no funds. With regard to the first of these, Colegio San Andrés came to the rescue. School classes ended at 2.40pm, so from 3.15pm to 10.00pm and on Saturday mornings the building functioned as the *Instituto Pedagógico Diego Thomson*, the name being a fitting tribute to the missionary pioneer of Peruvian Independence days who had among other things founded the first training college for teachers in Peru. Two Swiss missions provided financial help and some qualified personnel, including the Deputy Principal, Mr Fritz Giese. They were also instrumental in inviting University professor, Dr Patrón Contreras, to be the Institute's first Principal.

By the time classes began in March 1986, Colegio San Andrés had made even further provision for the needs of Diego Thomson. With the authorisation of the Foreign Missions Board, the residential block of flats beside the school had been incorporated into the main building and converted into two laboratories, a computer centre, a printing office, a staff room and staff toilets. Not only did the home Board finance the conversion programme and accept the need to pay rents elsewhere for missionary staff who would otherwise have occupied the flats, but they also sent out a leading elder of the Church, Mr John O. Sutherland, to supervise the work. A recently retired Principal of an Agricultural College, his skills in construction, education and financial matters were greatly appreciated by Alan Fraser and his staff. In view of the great gains in space, the school ceded to the Institute for their use as offices the former staffroom and staff toilets. A modest rent was charged to cover the additional expense incurred by the school.

The 1986 session began with over 100 students in attendance. Four and a half years later when the Institute moved to premises of its own, over 500 students were enrolled. It wasn't always easy for two large families to share the same small home, but a broad view of the welfare of Christ's church in Peru was sufficient to overcome most difficulties. Alan Fraser, Piet Jonkers, Joop Wolters and Elizabeth Mackenzie all added to their duties in the Colegio by teaching part-time in the Institute, and the school increasingly provided facilities for teaching practice for Institute students. In this connection Joop Wolters fulfilled a valuable role as tutor to several students preparing as teachers of Chemistry and Biology. By the time the first graduating class received their degrees in 1990, the school had already contracted one of them as Biology teacher for the following year. Juan Carlos Alvarez, well-known to the boys as a student teacher, was not long in making his mark as an excellent and imaginative teacher, a keen participant in extra-mural activities and an enthusiastic Christian. His introduction of an Ecological Week into the school's calendar has proved valuable in creating a greater awareness of the need to protect Peru's threatened environment and conserve and promote her rich diversity of flora and fauna.

The Institute still had a hard path to tread in raising its academic standards, in becoming financially self-supporting and in establishing its reputation in both the evangelical and educational worlds. But the faith of its founders and the efforts of its personnel were being rewarded. Neil A.R. Mackay had lived long enough to know of the founding of Diego Thomson, though not to see its first graduation ceremony. No-one more than he would have been delighted to withdraw in 1990 the words he wrote in 1943: "There are Protestants and there are teachers in Peru, but with very few exceptions the Protestants are not teachers and the teachers are not Protestants." And the central role of Colegio San Andrés in helping to bring this about was a fitting climax to its first 75 years of service to the cause of Christian education in Peru.

Planning for the Future

Well-trained Peruvian staff of firm Evangelical convictions were now more readily available. Was it right then for Colegio San Andrés to remain under foreign control? The Free Church had for many years worked towards and gladly recognised the complete independence of the Evangelical Presbyterian Church, cooperating as requested on a fraternal basis. But some sixty-five years after its founding the reins of the school were still firmly in Scottish hands. A quaint anachronism? A short-sighted paternalism? A necessary evil? A wise precaution?

The Missions Board in Edinburgh was well aware of the importance of such issues, and had discussed them at length with present and former headmasters and teachers. In 1986 they reported to the General Assembly in the following terms:

> The Foreign Missions Board has on several occasions affirmed its commitment to the eventual complete peruvianisation of Colegio San Andrés, provided both its academic standards and biblical basis are safeguarded. National control of this nature would not, of course, preclude continued cooperation on the part of the Free Church of Scotland, along similar lines to that provided by the secondment agreement with the Presbyterian Church for pastoral missionaries.

They then added, however, a very significant statement, on the basis of soundings taken "from a wide range of opinion in Peru and Scotland". This indicated that:

> neither the parents, former pupils nor the Evangelical community at large would favour any change of status which would lessen the contribution, especially in terms of personnel, made by the Free Church of Scotland.

It was agreed that the best way ahead, following the pattern adopted by other private schools and various Christian entities in Peru, would be the eventual formation of a Civil Association which would be legally responsible for Colegio San Andrés. As a first step towards such an *Asociación San Andrés*, the Board in 1987 appointed a *Consejo Directivo* (Advisory Board of Directors), with three Free Church Missionaries, three members of the Evangelical Presbyterian Church and three members of other Evangelical churches. This Advisory Board of which the missionary Headmaster was a full member, and all of whose meetings were attended by the Peruvian Director, was expected to:

> undertake such responsibilities as approving the budget, making senior staff appointments (not the Headmaster and Director), planning the construction of a new school building, advising on the form and functions of the eventual Civil Association and in lending general support, encouragement and advice in the organisation and activity of Colegio San Andrés.

The first Chairman was Rev Pedro Arana, and other members, from a variety of professions, were either parents, former parents or former pupils of the school.

As events turned out, the Advisory Board in the first few years of its existence, dealt with one matter only − the proposal to provide Colegio San Andrés with new premises on a bigger, better site.

In 1968 the Mission Board had informed the General Assembly that it had authorised the Headmaster:

> to make a long-term study of a new school building project along certain lines indicated by the Board. While it must be admitted that by modern standards the present school is becoming out-moded, the study, being merely of a fact-finding nature, commits the Board to nothing.

The school staff would not have chosen the word "out-moded" to describe the facilities on offer. "Grossly inadequate" would better express their view of the cramped conditions where over 700 boys had to be satisfied with a playground measuring 38 metres by 27 metres. A miniscule library, no art or music rooms, no science laboratories other than a demonstration room, inadequate staffrooms, but above all, not even the smallest of playing-fields, were some of the deficiencies against which they battled. The one playground being in constant use for staggered intervals and Physical Education classes meant intolerable noise levels for adjoining classrooms, while the surrounding green areas of 1930 had long since fallen victim to unrestrained building and the roar of air-polluting traffic.

No further public statement emanated from the Board with respect to a possible re-siting of the school. But their minutes indicate that William Mackay had identified "an extensive site in a very suitable location". Two factors, however, were to lead to the abandonment of the project. The first was a terse reply in 1969 from the Church's Finance Committee that they "were not able to recommend that the project be proceeded with as the capital outlays involved were beyond the present resources of the Church." The other factor was expressed in a Board minute in 1970 after an interview with William Mackay: "In view of the present uncertainty as to political developments, active operations to find a new site should be suspended."

Alan Fraser was not long in office when he became convinced that Colegio San Andrés's obvious lack of facilities and space would lead to an inevitable erosion of prestige and ability to compete in the educational world of the late twentieth century. The many improvements already outlined, including some effected by Diego Thomson during its occupancy of the buildings, which ingeniously increased available office space, helped considerably. But Fraser kept insisting that these were only short-term expedients, and over several years bombarded the home Committee with detailed proposals as to how a new school might become a reality. He accepted reluctantly that the Free Church of Scotland, faced with recurring deficits at home, could not finance the project, and explored other possibilities. But Peru's worsening economic crisis meant an endeavour to raise funds for buying land by selling the residential flats beside the school was unsuccessful (which led to their being converted for school use). An offer by Diego Thomson to buy the whole property over a period of years also foundered when hoped-for funds from Germany failed to materialise, and the Institute decided to buy a smaller property.

Undeterred, Fraser kept on looking for suitable land, from 1987 in close consultation with the new Advisory Board. A most remarkable recognition by the Peruvian Senate of Colegio San

Andrés's record of service to the nation resulted in 1988 in a large tract of land on a desert hillside in the southern suburbs of Lima being made available to Colegio San Andrés for building a new school. Considerable funds were needed to develop it, but when in that same year Alan Fraser returned permanently to Scotland, he was hopeful that his long-cherished dream was nearer than ever before to becoming reality.

New life in the old school

In 1986 Mr Julio Ardiles, a chartered accountant, was elected Chairman of the Colegio San Andrés Parents' Association. Alan Fraser was only in his first year as a San Andrés teacher when, thirteen years previously, Luis Enrique, the Ardiles' oldest boy was matriculated in the second grade of Primary. He had been unsuccessful in his attempt the year before, but his parents were insistent that they wanted him in San Andrés because of its reputation for discipline and character-building. The friend who had recommended the school warned them that it was Protestant, but though that did not appeal to them, neither did it deter them.

Some time later their little boy surprised them one day as they gathered round the meal table by asking them why they didn't pray before the meal as his class at school did with their teacher. Intrigued and interested, his parents confessed that they didn't know how to pray, and asked him to do it for them.

A seed was sown in Mrs Luzmila Ardiles' heart, for she knew that their comfortable income and social lifestyle were not bringing them true happiness or family harmony. Visiting the school, she spoke to a long-serving Christian teacher, Mrs María Carrera, about her spiritual concerns, and received an invitation to attend a Bible Study Mrs Carrera held for interested mothers. The Bible Study led to attendance at a Scripture Union camp for mothers and children, and then to attendance at the Protestant services held in San Andrés church that before had seemed so alien. Later, Mrs Ardiles and her three children began to attend the Pueblo Libre Presbyterian Church, pastored at the time by Rev Pedro Arana, and there they all eventually professed faith in the Lord Jesus Christ.

Mr Ardiles was glad his family seemed to be happy in the Evangelical church, but religion, he felt, was not for him. The Catholicism into which he had been born may not have meant much to him personally, but it was part and parcel of the fabric of Peruvian society and he saw no need to change it. But the minister of Pueblo Libre church was friendly and insistent. He urged him to face up to fundamental questions about God and eternity, and to shoulder his responsibility to provide a sound spiritual foundation for the children God had given him. Eventually, after refusing repeated invitations to come to church, Julio Ardiles surprised everyone by putting in an appearance at a special service on 31 October 1979. It was Reformation Day, commemorating Martin Luther's celebrated publication of his 95 Theses on the church door in Wittenberg and the guest preacher, from the Christian and Missionary Alliance, spoke on the great watchwords of the Reformation − Scripture alone, grace alone, faith alone. As Mr Ardiles listened, his amazement grew. "If what this man's saying is true," he found himself thinking, "what we've been taught is wrong."

As a result of that visit, he took the only course open to him. He began to read the Bible for himself, and it was not long before he took his place beside his wife and children as a believer in Christ and a communicant member of the church. Hard times lay ahead for the family as with many others they suffered redundancy, unemployment and successive robberies, but "though the rain came down, the streams rose and the winds blew and beat against the house, yet it did not fall, because it had its foundation on the rock." When Julio Ardiles took up office as Chairman of the Parents' Association, it was as an elder of the church, soon to spearhead an extension congregation in the newer residential area of the city to which they had moved. In 1987 his daughter, Anita, began her Primary teaching studies in the Diego Thomson Institute operating in Colegio San Andrés, and in 1988 his younger son, Tommy, was elected Head Prefect of the Colegio. Even then the intertwining of their family life with Colegio San Andrés did not end, for in 1992 Anita married a young Free Churchman, Angus Lamont, whom she met when he came from Scotland the previous year as a short-term volunteer to the school.

Little wonder that the Ardiles family thank God for Colegio San Andrés, and urge it to seek excellence in every sphere, never losing from view its fundamental mission to glorify God and proclaim Jesus Christ as Lord and Saviour.

But as Julio Ardiles laid down office in 1988, so too did Alan Fraser. Developmental problems faced by their youngest child had already necessitated his wife and children taking up residence in Scotland. He himself had stayed on for several extra months to work on behalf of the new school project, but now, sadly, he knew he had to go. When he had first indicated his impending resignation, no successor lay to hand in Lima, so for the fourth time in the school's history, the Foreign Missions Board had to scrutinise the Church's ranks for someone who could step into the breach. By reaching back some years into the past they found their man, and Alan Fraser was free to leave. Before long he was making his way to the Isle of Lewis, to take up his new post as Deputy Rector of Stornoway's Nicolson Institute.

10

Standing Firm

On 13 June 1987 the Peruvian Senate passed a resolution in the following terms:

Colegio San Andrés, formerly Colegio Anglo-Peruano, will shortly celebrate 70 years of professional labour on behalf of the youth of Peru.

Among its teachers are included distinguished political figures of different periods, who have enhanced the prestige of the institution, which continues to prepare many generations of valiant men of science, diplomats, military leaders who down through the years have brought great honour to the country.

We congratulate Colegio San Andrés and its teaching staff in the person of Dr José Vidal Coello, its present Director.

Yet at that very time when the highest legislative body of the nation was commending Colegio San Andrés, Dr Alan Fraser was informing the Foreign Missions Board that by 1988 family needs would oblige him to resign his headmaster's post. Decisions had to be taken, and by April of that year a replacement was on his way. This was John MacPherson who, with his wife Catherine, had first begun his connection with Colegio San Andrés in 1959. Since 1977 he had been Free Church minister in Dornoch, Sutherland, but through his membership of the Missions Board and his editorship of *From the Frontiers* had been able to keep closely in touch with developments in Peru in general and San Andrés in particular. Though very happy in his pastoral work in Dornoch he agreed to return to Lima as a temporary measure until a younger headmaster could be found. Travelling on the same flight with him and his wife was Miss Ruby Rennie, a young English teacher from Lochgilphead, at the time a member of Ayr Free Church. Not that her arrival would improve staffing numbers in the English department, since Janis Brand was ready to leave as soon as her replacement arrived. Though having to take immediate charge of the English department in a school and a country completely foreign to her, Ruby Rennie proved equal to the task and was soon working hard, not only in her own programme of teaching but also in the vital field of staff training.

Inflation run riot

An unusually tall San Andrés teacher was friendly with an unusually short colleague who taught with him in the same night school. The former was nicknamed "Cost of Living" and the latter "Pay Rises" — a fitting commentary on life in Peru in the late eighties and early nineties. When the young eloquent leader of APRA, the people's party, swept into power in the 1985 elections, many, including not a few Evangelicals, were hopeful of better days for Peru, in the grip of economic decline and mounting terrorist violence. Even more did this seem to be the case when, at his installation as President, Alan García read some verses from the Bible belonging to the founder of the party, Haya de la Torre, a Bible that had been given him by John A. Mackay. But as the economy continued to decline, as the President set Peru defiantly at odds with the world's banking system, depriving the country of credibility and credits, as evidence increased of Government officials just as dishonest as any others in spite of their high *aprista* ideals, as the bloodthirsty Shining Path terrorist movement left ever greater destruction in its wake, disillusionment set in. An inflation that rose uncontrollably to 7,500% in 1990 destroyed the value of savings and salaries, and made a mockery of budgets.

MacPherson found himself thrown into the maelstrom of financial administration in inflationary and recessionary times. He could no longer count on the experience and calm Christian confidence of the previous administrator, Florence Donaldson, who had retired in 1985 after thirty-four years of missionary service in Peru. But the new administrator, Elizabeth Villalobos, and the part-time accountant, Maritza Terrazas, were unwearied in their efforts to keep abreast of the ever-changing situation, and in calculating virtually every month what the revised fees and salaries ought to be. Not that one could simply raise the fees to cover increased costs. By government legislation, parent and teacher representatives had to have a voice with the Headmaster and Director in deciding any rise of fees. Since many parents and most teachers were suffering financial hardship, higher fees meant that the Headmaster was pounded by the parents, and lower fees that he was berated by the teachers. He found himself in full sympathy with the headmaster of another Evangelical school who confessed that each month's bargaining session left him utterly drained and condemned to a sleepless night, and with the headmaster of a prestigious foreign-based school who compared himself to a battered shuttlecock, knocked back and fore by equally determined parents and teachers.

And yet each year the books balanced. Careful housekeeping helped. Increased scholarship assistance from the school and interested friends met the needs of many parents made redundant or with frozen salaries. Christian friends abroad, aware of Peru's economic crisis, sent gifts for educational equipment, thereby helping to maintain standards that might otherwise have plummeted. The British Embassy also made welcome donations of equipment, with Her Majesty's Ambassador, Mr D. Keith Haskell, going far beyond the call of duty in his personal interest in and encouragement of the school and its staff. Efforts to promote harmonious relationships between parents, teachers and the school authorities were generally successful, and Parents' Association meetings, which could have degenerated into slanging matches, and often did so in other schools, were nearly always peaceful. Groups of teachers and groups of parents meeting together for prayer undoubtedly brought God's blessing on the school in difficult days, and gave to those involved a sense of common purpose.

Bombs, bullets and burglaries

In the Fraser family's luggage on their return to Scotland were many souvenirs of Peru in the shape of superb textile, leather and silver handicrafts. Less attractive to the eye was a misshapen piece of mangled metal, an eloquent reminder of the harsh realities of Lima life as the Marxist revolutionary movement, Shining Path, made its violent presence increasingly felt throughout Peru. The mangled metal was part of a bomb that had hurtled from several hundred yards away into the school playground, when terrorists tried unsuccessfully to blow up the Joint Military Command Centre nearby.

It is not surprising, in view of their economic distress and sense of utter helplessness engendered by the failure of successive governments to improve their lot, that some of Peru's disinherited rural and urban poor should look to the Communist Party of Peru to champion their cause. Scorning the official Peruvian Communist Party, this new group, under the leadership of philosophy lecturer, Abimael Guzmán, and with the name of Shining Path, initiated in 1980 its bitter armed struggle against the State. By 1992 well over 25,000 people on both sides of the conflict had lost their lives, and while the burden of guilt lay squarely with Shining Path, all too often the police and armed forces responded with indiscriminate brutality. A long-serving teacher of Colegio San Andrés, a native of the Ayacucho department where the terrorist movement began, had cause to know this only too well. When the terrorists on one occasion stormed a village, her nephew, the local headmaster, managed to phone the nearest army barracks. When the soldiers arrived, the terrorists had fled, but the military rounded up various local inhabitants, including the headmaster and his brother, another teacher. In spite of his identifying himself as the person who had telephoned for help, the whole group were summarily shot as terrorist sympathizers. A half-hearted apology some time later did little to assuage the grief of widows and orphans, or to win over the population to the side of the authorities. Terrorist activities were responsible for another disruption to normal school life. Ever since Shining Path burst on the national scene, they accompanied their massacres and assassinations with the blowing up of electricity pylons and power lines. They liked to choose special dates for such publicity-generating acts, such as their leader's birthday, or the anniversary of the founding of their party, or "Heroes' Day" commemorating the mass killing of *Sendero Luminoso* prisoners in a Lima jail in 1986 or the first seconds of a New year. But it could happen at any time, plunging whole regions, especially Lima, into darkness. This dislocation of the city's electricity supplies was compounded by disastrous droughts in the *sierra*, leaving Lima's long-suffering inhabitants without light or water for hours or, in some cases, days on end. More serious still, the resultant lack of hygiene and proliferation of contaminated water supplies proved a ready breeding ground for disease, and in 1991 Peru had to endure its first outbreak of cholera for nearly seventy years.

In Colegio San Andrés the constant interruptions to the electricity supply played havoc with the computing classes, the use of much educational equipment, the secretarial and administrative work, and staff and some pupil toilets on the first floor, which relied on water being pumped to them. During a particularly bad period in 1989 the Diego Thomson Institute lost many hours of classes when the supply was cut off during evening hours. Clearly this could not go on, and estimates were received for the purchase of a generator to cover emergencies. The cost of one powerful enough to meet all the school's needs was very high, just at a time when the Headmaster was doing his utmost to improve staff salaries, and a slight improvement in the situation in 1990 and 1991 led to no purchase being made, and staff and pupils learning to adapt to the difficulties as they arose. The Director's proverbial punctuality was often put to the test when, with the bell inoperative, he strode through the corridor, blowing his whistle at the end of each class. In 1992, however, the situation was as bad as ever, and the school was compelled to use up part of its scarce resources and buy its own generator. It had also proved necessary, since the cholera outbreak, to forbid the pupils to drink the regular water supply — no easy task for Primary children after running themselves dry under a hot tropical sun. Supplies of bottled water to every classroom were another item that inflated expenditure even further.

But the much greater incidence of violence was not the result of terrorism alone. An army of people, unemployed, under-employed or miserably paid, unless held back by moral restraints, will not hesitate to turn to assault and robbery, and the law-abiding population of Lima became increasingly the target for such behaviour. In an article, *Where Thieves break through and steal* in an occasional bulletin for interested friends entitled *Inside Colegio San Andrés*,

John MacPherson gave some idea of how this affected the school:

> In the first place, we have straightforward stealing, some by pupils, some by outsiders who succeed in slipping unnoticed into school premises. Over the past couple of years or so we have lost such articles as: fire extinguishers, the Peruvian flag in the Assembly Hall (twice), toilet seats, wash hand basins, fluorescent lights, library books, scales, chemicals and microscopes from the science labs, nine cassettes from a set of a hundred in the music room, two pairs of running shoes ...
>
> On the other hand, we live with the danger of terrorism, particularly in its most recent phase which is concentrating on selective assassinations in the cities. Two World Vision directors were murdered a few weeks ago, while in June our newly-elected Chairman of the Old Boys' Association was gunned down as he was entering the textile factory of which he was the manager. Since very few of our pupils come from really wealthy homes, the danger of kidnapping is slight, and we don't have the concerns of some other schools. For example, at a football match last week, the P.E. teacher of the other school told me that the dozen or so men on the touchline were not. parents, but bodyguards of some of the players. But all the same we have to take various precautions. The school doors are always locked, and visitors have to be scrutinised and admitted by the porter permanently on duty. More and more windows and stairways are barred. Our long-serving wooden door into the playground has had to be replaced by a strong metal one. By now the place looks more like "St Andrew's Fortress" rather than "St Andrew's School".

Perhaps the fact that the school's finances were in Scottish hands explains the further comment that "iron gates and bars don't come cheap"!

In commenting on this whole situation, MacPherson went on to say:

> We needn't be surprised at some people's desperate efforts to steal when we know of the soul-destoying poverty in which they live. The daughter of one of our secretaries was assaulted the other day by a young man clutching a broken bottle and demanding money. She exploded in anger, asking him why he chose her since she'd already been robbed the week before, was now penniless and on her way to look for a job. The would-be

thief confessed that he too was unemployed and because he was starving had turned to crime (no unemployment benefit here). He accompanied her in her search, and she had the opportunity to tell him of a better way to live.

Teachers for the task

Most Diego Thomson students were training to be Primary or Kindergarten teachers, and this gave hope of a good supply of Evangelical teachers in these specialties in years to come. Even in Secondary, the proportion of Evangelical teachers was gradually improving, with the assistance of CEAP which was trying to maintain a register of Evangelical teachers, and of *Radio del Pacífico*, the local Evangelical radio station, through which vacant jobs could be advertised. But still the problem persisted of teachers obliged to work long hours elsewhere, making missionary help invaluable. And still the parents kept urging the Headmaster to obtain teachers from abroad, especially native English teachers. The response from the home Church continued to be disappointing, but in 1989 another country was added to the list of those that came to the rescue when Scotland was unable to do so. Rev Marcos Florit, a Presbyterian minister from Barcelona, had spent a year in post-graduate study in the Free Church College in Edinburgh. On his return to Spain, the appeal he had heard in Scotland for a chaplain for Colegio San Andrés kept returning to his mind, and eventually he and his wife, Patricia, offered for service in Lima with the Free Church of Scotland. The provision of such a person, able to follow up expressions of spiritual interest among pupils and parents in a way that a headmaster, tied up with administration, never could, was the fulfilment of a longing expressed by several previous headmasters, and Marcos Florit was able to share their vision, in addition to taking over responsibility for the programme of Religious Education.

Changing times demand flexible responses from the Church that is committed to evangelism and mission. If the Free Church's provision of missionary teachers in 1987 was, in Alan Fraser's words, "downright ridiculous", then it was time to consider other ways of providing personnel support. The ease and relative cheapness of international air travel meant that far more church members and interested friends than ever before could fly from Britain to Peru, and so the Headmaster and the Foreign Missions Board worked together on a scheme of short-term assistance for Colegio San Andrés. Various individuals covering their own expenses, sometimes with the help of their families or local congregations, went out as volunteers for periods as short as six weeks or up to a year and more. Their main contribution was in the English department, taking groups of boys for conversation and generally assisting the class teachers. Even people who spoke no Spanish could be of excellent service in this work, though those who knew some Spanish or had other abilities could cooperate in many different ways. Volunteers, all recommended by their local churches and approved of by the Headmaster, Director and Head of the English department, came from different countries and denominations. Apart from Scotland, there were representatives from England, Wales, Northern Ireland and Australia. In addition to Presbyterians from Scotland and Northern Ireland, there were Methodists, Anglicans and Baptists. In age they ranged from the early twenties to the late sixties. Some were teachers, but others were students, a secretary, a systems analyst, a computer programmer, a music instructor and a personnel manager.

John MacPherson was well aware of the drawbacks inherent in such a scheme, and that one long-term teacher with a clear missionary call could accomplish more than a dozen short-term recruits. But he gave it enthusiastic backing, publicised it in missionary publications and spent considerable time on several visits to the homeland interviewing possible candidates. He believed that such Christian service overseas would greatly benefit the people concerned, and would be of immense value in stimulating informed missionary interest in their home congregations. This was clearly demonstrated in instances such as that of Stranmillis Evangelical Presbyterian Church in Belfast, one of whose members, Campbell Brown, spent eight months helping the school. The congregation swung into action with generous financial support, regular and specific prayer and sustained correspondence from the Sunday School, youth fellowship, members, elders and minister. On his return they gave ready listening to his reports and recommendations and encouraged him in his visits to the other congregations of the denomination.

Many of the parents expressed deep appreciation of the volunteers' willingness not only to pay their way in order to help maintain the school's English teaching standards, but to venture to Peru when the country's image in the world press was the devastatingly negative one of inflation, poverty, violence, terrorism and drug-trafficking. But they made clear again and again their great desire that the Free Church of Scotland would be able to recruit from among her own members or other sympathetic bodies full-time teachers, especially of English, thoroughly committed to the spiritual and moral standards for which Colegio San Andrés had always stood.

The reflections of one of the volunteers in *Inside Colegio San Andrés* are illustrative of what such an experience can mean. The writer is Fiona Alty, a systems analyst with retailers John Lewis in London:

> Having had no previous teaching experience (my work has involved training others, but I soon realised that was very different), I found there was a great deal to learn and adjust to in everyday school life: administration (of which Peru and its schools have more than their fair share), discipline, etc; and actually taking classes was quite different from what I'd expected. (I think I'd rather naively assumed that my pupils might want to learn.) When I first looked at the syllabuses and worried about how I was going to make the material last all term, I hadn't taken into account the amount of time required to maintain law and order in the classroom, especially in a foreign language.
>
> Once I had got into the swing of things, I found my timetable fairly light and had some spare time. "By coincidence" one day when I went to speak to Jorge Terrazas, the Secondary Supervisor, he was trying to solve some Geometry problems and asked me for some help. That was the first step on a path that led me into spending any free time coordinating the production of a Geometry text-book for the maths department. Jorge had been sent a book from Germany containing the problems and solutions but none of the working-out: the aim was to produce a teachers' manual which showed how the solutions were reached. My own Geometry is limited to (not very recent) O-level Maths, but I found I could dredge up a fair bit from memory, and with the help of Jorge's fifth year class we were able eventually to

complete the task — an interesting inter-disciplinary exercise containing elements of English, Spanish and German in addition to mathematics and computing. We set ourselves the deadline of the Open Day in June, and in spite of a number of power cuts in the final weeks which hindered the process of copying and checking we succeeded in publishing our "first edition" (two copies each of the teachers' and pupils' books) with a few hours to spare. I certainly hadn't expected to be doing anything like this when I arrived, but it was very satisfying to help produce something which the school can continue to use.

I enjoyed my time in San Andrés immensely, although when I think of some individual classes and pupils I find it difficult to explain why! It is true that there are many difficulties here which we don't experience at home. There are constant reminders of the political and economic instability — the nurses and teachers (in State schools) have been on strike for months — and the cholera epidemic which began just before I arrived gave us something else to worry about. But in other ways life here is very normal, and I feel confident that God can look after me as easily in Lima as in London. Working here has been a complete and refreshing change — certainly not easy (as I was warned in advance !) but stretching and stimulating. I'm very glad I had, and took, the opportunity to come, and I am going to miss the school. It's difficult to put into words all the experiences of the last few months, and there is lots more that I haven't touched on: the sense of community in the school, embracing not just teachers and current pupils but parents and old boys; the opportunities the school has to meet needs — financial and spiritual — of pupils and their families; its constant quiet witness to the truths of the Gospel. But rather than say more, I'll give you some advice: come, if you can, and see for yourself!

New school project

During his last few months in Peru, Alan Fraser worked hard on the details of the new school project, especially with regard to possible sources of funding. Aware that the Free Church of Scotland could do little more than give token help, he soon realised that Peru's shattered economy ruled out of the question such expedients as bank loans or a mortgage on the existing property. Many former pupils and parents who in normal times might gladly have donated to the project were themselves in financial distress. The school itself, through entry fees paid by new pupils, could provide some income each year, but that fell far short of the capital sum needed to launch the project. Alan Fraser, therefore, and on his return to Scotland, Pedro Arana as Chairman of the Advisory Board of Directors, made contact with a wide range of bodies interested in missionary work or development programmes or Christian education in developing countries. They soon discovered that funds are readily available for feeding the hungry, housing the homeless, providing free education or similar humanitarian activities, but that the building of a school for fee-paying children fell into a very different category. In the light of other pressing priorities, very few agencies or churches saw enough strategic importance in Colegio San Andrés to invest in its future usefulness.

In the meantime projected costs were received for servicing the site. Because of its location, estimates for water, sewage and electricity connections along with the building of a perimeter wall, were extremely high, far beyond available funds. The Advisory Board felt convinced, however, that God's call was to persevere with the project, even though progress might be slow. While they waited, an unsought-for opportunity arose for requesting another site, much more centrally located in an already fully serviced area of the city. This was granted by the Government, but immediately objected to by a neighbouring proprietor. After protracted negotiations, the school lost its title to the land, and the Advisory Board had to reassess the project. In 1992 they decided, while awaiting an improvement in the Peruvian economy, to invest the funds they had slowly been accumulating in improving the facilities on the present site. New buildings, incorporating additional play space would go some way towards modernising the school's educational infra-structure, though in the long term still only a temporary expedient.

So 1993 began with the first phase of remodelling the present premises under way, the plans being drawn up by a Jewish former pupil Marcos Kaliksztein, eager to put his skills as an internationally-known architect at the disposal of his old school. A three story building to house the first three grades of Primary, including toilets (for girls as well as boys, in order to implement in 1994 the desire to reintroduce co-education in the school) and a play area on the roof is being constructed. Improvements to the English, Science and Art departments are being planned, and also to the library, to be named the *John A. Mackay Library* in honour of the school's founder. At the same time one of Peru's most successful businessmen, a former pupil of Colegio San Andrés, has agreed to chair a small group of financial experts who will advise on the best ways of using the present premises, when the time is ripe, to finance the new site and buildings so greatly needed.

Support groups in Scotland

The June 1985 issue of *From the Frontiers* contained a news item headed, "Lewis support sought for Lima school". It reported:

At a recent meeeting in the Stornoway Free Church, about 50 people, half of whom were teachers, gathered to hear about the history, development, Christian potential and current needs of Colegio San Andrés. The speaker was a former teacher of the school, Rev John M. MacPherson, now minister in Dornoch. Except for the war years, the school has never had so few teachers from Scotland as at present, and the Foreign Missions Board is arranging various meetings of this type to inform Free Church teachers in particular about the purpose and challenge of Colegio San Andrés, and to enlist their support for it in its missionary task. Mr MacPherson suggested a wide range of ways in which Christian people in the homeland could more actively support the school ...

The report went on to say:

At their last meeting the Foreign Missions Board felt rebuked to be told that when Miss Elizabeth Mackenzie took her final (as it seemed — she was later able to return) farewell from Peru, several Peruvian teachers and parents asked, with obvious disappointment, if the Church in Scotland had decided not to send any more of their members to serve in Colegio San Andrés. They were assured this was not the case, but it would be preferable to prove it in deeds as well as words.

Two years later John MacPherson was able to report in the following terms:

> About two years ago there came into being the Lewis Free Church Missionary Support Group with the express aim of supporting and encouraging the work of Colegio San Andrés. In the fulfilment of this aim it has been extraordinarily successful, with the result that at a time when the number of Free Church teachers in the Colegio is at its lowest level ever, the few who are there have rarely felt so closely remembered and encouraged in their task.
>
> In addition to the vital ministry of prayer, the group corresponds regularly with missionary teachers, and contributes generously towards various needs within the school. As a result, video equipment has been purchased, useful educational magazines are being regularly sent to the staff, and bursary help has been provided for needy pupils.
>
> In the course of their most recent meeting an impressive illustration of the gracious providence of God emerged. At their January meeting the group members agreed to provide bursary help for a pupil in need, though unaware of who that might be. Two days later the grandfather of a pupil died suddenly, leaving the boy bereft of the economic support that was maintaining him in a fee-paying school. When the mother eventually came to the school in considerable distress, asking what help could be given her son, it was to be told by Dr Fraser that "before they call I will answer". Christian teachers in a far-off Scottish island had, uninformed of her situation, promised the needed finance, and now she and her son, both believers, would be provided for. A letter from the mother, full of trust in God and thanks to his servants, was read out in the meeting and will undoubtedly prove a stimulus to further support.

During the next two or three years similar support groups were formed in the Inverness/Dingwall area, in Aberdeen and in the Glasgow/Edinburgh area. Their remit was widened to take in other educational institutions in which the Free Church has a special interest: Chhapara Christian School in Central India, Dumisani Bible School in South Africa and the Annie Soper Christian School in Moyobamba, Peru. The personalised and practical support of such groups proved a timely reminder to the hard-pressed Christian staff of Colegio San Andrés that they retained an important place in the missionary concern of the people of the Free Church of Scotland.

157

Support came, too, from the children and young people of both the Free Church of Scotland and the Evangelical Presbyterian Church of Ireland. During session 1986-87 they launched a Youth Project, the aim of which was to raise funds to buy a new minibus for the school, to replace the 23-year-old one still in use. The response was excellent, so much so that the Headmaster was able to add school funds and buy a 29-seater bus. The chassis was imported from Brazil, and after seemingly endless customs formalities, eventually reached the school. After some time the bodywork was added by a Lima coach-builder, and in July 1990 the bus's inaugural journey took San Andrés teachers on an excursion into the country.

But this was Peru in troubled times. In the month of October the Biology teachers took a fourth year secondary class on a field trip into the mountains. While they were scouring the countryside for flowers and plants, the driver and his assistant were accosted by four armed men, tied up and abandoned in an empty shack in a nearby shanty-town. By the time they got free, the bus was gone without a trace. Having covered a mere 130 miles, the hard-won result of thousands of Scottish and Irish children's sacrificial efforts had disappeared for ever.

Were the culprits terrorists, intending to load the bus with dynamite to blow up some prime target? Would they use it for transporting their "liberation troops"? Had it fallen into the hands of drug-traffickers, to assist in their lucrative jungle operations? Or were the thieves simply common criminals, speedily dismantling the vehicle for a quick profit? Fortunately, the insurance company accepted that there was no proof of terrorist involvement — not covered by the policy — and paid out the replacement value. By then import duties had been reduced by the new Government, and not only was a similar bus bought, but being a more economical Nissan than the earlier Mercedes-Benz, left sufficient funds for the now 28-year-old van also to be replaced. Crime doesn't pay, but in this case God overruled it for good.

Old Boys and their Alma Mater

One of the striking and more pleasing features of John MacPherson's four years as Headmaster was the spontaneous

158

contact made with their old school by hundreds of former pupils. Some came along to greet an old teacher. Others came wanting to matriculate their sons or grandsons. Each year groups celebrating the twenty-fifth or fiftieth anniversary of their class graduation came to discuss how best to commemorate their schooldays. They might have a lesson as in the old days, conducted by a former teacher, as when the 1939 class invited their one surviving Peruvian teacher to address them, Dr Estuardo Núñez, President of the *Academia Peruana de la Lengua* and one of the country's most distinguished literary figures. They would often ask for "an assembly like we used to have" with the Bible and prayer at its centre, even though some would appear to have little real sympathy for the message of the Gospel. There would be dinners such as the one where a retired General from the 1940 class, a former military attaché in Washington, when asked by MacPherson what he remembered most from his schooldays, quoted the whole of Psalm 23 which he had learned as a Primary pupil. And with very little prompting, if any, the silver jubilee or golden jubilee classes would express their gratitude through valuable donations to the school − lockers, loudspeaking equipment, overhead projector, library books and so on.

Sometimes former pupils came for a very specific reason. They might have made a professional or financial success of their lives, or they might on the other hand be passing through deep economic or matrimonial or moral trouble. They knew their school stood for unchanging spiritual and moral values, and, perhaps uncertain of what their reception might be, made a tentative phone call or a brief visit. One with a broken marriage and unemployment after years of managerial status told of his hesitant return to the very Bible the school had given him years before and sought further guidance. Another recounted his participation in Scripture Union camps thirty years before and asked if he could come back to the local church services. Another came to say he had been brought to faith in Christ long after leaving school, and now wanted to transfer his sons to his own old school with the Gospel at its heart.

But the route by which former pupils came to recognise that the fear of the Lord *is* the beginning of wisdom often did not pass by the Headmaster's door. During a two-hour wait in a dingy, seatless corridor of the Ministry of Education in 1988, the Chairman of the Parents' Association, Mr Hugo Bustamante, recounted an experience to John MacPherson that lightened the burden of their weary vigil outside the door of the Director of Private Education. Their younger son had struck up a friendship with a boy in his class, so he and his wife decided to invite the other boy's parents for a meal. In the course of conversation the Bustamantes indicated that they were members of an Evangelical church, which evoked a belligerent response from Mrs Ramírez, their guest. Did they believe that the Pope was antichrist, as she had heard some Protestants say? The Bustamantes steered the conversation away from such debatable issues, and succeeded in establishing a friendship with the Ramírez family. An open invitation to church was eventually accepted, leading to a profession of faith in Christ on the part of the parents and their sons. For Mrs Ramírez a whole new world opened up, involving active participation in a network of ladies' Bible Studies and a strong desire to invite other San Andrés mothers to attend. For Mr Ramírez, the manager of a textile factory, it meant that seed sown in his heart and mind when he was a pupil himself in Colegio San Andrés, had finally flowered after lying dormant for over twenty-five years.

But for every former pupil who found new life in Christ, many more showed only a nostalgic or formal appreciation of the Christian message they had heard in school. And as John MacPherson, Marcos Florit and Pedro Arana discussed often how this might be remedied, they decided to act on a suggestion made by a former pupil. Enrique Ramírez, an architect and part-time Art teacher in the school, proposed that some of the talks given at morning assembly be recorded and made available for former pupils who might like to hear again what as boys they had perhaps paid little attention to. And so in 1991 the words with which every assembly begins, "Good Morning, boys" were stamped on a cassette, and 600 copies conveying a typical week of morning assemblies began to circulate among former pupils and parents. And Marcos Florit's singing between each talk was an appropriate introduction to yet another important change that a few weeks later was to take place in Colegio San Andrés.

A new chapter

On the retiral of Dr José Vidal, 1992 saw the new Director, Mr Jorge Terrazas installed in office. But another change was in the offing. When he accepted the post of Headmaster in 1988, John MacPherson had made it clear that he viewed it as a temporary measure, perhaps for about two years. The two became three, and the three four, but now he and his wife knew that for family reasons they had to leave Peru. The Foreign Missions Board had contacted and interviewed several possible candidates for the post, but none was prepared to accept it. As time went by, it became increasingly clear that a suitable replacement was already in Lima, so in 1991 Rev Marcos Florit agreed to assume the headmastership from the following year. Although a member and a missionary of the Free Church of Scotland and a fluent English speaker, Marcos Florit was the first non-Scot in 75 years to take control of the school, except for the Englishman Stanley Rycroft's two spells as Acting Head. The task was a formidable one, for most parents and former pupils regretted the severing of the direct British connection, but a visit from the Chairman and Secretary of the Scottish Board went some way to reassuring them on that score.

The significance of the Scottish connection was put in a rather different light by another visitor, Dr Pastor Rondinel, who had taught for over forty years in the school. Being a very gifted chess player, he had ensured that every pupil who passed through his hands could master the game, and had piloted the school team to various tournament victories. Now retired, he came with anniversary greetings, and on seeing several refurbished offices, each with its computer and telephone extension, remarked that he had worked with six Scottish headmasters, but had never seen such prodigal spending before!

Florit and Terrazas had little time to ease themselves into their new responsibilities, before being launched into the seventy-fifth anniversary celebrations. These included an art exhibition in the National Museum, all the artists being distinguished former pupils; a weekly radio programme throughout the year on *Radio del Pacífico*, presenting the school, its message and its activities; a choral concert in a central Lima theatre, with most of the choirs conducted by teachers or former pupils; and a sporting activity that highlighted how far the Evangelical Church had progressed in 75 years. In 1917 the Anglo-Peruano would not have found another Evangelical boys' school in Lima able to field a football team against it. Even in 1967 a six-a-side football tournament for Evangelical schools would have attracted few participants. But in 1992 San Andrés was able to sponsor such a tournament for Evangelical schools in the full confidence that a large number of them would be able to take part.

One of the most remarkable television series in Peru during 1992 was an interview programme in which leading figures in many different fields of Peruvian life were invited to take part. Not that a show of such a nature is remarkable in itself — rather was it the fact that the host was 92-year-old Luis Alberto Sánchez, former Vice-President of Peru, former Principal of San Marcos University, distinguished author and journalist and close friend of Dr John A. Mackay. As a tribute to Colegio San Andrés on its 75th anniversary Sánchez invited Rev Pedro Arana, Chairman of the Advisory Board of Directors of the School to share one programme with him. While much of the discussion ranged over philosophical matters and political issues (Arana and Sánchez had served together on the 1979 Constituent Assembly), Arana took the opportunities given him to state clearly the school's spiritual aims and commend to his viewers the Christ of the Scriptures. He handed over to Dr Sánchez a copy of a new edition of John A. Mackay's best-known work, *The Other Spanish Christ*, and the camera focused on it as Sánchez recommended all his viewers to read it for themselves.

A presentation of that same book constituted the first in a series of three meetings addressed by Professor Samuel Escobar of Eastern College, Philadelphia, a former teacher and former parent of Colegio San Andrés. On the other evenings he addressed the topics: "The Evangelical contribution to national education" and "Education for the twenty-first century". As it celebrated its own seventy five years of life, the School made clear its intention not only to look back with gratitude, but to look around it with a spirit of service to the nation, and to look ahead with fresh commitment to its God-given task.

And so, as the latest chapter in the school's history began, the two men at the helm publicly declared in the Anniversary programme:

> The celebration of this 75th Anniversary does not seek to be a proclamation of the School's own achievements, but a testimony of thankfulness, above all to God who has prospered our work, and also to all those who throughout its history have placed their trust in the School.
>
> To God be the Glory!

11

Religious or Biblical?

Three quarters of a century of San Andrés history have been charted. Successes and failures have been outlined. But here and there issues have been touched on that call for more detailed discussion, questions have been raised that require fuller answers. These all concern objections levelled against the school or obstacles that had to be overcome along the way. In some cases they lead necessarily to a consideration of principles central to all Christian missionary work and to educational missions in particular. They can be summarised as follows:

- the hurdle of religious objections
- the accusations of spiritual ineffectiveness
- the fear of social elitism

A Protestant school in a Roman Catholic society

Every day since the school's inception, morning assemblies have been held, one for Primary and one for Secondary pupils. Central to these assemblies has been the reading of the Bible with an explanation of its meaning. Every week each class receives one or two periods of Religious Education, lasting forty or forty-five minutes. Yet in all that time only the scantiest references to Protestantism or Roman Catholicism would have been heard. Distinctive beliefs or practices of Roman Catholicism which conflict with the Protestant understanding of Christianity are almost never alluded to — the doctrine of the mass, the infallibility of the Pope, the place of tradition alongside the Bible, auricular confession, the celibacy of the clergy and others. If boys ask questions, as they often do, about the two religious traditions, they are always pointed to relevant passages of the

164

Bible, and advised to make up their own minds on the basis of what God's Word says. In fact, the strongest direct attacks on Roman Catholicism heard within the walls of Colegio San Andrés have come from parents, themselves Catholic, who give their reasons for not wanting to send their children to schools run by priests.

Does this represent a departure from the convinced Protestantism of the Free Church of Scotland? Would successive generations of Evangelical teachers in Colegio San Andrés have felt uneasy in the presence of John Knox? Was the school not founded in the belief that the Roman Catholic Church had failed to bring the Gospel to the masses of Latin America?

No missionary teacher has ever been sent out by the Free Church of Scotland without a wholehearted commitment to Evangelical Christian belief, and without having come to a thought-out rejection of many of the central tenets of Roman Catholicism. Peruvian Evangelical staff, in daily contact as they always have been with Roman Catholic doctrine and practice, are usually well aware of what distinguishes their beliefs from those of the Roman Catholic Church and fully appreciate why one of the main dates in the calendar of many Evangelical churches in Peru is Reformation Day, which emphasises the cardinal doctrines of Protestant Christianity as they were rediscovered by Martin Luther and other Reformers. But though this is true, what are considered to be fundamental errors of the Catholic Church are rarely brought to the fore, and outside the history classroom, Rome's record of violent persecution, political intrigue, illicit accumulation of wealth and toleration of scandalous immorality is never referred to. Books which compare Roman Catholic doctrine with the Bible are available in the school library, but none on the lives of popes or the political machinations of the Roman See.

No headmaster would ever have found it difficult to explain the school's policy on this issue. They saw it as a vital part of the school's Christian testimony to show respect to others, whatever their religious or political views. Ordinary courtesy demanded a recognition of the fact that the vast majority of pupils, parents, Government officials and everyone else who ever visited the school professed the Roman Catholic faith. In the years before the Ministry of Education authorised specifically Evangelical programmes of study, the school's curriculum of Religious Education followed as closely as possible the one drawn up by the Government, omitting only those elements of Roman Catholic dogma unsupported by the Bible. For many years the official Government examiners of Religious Education were priests or others specifically approved by the Roman Catholic hierarchy, to whom every facility was afforded to check the teachers' programmes and assess the boys' religious knowledge.

But it was not just a question of courtesy. Each headmaster and all his Christian staff believed strongly that the best antidote to error is the teaching of truth. If the worship of images is wrong – and no Peruvian could fail to be familiar with the practice, given the prevalence of processions such as that which renders homage in Lima every October to the "Lord of Miracles" – then let the unadorned teaching of the Bible show it to be so. Every Primary pupil learns the Ten Commandments in their biblical form, not the mutilated version common in Roman Catholic catechisms, which omits the second commandment condemning the use of images. That alone, without further polemics, is sufficient to show children God's will on the matter. If the Pope's status as infallible successor to Peter is mistaken, then the biblical picture of the all-too-fallible Peter, "a fellow-elder" with other elders, and married into the bargain, speaks for itself without any reference to the papal office being required. If the perpetual virginity of Mary and her role as mediatrix who can be addressed in prayer, is incompatible with the uniqueness of Jesus Christ as Lord and Saviour, that can be shown by a straightforward rehearsal of the relevant biblical data, while maintaining silence on what Rome teaches on the matter.

This policy is well illustrated by comments in Alexander Renwick's 1927 Report:

> In the Secondary department I undertook personally the religious instruction in four of the classes, taking in the Second Year the "Life of Christ", in the Third Year the "Life of Paul", and in the Fourth and Fifth a course on "Christian Evidences" which aimed at saving the rising youth from the pit of infidelity or sheer indifference into which so many fall when they lose faith in Romanism. In spite of the difficulty of grappling with the language, it was a most enjoyable experience, especially in

the Fifth Year, where very great interest was displayed. I made no attacks on the Roman Catholic faith, believing that it was better to allow the Word of God to do its own work. One day, however, towards the end of the session, the Fifth Year boys made an eager and unanimous request that I should explain to them the differences between Romanism and our Evangelical faith. A week later the Third Year did the same and thus I had an opportunity of doing courteously what could not have been done at all if these matters had been fiercely and tactlessly thrust upon them at the first.

Renwick's 1940 Report is also interesting in this regard:

During the examinations in December I received a visit from a lady who occupies a high position in the Ministry of Education. She had been sent to attend to certain matters in connection with the examinations, and as I knew she was a perfervid Roman Catholic, I wondered what she might do, for I know she had insisted on rigid Roman Catholic dogma in other schools. To my great relief I found her most complimentary as to what she had heard about our school from some of the examiners. Then she reminded me of what I had said to her some years ago when she came to us about a certain matter before she got her official appointment. I had said, "If every boy in school were a true Evangelical Protestant, I would indeed be glad; but you can take it from me that I shall never use my position to compel anyone to accept my religion by force and against his convictions." I knew she had spoken to several about this declaration of mine, but I was indeed surprised when she told me personally that these words had produced a deep impression on her. It is an example of how foreign our ideas of religious freedom are to many people who cannot imagine that we would not use compulsion to spread our beliefs.

In a similar way, although the school has been founded by a Presbyterian Church, and maintains close links with the Presbyterian congregation which functions alongside it, no pressure is ever applied to coerce attendance. Boys and their parents are cordially invited to attend church activities and there are always some who voluntarily do so. If they continue their participation, they will naturally become familiar with Presbyterian distinctives, emphasised by the Church though not by the school. There the aim has always been to introduce the pupils to the Christ of the Scriptures in the hope that they will acknowledge him as Saviour and Lord, and then, through the Scriptures, come to a full understanding of biblical faith and its implications for life and worship.

Suspicion and hostility

Neither the most respectful attitudes towards others of different creeds nor the most strenuous efforts to maintain a low profile and avoid unnecessary confrontation could disguise the fact that the Evangelical faith taught in the school was at direct variance in many points with the traditional dogmas of the Roman Catholic Church. And they certainly did not prevent the Church's hierarchy from being implacably opposed to the very existence of the Anglo-Peruvian College. The school was Protestant: that alone was enough to damn it. Particularly galling to the Church authorities was the fact that so many Roman Catholic parents willingly, even eagerly, chose to send their children to the Anglo-Peruano, while themselves remaining within the fold of the Catholic Church. This led to regular denunciations of Protestant schools from the pulpits, circulars from the Archbishop of Lima threatening the direst ecclesiastical censures for recalcitrant parents, and repeated campaigns of vilification in both the Catholic and secular press. Jesuit historian, Jeffrey Klaiber, in his comprehensive survey of the Roman Catholic Church in Peru, *La Iglesia en el Perú*, acknowledges this. He calls John A. Mackay the most distinguished Protestant missionary of that period, "more open to dialogue than the average missionary of his day", yet describes how the Archbishop of Lima condemned him as a Protestant propagandist in San Marcos University and also forbade all Catholics to have anything to do with the YMCA. John A. Mackay reported in *The Instructor* in 1917 of "a savage article, later widely circulated as a pamphlet. It stated that parents who send their children to a Protestant school had as little regard for their welfare as if they were to hurl them down a precipice or send them to a house of prostitution." In his 1923 Report he informed the home Church:

> At the present moment the Roman Catholic Church possesses greater power than it has done for a generation and more. Persecutions of Protestants have recently taken place in different

parts of the Republic. Everything points to the fact that our College is regarded by the Church as one of the chief obstacles to the realisation of its aims. In the course of the past year a number of attempts have been made to deal us a death blow, but in vain. After it was attempted to compass our destruction through three State departments, those of Education, Government and Public Health, the Archbishop of Lima has now decided to found an English school for boys in the capital.

In the light of both the opposition being aroused and the growing success of the institution, Mackay threw out a challenge to the home Church as also to himself and his colleagues:

Let our College become the rallying-point for a Peruvian Reformation!

During Renwick's headmastership, Protestant schools in general, and the Anglo-Peruvian in particular, were subject to periodic attacks. One of these has been referred to in the opening chapter, but there were others, as is evident from Renwick's 1932 Report:

Last Good Friday, one of the priests preached to a crowded congregation in one of the city churches "the three hours sermon", which is a feature of that day. It was largely an attack on the Protestant organisations working in Peru. He warned his audience against the Anglo-Peruvian school as being a dangerous institution, both religiously and politically. The sermon was broadcast by radio, but instead of injuring us, it seemed to do us good, for our enrolment increased by fifty as compared with the previous year.

In 1934 the Ministry of Education informed all private schools that only a priest could teach Religious Instruction. After some fruitless correspondence on the subject, Renwick went directly to the official concerned. The courteous reception he received demonstrated that the directive, ostensibly a Government one, emanated in reality from the Church hierarchy. The esteem in which the school was held, he was assured, meant it could continue with its own programme of moral and religious education.

This did not prevent routine fulminations against the school, and various attempts to have it closed, or at the very least, restricted in its activities. Renwick tells of one such attempt in

1941, which had a different effect from the one intended:

> Just before our enrolment began in March, the Catholic Action organised a series of widely advertised public meetings to attack Protestantism. Some notable personalities were induced to address these meetings. I was publicly denounced by name, along with others, and was held up as a man whose work ought to be combatted. At the same time there was posted up in nearly every Roman Catholic church in Lima a notice warning all parents of the severe ecclesiastical penalties which would fall upon them if they dared to send their children to our school or to the Lima High School for girls (American Methodist). All such parents would be excommunicated forthwith as being guilty of a grave sin, and their children would be denied communion.

> I am not aware that even one boy was removed from this institution because of the threats. Instead, our school grew as never before. Our enrolment reached the record figure of 599, and we had to turn away as many as fifty boys for whom there was no room in the classes.

> Some time later, to our great surprise, the National Radio Company of Peru launched a violent attack against us in their "Children's hour". It accused us of having turned the school into a gambling den — that not only were games of chance, like roulette, fomented, but that we actually had a secret hippodrome where the boys spent on betting the money given them by parents to deposit in the school savings bank. (As a matter of fact, we have no savings bank.) We were accused of corrupting the youth of the country, and it was declared that the Ministry of Education would probably close down our school - and much else of the same kind.

On this occasion the accusations were so ludicrous that a public outcry ensued. The Radio Manager felt obliged to dismiss the announcer, and broadcast fulsome apologies. In both the Senate and Chamber of Deputies the matter was raised with a demand that the Minister of Government conduct an investigation and bring to task those responsible. The main speaker in the Chamber of Deputies, a former Minister of Education, declared:

> My sons studied for six years in the Anglo-Peruano, it has on its staff some of the best men of letters and science in Peru, and the Headmaster has laboured to the general satisfaction of the country during many years.

In the Senate one speaker protested strongly against such an attack on:

> a school which has merited every confidence for its zeal and for the care with which it has respected Peruvian national interests. It does not need much subtlety to understand whence have come such invectives against this school. It is no doubt a hidden sectarian interest which has secured for its service the complacent and uncontrolled voice of the National Radio Company.

As a result of all the furore, the Ministry of Education sent an Inspector to the school, whose report described the Anglo-Peruano as:

> One of the most efficient schools in Lima which, for its discipline, its efficient teaching and its pedagogic organisation merits the ample approval of the Ministry of Education.

While Renwick described the unprovoked attack as "very painful", he acknowledged the beneficial outcome and quoted feelingly Paul's words: "A great door and effectual is opened unto me, and there are many adversaries."

Neil Mackay and James Mackintosh both experienced serious attempts to nullify the school's evangelical witness, focusing each time on the question of Religious Education. In 1943 Neil Mackay reported on an intensification of Roman Catholic persecution of Evangelicals throughout the country. Fanatical groups gathered near the school, denouncing it as a heretical institution.

> In another quarter of Lima noisy groups, led by a priest, gathered outside a Protestant meeting-place and filled the air with insults and threats. The local Catholic weekly paper published articles in which it was openly stated that bands of young men had accepted the mission of going round the different districts of Lima to break up Protestant meetings, and that they were doing it with such zeal that they had no time for their meals.

At that time Neil Mackay received a letter from an Evangelical parent in one of the more distant regions of Peru, which highlighted the problems faced by many non-Catholic parents:

> For religious reasons the children of Protestant parents in State schools are the object of the antipathy, sometimes even the

hatred, of their teachers. The Headmaster of our school has given my son an official certificate of poor conduct, while others who are known to be badly behaved are given good conduct certificates.

In many other State schools, Evangelical children were failed in the Religious Education course, however well they might have studied it, because they did not attend mass in the Catholic Church. Given the rigidity of the national education system, fail marks in any subject or in conduct could severely prejudice pupils' future careers, and Evangelical parents were greatly concerned. The parent who wrote Neil Mackay had decided, in spite of the financial hardship and family distress involved, to send his thirteen-year-old son to Lima, trusting that Colegio San Andrés would provide bursary help and also the care and counsel that a country lad would need when thrust on his own into the pressures and temptations of city life.

The climax to the opposition came when some members of an Evangelical congregation who were having their annual outing in a small wood on the outskirts of Lima were arrested for singing hymns. At this point the National Evangelical Council decided to take action. Their documented evidence of cases of persecution all over the country surprised many congressmen, and led to parliament insisting that freedom of religion be respected in Peru. The general situation improved for a time, though events in the Religious Education sphere kept Mackay concerned for much longer:

At the beginning of the year the school was threatened with a grave crisis. The Ministry of Education published the new syllabi which had to be accepted by all schools, and it was immediately evident that we could not teach the programme of Religious Education, which was permeated with Roman Catholic doctrine. Indeed, in some parts it was little more than Catholic Action propaganda.

Murdo Nicolson hurriedly prepared an alternative programme. Mackay drew up a plan of action which involved presenting that programme to the National Council of Education (a body with strong Roman Catholic representation) and asking for it to be approved. In the likely event of refusal, the syllabus would be presented again with the petition that it be approved for use among Protestant pupils and sympathisers. This would almost certainly be granted, in which case a meeting would be called of all parents, when any not in sympathy with the school's position would be given the opportunity to withdraw their children. Mackay felt confident that very few, if any, would take that step. In his dealings with Government officials Mackay made clear that if religious freedom were denied the school, he would not hesitate to close it, an action which would have been greeted with dismay in many quarters of Lima. As it happened, the crisis was averted, with several factors playing their part. One was a State visit to Peru by the Vice-President of the U.S.A., which made the authorities anxious to avoid any controversy on religious liberties. Another, as Mackay explained, was:

the series of favourable reports on our Religious Instruction which the official examiners have sent to the Ministry of Education throughout the years. Some of these men have been hostile to us, and have arrived at examination time intent to do us harm, but they have gone away impressed by the amount of solid knowledge of the basis of the Faith that the boys have exhibited, and some have openly admitted that the Colegio is the only school in Lima where such instruction is to be found.

But it had been an anxious few months, and in the 1986 Mission History Survey already referred to, Neil Mackay still remembered as the greatest encouragement of his missionary career "the Government's giving in to my threat to close the College and their permission to use our own syllabus for Religious Instruction".

In view of the constant accusations levelled against the school of enticing Roman Catholic children under false pretences, Mackay pointed out in his 1944 Report that he made it:

an invariable rule to discuss our standpoint on Religious Instruction with each parent who seeks to place a child in the school, and I make it quite clear that we will not accept the boy if there is any objection to our syllabus or method of teaching. Up till now there has not been one single withdrawal on this account.

This policy has been maintained until the present day, though broadening the scope of the interview to include the whole Evangelical basis and ethos of the School. At the same time parents are assured that no boy will ever be pressured or compelled to become a Protestant or to attend any Evangelical meetings outside school hours against his parents' wishes. The response is uniformly one of ready acceptance of the School's position.

For five years an uneasy calm prevailed, but in 1948 and again in 1956, fresh attempts were made to silence the school's Evangelical testimony. On both occasions Government decrees were issued, demanding not only that the official Roman Catholic syllabus for Religious Education be followed in every detail, but also that all teachers of the course should either be priests or approved by the Church authorities. Illustrative of the problem was the decree sent out in 1955 by the Minister of Education, which contained the following articles:

> The teaching of the Catholic, Apostolic and Roman religion is based on constitutional principles, and it is the duty of the Ministry of Education to ensure that this teaching is properly given.
>
> Article 372 of the Organic Law of Public Education does not permit the teaching of dissident religions.
>
> The course of Moral and Religious Education must be taught in all private schools in the country in total agreement with the existing programmes, omitting and changing nothing.
>
> The course will be taught in these schools by suitable staff, as required by Article 281 of the Organic Law of Education.
>
> If these regulations are not observed, the offending schools will have their licence to operate cancelled.

Since the three Protestant Secondary schools that operated in Lima at that time (San Andrés and two American Methodist schools) refused to comply with such directives, further pressure was brought to bear on them. For example, early in 1956 the National Office for Catholic Education reminded all headteachers that "all practising Religious Education teachers were obliged to have a licence from the Archdiocese of Lima in order to continue teaching." In May of that year headteachers were warned that all R.E teachers who had not already attended and passed the training course required by the Archbishop of Lima and organised by the National Office of Catholic Education (ONEC) and the Catholic University were obliged to attend another one that month. An additional circular from the ONEC not only asked for personal details of R.E. teachers, including their home address, but demanded the same information about the headteacher and all members of staff.

Since revolutions or sudden changes of government are fairly common occurrences in Latin American countries, James Mackintosh and his colleagues knew that up to a point they could drag their heels with regard to unacceptable legislation. After all, today's Minister, or even President, could be tomorrow's jailbird. But more definite action had also to be taken. On both occasions memoranda were drawn up, setting out the school's policy on religious education and on freedom of conscience. Appeal was made to the Atlantic Charter and to Peru's being a signatory of the United Nations Declaration of Universal Human Rights. Influential groups of parents, most of them Roman Catholic, presented documents asserting their total satisfaction with every aspect of the school's teaching and discipline. Parents were invited to sign a statement expressing their agreement with the method and content of Religious Education in Colegio San Andrés, and none refused.

In the end, the school's friends proved more influential than its enemies. So many former pupils and former and present parents were among the country's leaders and decision-makers, and were deeply appreciative of the school's contribution to Peruvian life and determined that the calamity of its closure should be averted, that even the highest echelons of ecclesiastical influence were unable to achieve their aim. Thus, some years earlier, in 1950, when the Pope made the bodily assumption of Mary an infallible article of faith for Roman Catholics, and all schools were ordered to celebrate a special mass in honour of the occasion, San Andrés refused. The delegates from the Archdiocese were highly incensed and went away threatening reprisals, but though some antagonism was experienced during the end of year examinations, no hostile action was taken.

In 1956 a change of government brought in as Minister of Education Peru's most distinguished historian, Dr Jorge Basadre, who had often visited the school and addressed the pupils. He invited the British and American Ambassadors to discuss with him the issue of religious freedom in Protestant schools, and while explaining that he had to proceed cautiously in the matter, assured the British Ambassador that as long as he was in office as Minister, nothing would happen to Colegio San Andrés. And half a mile away the school's Christian teachers gave thanks that "the Lord is enthroned as King for ever, and blesses his people with peace."

"Aggiornamento" comes to Peru

In 1962 Pope John XXIII called the Second Vatican Council. The Roman Catholic Church, he said, had to come to terms with the modern world, including Protestants and other non-Catholics. Far-reaching changes were proposed, some of which, such as the celebrating of the mass in the language of the people and the impulse given to Bible reading, were to make a striking impact on Roman Catholic worship, if not everywhere, at least in many places. While fundamental Roman Catholic doctrine remained unchanged, there began to be experienced a clear shift away from former confrontational attitudes, as Catholics were urged to view Protestants not as "heretics" but as "separated brethren". It could hardly be expected, in a country as solidly Roman Catholic as Peru, where the Latin American branch of the Inquisition had had its centre and Protestants had had to suffer centuries of discrimination and persecution, that attitudes would change overnight. But throughout the sixties and seventies cases of outright hostility dwindled considerably, and Evangelicals found themselves accepted, sometimes grudgingly, sometimes generously, by the Roman Catholic majority.

It is true that the rapid growth of Protestantism was not welcomed by the Church hierarchy, as was seen in the extraordinary events surrounding the 1990 General Election. In the first ballot the virtually unknown Presidential candidate, Alberto Fujimori, came a close second to the celebrated right-wing novelist, Mario Vargas Llosa. Fujimori, though Catholic, had suceeded in gaining a large measure of Protestant support, and an unprecedented number of Evangelicals had been elected from his party's lists. The Church hierarchy were appalled at the prospect of so much Protestant pressure on the levers of power, and conducted a campaign against Fujimori, which included a special procession of the Lord of Miracles, normally held only once a year. Scurrilous pamphlets attacking Catholic beliefs and practices were adduced as evidence of Peru's Catholic heritage being under threat, though anyone with the slightest knowledge of biblical terminology could see that most of the offending literature could never have been composed by Evangelicals. In the weeks before the second ballot Peru was treated to the ironic spectacle of the Catholic hierarchy supporting Vargas Llosa, who made no secret of his being an agnostic, and Fujimori doing his utmost to affirm his Catholicism and distance himself from his erstwhile Protestant supporters, yet being cold-shouldered by the Church to which he professed such allegiance.

Though in some quarters passions ran high, and an anti-Protestant backlash might have been feared, things calmed down fairly quickly. In Colegio San Andrés there was no disturbance of the religious harmony that had prevailed for over thirty years; indeed, Catholic parents who referred to the issue made light of it as typical pre-election mud-slinging, and tended to make hopeful remarks about the advantages that might accrue to a Protestant school from there being over twenty Protestants in Parliament. Many of them knew that these included one former pupil, several former and present parents and even the Deputy Vice President, Dr Carlos García, whose two sons had studied in San Andrés. Any such thoughts would soon be banished when President Fujimori sidelined his Protestant supporters, and even more so when in April 1992 he dissolved Congress and suspended the Constitution.

Politics apart, many thinking Catholics had been deeply concerned about the state of their Church even before Vatican II. They knew that for millions of Peruvians their Catholicism was little more than a social convention, that processions and ceremonies were often merely a veneer for old animistic worship, that religion was all too often divorced from reality, and that priestly vocations were diminishing so rapidly that the whole ecclesiastical edifice would collapse without the support of large numbers of foreign clergy. In the *Maryknoll* of February 1960 Father Charles Rankin was reported as saying:

What is needed in Latin America is to resuscitate a corpse. Maybe that sounds too strong, but the Church is a shell, whose religious vitality and dynamism has been sucked out and overwhelmed. It is no longer influential in the life of the people. The faith is taken as a social heritage or a tradition. It is too tied up with Hispanic culture.

One of the gravest problems for the Roman Catholic Church is spelled out by Professor Klaiber in his history of the Peruvian Church:

> In 1820 there were about 3,000 priests in Peru for a population of approximately 2,000,000. But in 1984 a population of 18,000,000 was being served by 2,265 priests ... Actually, the crisis is worse than the statistics show, because the numbers of Peruvian clergy have fallen since Independence, while the foreign clergy, who have come to fill the gap, have increased. In 1901, for example, 82% of the Peruvian clergy were native, but in 1973, only 38.8% were Peruvian born.

In the light of such statistics and the nominalism of the great majority of professed Roman Catholics — and similar figures can be produced from all over Latin America — it has become increasingly meaningless to speak of the Catholic Church as the truly native institution in contrast to the alleged foreignness of Protestantism.

Thus it was that many in the Roman Catholic Church realised that the task of winning the masses of the Peruvian people to an intelligent understanding of their religion was vastly more important than engaging in sterile conflict with Protestants. Institutions such as Colegio San Andrés, once viewed with great hostility, were increasingly left in peace, as many Roman Catholic priests and nuns engaged in activities that formerly had been totally alien to them. Some, in the renewal movement, encouraged Bible reading and charismatic experiences. Others, influenced by liberation theology or by regret for the Church's previous identification with the rich at the expense of the poor, gave themselves sacrificially in service to the underprivileged. One of the earliest priests to devote himself to a wholesale programme of help for the poor was a former pupil of the Anglo-Peruano, Padre José Frisancho. Appalled by the increasing number of homeless people in Lima, he founded in the nineteen fifties his *Ciudad de Papel* (Paper City). This was a housing development on the desert coast south of Lima, financed largely by waste paper collections organised by Padre José and his volunteer helpers, and followed over the years by several other housing estates. Every year until his death, San Andrés was one of many schools which contributed to the scheme with its own waste-paper collections. Though Padre José remained true to the Catholicism in which he was reared, he always spoke gratefully of the biblical training he received in the school, and attended when he could the annual meetings of the Old Boys' Association. Several former pupils were among those who gave regular donations to help forward his charitable work.

Some of yesterday's battles no longer need to be fought. But the need to present Jesus Christ to the youth of Peru, freed from the shackles of dead traditionalism, as the only Mediator between God and man, as the once-for-all Sacrifice for sin through faith in whom they can be made right with God, is as pressing as ever. The school bears the apostolic name of Andrew, who, when he heard John the Baptist speak, followed Jesus. That remains the school's supreme aim: so to speak, so to teach, so to live, that boys and their families will follow Jesus.

179

12

Education versus Evangelism?

At its General Assembly in May 1916 the Free Church of Scotland commissioned Rev John A. Mackay to begin missionary work in Peru. The following month a letter appeared in *The Monthly Record* from a northern minister, strongly decrying "this mistimed furore for missions". He wrote of large numbers of Free Church congregations without pastoral care, and asserted:

> The Indians of the Orinoco now have a better chance of getting a full-fledged Free Church pastor than the people of Keiss or Ardnamurchan

who, he claimed, would be "puzzled and pained" by such neglect of their spiritual needs. He went on to say:

> I discern a seamy side in this missionary frame of mind. It seems to me to operate side by side with a very cold respect to the old mother Church, whose calamities are not yet overpast; it seems to exist in combination with a disrespect to the mingled prestige and humiliation of the evangelical cause in Scotland. The keeping alive of this sacred flame in the old country is the main work of the Free Church at the present time, and this consideration should have due weight. There are glamour and romance connected with that old cause quite sufficient to satisfy any aspiring man.

Such anti-missionary sentiment was not, of course, typical of either the Free Church leadership or general membership. The editor of the magazine, while expressing sympathy for the concerns of the letter writer — who happened to be his own brother — insisted that "there is nothing better established than that the expansion of a church on missionary lines has invariably led to a quickening of her home life." And the following month saw a letter from a Glasgow minister, deeply disturbed by the "chilling arguments against this South American enterprise from which some of us are expecting so much." In response to the declaration of the first writer that "missionary ardours" should be treated "in a calm, judicial spirit, and with regard to previous questions and competing interests", he asked with fine irony:

> What if Paul had been so treated? Imagine a committee of brethren, sitting on him, treating his missionary ardour in a calm, judicial spirit, weighing all arguments for and against his enthusiastic proposals, looking at the whole question from every point of view, especially with regard to "previous questions and competing interests"!

And in the light of the late twentieth century growth and vibrancy of the Christian church in Latin America, Asia and Africa, set alongside the decline of the church in Western Europe, the writer's words in 1916 take on a prophetic ring:

> It is the nations that will be born in a day that will bring new life to the nations that were born so long ago, and that are fast withering into decay and death through denying the Lord that bought them. To me there comes now and then a vision of a glad day that will yet dawn, when from north, south, east and west evangelists will come who will bring new life to an effete and dying Church here at home. When the Church gives herself more zealously to the evangelisation of the world, there will be a healthier religious atmosphere and a finer spiritual tone in our Church life at home.

Though the latter view of foreign missions was far more representative of Free Church opinion than the one that saw them as "a rival enterprise", there was undoubtedly a body of opinion that questioned the value and even the legitimacy of schools as a missionary agency. The remarkable success in its early years of the Anglo-Peruvian College meant that such feelings rarely received a public airing, but they surfaced in the foreign missions debate in the 1929 General Assembly. In view of the imminent expiry of the lease for the school building and the continued demand for more places, the Headmaster had asked the home Church to sanction a £20,000 loan from foreign missions capital in order to build a new school. The

Foreign Missions Committee, though not unanimously, agreed to support the request, and pleaded with the Assembly to do the same. The door was open for objectors to the work and they took their chance.

One speaker moved "that the Assembly pass from the present scheme of building a new college in Lima, and in lieu of the present educational policy, devise some humbler and more evangelical line of effort." He asserted that "up to date they have not made a single convert"; that "the boarding department has fizzled out"; that the religion taught in the school was "very brief, very diluted and emasculated"; and that "the Foreign Missions Committee are wallowing in a debt of £4,000 and now they proceed calmly to propose that they should incur another liability of £20,000."

The intemperate language of this speaker meant that his motion failed to find a seconder, but various other delegates spoke more weightily against the Committee's proposal. The amendment that best represented the mind of those who opposed the Church's involvement in educational missions was put forward by a minister from the island of Skye who explained clearly his biblical understanding of the matter:

> What is the Scriptural order? It is this: Go on with the Gospel. Then when a Christian community has been created and converts gathered in, there is the necessity in most countries of providing educational facilities for the children of these converts. The Gospel will make room for education, but in my opinion, education will never make room for the Gospel. The reason why they cannot get on with Gospel activities in the Lima school is just this, that once they begin direct aggressive evangelical work in Lima, the school is doomed, the children will be withdrawn.

On the basis of these views he moved that the Foreign Missions Committee be instructed:

1. To endeavour to secure the transference of the College, together with the new site purchased by the Committee, to some evangelical body with resources sufficient to ensure its continuance.
2. In default of the above, to make the necessary arrangements for the winding-up of the College on the expiry of the present lease.

3. In either of the above alternatives to handle the case with as little financial loss to the Church as possible.
4. To consider the possibility of beginning a direct Evangelical mission in Lima which might or might not necessitate a school in connection with its development.

The debate went on for hours. The seconder of the amendment claimed that "in the Lima school there is no preaching whatever ... the sooner we shift out of Lima the better." Another speaker stated that he was "opposed to education being put in front of the preaching of the Gospel, and also to the spending of money in that place."

There was, of course, much said in favour of the Anglo-Peruano and of the staff of the school. Indeed, such arguments carried the day, though more than a third of the Assembly delegates voted in favour of the amendment to close the school. Six of these felt so strongly about the issue that they recorded their dissent from the Assembly's finding. But never again, after that momentous debate, was any concerted attempt made to call into question the value of the school in the Church's missionary strategy. Some may have been distinctly unenthusiastic and, if they were ministers, would convey that lack of enthusiasm to their congregations. Others might occasionally speak or write unfavourably about some aspect of the school's work. And still others would continue to hold that the only valid model for a Christian school was as a service to the children of believers, not as a means of influencing society or of reaching unbelievers with the Christian message. But from 1929 onwards there was no doubt that the Free Church as a whole saw Colegio San Andrés as a valid missionary activity, deserving of the Church's support.

How should educational missions relate to the preaching of the Gospel and the planting of churches? Does the former conflict with the latter? The development of Colegio San Andrés provides some interesting answers to such questions.

The nature of Christian education

From time to time visiting evangelists or evangelistic teams have asked permission to conduct campaigns in Colegio San

Andrés. Over 800 boys give ample scope for "decisions for Christ". If permission is refused, as may well happen, the evangelists and their local sponsors are probably confirmed in their view that Presbyterians are uninterested in evangelism, and that the school is nothing more than an educational institution.

Some years ago, in a discussion on the future of Colegio San Andrés, an elder of the Evangelical Presbyterian Church spoke in favour of its being handed over to his denomination. "In that way", he said, "we'll have extra funds to help pay our pastors' salaries."

But being a missionary school has never meant that Colegio San Andrés has seen its pupils as merely targets for evangelism, nor its parents, especially the better-off ones, as a convenient source of income for the Church's needs. In his 1985 Report, Dr Alan Fraser describes a Christian school as one "controlled by a biblical perspective on life." In an article in *The Monthly Record* in 1978 he had already amplified that concept:

> A Christian school is not a school with an extra amount of religious activities, or a school geared for the production of the future leaders of the church; nor is it a kind of monastic institution that attempts to shut the world out and forget about the evil that is in the heart of every man. It is rather an educational establishment run in accordance with biblical norms, seeking to present to the children a Christian world view.

In practice this means that the school strives to carry out all its activities to the glory of God. However unsuccessful it may be at times, it aims to permeate every aspect of life with Christian values, whether it be the teaching in the classroom, the exercise of discipline, the participation in sport, the relationship with parents or the administration of finance. And as Alan Fraser points out in his *Profile of a Missionary Teacher*, the Christian teacher who serves God in a land other than his own is "one who sees his chosen profession as his primary field of service to God, and who is not a teacher merely to gain entrance to a country in order to do missionary work in the church."

This does not mean, of course, that there is no evangelism in a Christian school. For the Christian all of life is evangelism, and while the teacher's desk must not be converted into a

184

pulpit, opportunites abound for the direct communication of the Gospel. There are, in fact, wide-ranging possibilities of Christian service, and these are spelt out in an informational leaflet on the school, which indicates the basic aims of Colegio San Andrés: to provide an all-round education founded on biblical principles and of the highest attainable academic standards; to make known the Gospel to pupils and their families drawn from all classes and confessions; to promote a Christian attitude of love and compassion, bearing in mind the many disadvantaged in Peruvian society; and to help the growing Evangelical church fulfil its God-given mission in the nation.

The Church weakened by institutions?

In the nineteenth and early twentieth century heyday of Protestant missions, schools and hospitals sprang up in scores of countries. In their wake came churches, often using the premises of the institutions, relying for their leadership on educational and medical staff and drawing most of their members from pupils or patients and their families. Outside hostility to the Gospel, the lack of trained local leadership and the poverty of the converts justified such a policy. But it had its own problems. Congregations could become dependent on the institutions, they tended to lack impetus to growth, they seemed so often a very small affair in comparison with the highly regarded institutions which absorbed so many resources, both in finance and personnel.

Some Free Church missionaries, involved exclusively in pastoral and evangelistic ministries, sometimes felt that their work, so central in Christ's missionary command to his church, was being overshadowed by undue emphasis on schools and hospitals. One went so far as to describe the institutional work as "not only inadequate but harmful to native church development." Another, Dr David Ford, in a frank and perceptive study, *Has the Free Church Mission in Peru been a Success?* while expressing his appreciation of the sacrificial work of teachers, doctors and nurses, correctly pointed out the fewness of missionaries directly involved in church work as compared with those in diaconal ministries. He states: "The diaconal ministry has absorbed the time of most of the missionaries and been

185

expensive." With regard to Colegio San Andrés, he illustrated the point by referring to the £20,000 paid out in 1929 for the new building.

In spite of the fears of some, most Free Church missionaries considered the school to be a valuable instrument for the establishment of Christ's kingdom in Peru. On his way to begin pioneer church-planting work in Cajamarca, Rev Calvin Mackay spent some time in Lima. Aware of the fears in the home Church that the requirements of the school were hindering the preaching of the Gospel, he wrote at length in *The Monthly Record* of March 1920, praising the Anglo-Peruvian College as a missionary agency, and urging the Church to wait patiently for future blessing. He suggested that:

> the school may be a *sign*, testifying to the reality and truth of the Christian religion, just as the miracles were signs in the early days.

In 1926 Dr Kenneth Mackay, en route to his medical and pastoral work in Moyobamba, had to attend to some official duties in Lima. Of the school he wrote:

> I have been several times to the College and have been very much impressed with the greatness of the effort and the peculiar difficulties as compared with schools at home ... I have almost a feeling of regret that I am not a teacher and giving a hand with the College.

Several decades later, the three ministers who successively pastored the San Andrés congregation, now totally independent of the school, and incorporated into the Evangelical Presbyterian Church of Peru, spoke often of the enormous potential for good of Colegio San Andrés. Rev Fergus Macdonald, Rev George Thomson and Rev Alejandro Tuesta all recognised that Colegio San Andrés had been a key factor in the development of their congregation and the planting of other Presbyterian congregations in Lima. Special services to which new entrants or final-year students and their families were invited proved a fruitful means of joint pastoral and evangelistic outreach. Former pupils of the school serve as ministers in congregations of several Evangelical denominations in Peru, while others, along with parents or former parents, are active as members, deacons or elders. At an ordination of four deacons in the San Andrés Presbyterian church in 1990, three were former pupils of the school. One of the new members that same year, also a former pupil, recalled how his personal commitment to Christ came very simply as his third grade teacher explained in the Religious Education class the meaning of one of Christ's parables. In 1992 a family was received into membership in the Pueblo Libre Presbyterian Church in Lima, having first made direct contact with the Gospel when the wife accepted an invitation from a former pupil of the school to attend the San Andrés church. In Paul's words, "the eyes of her understanding were opened" and she understood why God had led them to matriculate their son in Colegio San Andrés.

It is understandable that missionaries committed exclusively to church planting and pastoral work, covering alone huge tracts of country where several men were needed, should have questioned the concentration of personnel in a school or a hospital. But most of those working there were professionally qualified Christians, who believed God had called them to exercise their particular gifts in those areas of church support. Were there no Colegio San Andrés, the majority of the missionaries would not have eased the burdens of their pastoral colleagues, but would have been exercising their vocation as teachers elsewhere.

Of course, this question of the value or otherwise of Christian institutions - schools, hospitals, agricultural or industrial training centres and so on − is no new one in discussion on missionary policy. Within the Free Church of Scotland herself it had led to earnest debate in the nineteenth century as the Church established a network of schools throughout India and several African countries. Staffed in many cases by people of outstanding intellectual gifts, the schools often rose to be colleges of higher education and even prestigious universities. But did they serve the Gospel? Did their very existence imply a lack of faith in the power of direct preaching applied by the Holy Spirit?

In *The St Andrews Seven* Stuart Piggin and John Roxburgh, in discussing this issue, quote the words of a successful itinerant preacher, Dr J. M. Macphail, who in the 1890s wrote with respect to India:

We itinerating missionaries can influence more men, but they (the teachers) can influence men more.

Just as in 1929, so in the latter decades of the previous century, the Free Church of Scotland agonised over whether or not to close some of its mission schools. It could expect storms of protest from nationals who had benefited from schools and wanted their children to do so too, but it also discovered that not all its directly evangelistic missionaries were as opposed to institutions as were some of the others or some of the home supporters.

But is there any need for conflict? All agree that the preaching of the Gospel is the prime task of the Church of Christ. Yet different methods of preaching the Gospel are appropriate in different contexts and cultures and at different periods. "I have become all things to all men," said the Apostle Paul, "so that by all possible means I might save some." (1 Corinthians 9:22) And the Holy Spirit has distributed gifts within the church for the carrying out of the great commission. Some are teachers, some are doctors, some are agriculturalists, some are pastors, some are evangelists. And through their harmonious labours in different spheres the overall work of the kingdom of God is advanced.

The belief that Colegio San Andrés has been a financial burden to the home Church, absorbing more than its fair share of scarce resources, has been a recurring one during the school's history. It has been based, however, on several misapprehensions, one being that the £20,000 made available in 1929 for the building of a new school represented a total loss, apart from the value of the property obtained, of missionary funds needed elsewhere. In its 1981 Report to the General Assembly, the Foreign Missions Board informed the Church:

> The school initially borrowed a very considerable sum from church funds, but paid it all back over the years.

In 1942 the Mission Treasurer, Dr Neil Mackay, referred to:

> the apparently widespread, but certainly unfounded, idea that the Lima College is an insolvent institution which causes financial embarrassment to the Church. The accounts will show that, on the contrary, the College relieves the Church of a considerable amount of financial worry and trouble, and that if it were to

188

cease to function, the consequences to the Mission as a whole, from a financial point of view, would be far from slight.

In the nineteen eighties soaring inflation and the devaluation of the Peruvian currency meant that the school's self-supporting policy (apart from the Headmaster's salary paid from Scotland) ran into difficulties where missionary teachers were concerned. The home Board agreed to compensate them for devalued salaries, and also to pay rents for missionary teachers once their former residences were incorporated into the school. But the school has never ceased to pay rent for its use of the building, and recent adjustments have brought it back to an almost entirely self-supporting status, including the salaries and most expenses of missionary personnel.

Scholarship in the service of the Church

On a drab Lima street, some ten minutes walk from Colegio San Andrés, an outwardly unpretentious house stands hemmed in between several down-at-heel properties. But behind the unimpressive façade there functions the Casiodoro de Reina Study Centre, so named in honour of the valiant sixteenth-century Reformer who translated the Bible into Spanish. The Centre is run by Moisés Chávez, a highly-trained biblical scholar and gifted teacher, whose great ambition is to provide for the church in the Spanish-speaking world the linguistic and exegetical tools it needs for understanding and teaching God's Word. With a Bachelor's degree in Theology from Lima Evangelical Seminary, two Bachelor's degrees, in Archaeology and the History of Israel, from the Hebrew University of Jerusalem, a Master's degree in Theological Studies from Boston University and doctoral studies in Old Testament Textual Criticism in Brandeis University, Moisés Chávez has produced the first Hebrew lexicon for Spanish readers in addition to a programmed text for the learning of Hebrew. He played a major role in a recent revision of the classic Reina-Valera Spanish Bible, and is currently working on programmed texts for the learning of Greek and Aramaic. His family first heard the Gospel through the evangelistic ministry of Calvin Mackay in the Celendín district of the northern Andes, and years later, in 1958, Moisés came as an eleven-year-old boy

189

to Lima to enrol as a Secondary pupil in Colegio San Andrés.

As a member, with his wife Amanda, of the San Andrés Presbyterian congregation, and responsible for the adult Bible Class and monthly seminars, Moisés believes strongly that Colegio San Andrés played a vitally formative role in preparing him for his future ministry. He recounts several incidents that took place in his schooldays:

> When I was on Second Year I once overheard a conversation between my History teacher, Mr Guillermo Arredondo (a former pupil of the school) and a colleague. Mr Arredondo told him that he had been asked to revise the Spanish of a certain section of the Bible for a new revision being prepared by the Bible Society. (This was at the request of James Mackintosh, a member of the New Testament revision team.) I was impressed that my teacher should have been asked to take part in a task of such magnitude. I felt that the Bible was something of great importance which merited the greatest respect, and from then on I held my teacher in the highest regard. The truth is that that conversation, brief though it was, made a great impression on me, and I never forgot a single detail of it.
>
> Some years later, on graduating from high school in 1963, I received, along with my classmates, a beautiful copy of the Bible in whose revision my teacher had played a part. It was the 1960 edition of the revised Reina-Valera Bible, and came to me as a gift from the National Bible Society of Scotland. It has grown old in my hands as the result of so much study. It's the Bible that went with me to Israel, it's the Bible that bears witness to my deepest experiences, above all that of knowing personally as my Saviour, Jesus the Messiah.

It was as a boy at school that Moisés Chávez discovered his vocation to be a writer. He tells of how his Spanish teacher in Second Year decided the class should produce its own newspaper, to be published on a notice-board in the main corridor. But first he asked them all to pretend they were the editor of this newspaper, and to write an editorial for the first issue. From these he selected two, and asked the authors to read them out to the class. By the unanimous vote of his classmates Moisés was appointed editor.

> I took my position as editor very seriously. We discussed what the name would be, and decided on *Tick-tock*. I soon knew what

a stencil and a duplicator were. In those days I couldn't imagine, even in my dreams, what it would be like to have a personal computer with automatic processing of the text. I had to count the spaces between the words and distribute them so that the end result would look like printed material.

School journalism became a passion with me, and took up too much of my time. After *Tick-tock*, I became editor of a daily newspaper, *Andresito*. By then I was taking to school the type-writer my mother had bought me with all her savings. One teacher even allowed me to type an exam, to the great envy of the other pupils.

Moisés Chávez's role as school journalist proved of great significance in 1961. Dr John A. Mackay, the school's founder and renowned author, was due to visit Lima, and of course *Andresito* had to cover the story. As a good journalist Moisés set about reading up all the background material he could find about his subject:

> From the school library I borrowed his book, *The Meaning of Life*. It made a great impression on me, and I read it over and over again. I decided I should have my own copy, and wrote to the publishers in Argentina. When they replied it was out of print, I borrowed it again from the library, and typed the whole book out myself.

Wherever John A. Mackay spoke or preached — in the school, the San Andrés church, the English-speaking Union Church, the Latin American Evangelical Congress, the University of San Marcos — the assiduous reporter followed him. He succeeded in interviewing him in his hotel, at the end of which Dr Mackay asked a favour of him. He had heard of the growth of shanty-towns around Lima and wanted to see them at first hand. Nothing daunted, the fifteen year old took his seventy-two year old mentor on broken-down old buses so that his heart might beat in sympathy with the victims of so much poverty and degradation. The letter that Moisés received from Dr Mackay on his return to the United States, in which he expressed his regret at not having seen him at his farewell in the airport, moved him greatly. It ended: "May God bless you in your studies and may you have a sense of his sovereign presence in your daily life, for the Christian vocation to which you are called." Many years later he was equally moved to receive a letter in which Dr Mackay wrote:

> I remember a little boy who used to follow me around every-where I went in Lima. It moves me to learn that that boy is now a member of the faculty in the Latin American Biblical Seminary in San José, Costa Rica, teaching Hebrew and Biblical Archaeology.

Not all Moisés Chávez's reminiscences are in the same serious vein. Though he never excelled in sport, he was persuaded by a classmate in his final year to join a sports club along with several other San Andrés pupils. On one occasion the club took part in a championship in the National Stadium, and in order to reach the finals needed someone merely to take part in the 400 metres hurdles. They persuaded Moisés, against his better judgment, that he should compete, even if he came in last.

> So I accepted, though I'd never run 400 metres, and had never jumped a single hurdle. In those days I was wearing glasses with only one arm, since the other had snapped off.
> Soon I was in the starting position. I'd never run in a race which began with a gun, and when they fired it my glasses darted off before I did. I ran after them, picked them up, put them on, and tackled the first hurdle, which left me with a bruised shin. When the other athletes had reached the finishing line, I was still trying to get over hurdles 150 metres away. But I didn't want to appear ridiculous giving up half-way in front of a packed stadium. So I kept going, and got over the last hurdle by sitting on it and climbing down.
> The spectators didn't care who arrived first. All their cheers were for the one who came in last, and for him alone the band played. My teammates carried me shoulder high along the track, and assured me my feat would never be forgotten.
> The matter didn't end there. At school the next day there was so much talk about Chávez coming in fifth in a great race at the National Stadium that the Headmaster heard of it. He was really quite moved and called me over to congratulate me. "And how many took part in the race?" he asked. "Five", I replied.

Influence for good

It is not difficult to point to former pupils of Colegio San Andrés, like Moisés Chávez, who are actively living out their

Christian faith in many different areas of public life, both in Peru and abroad.

But in the school's earlier history, specific instances of Evangelical commitment were less obvious, and Alexander Renwick was deeply pained by repeated accusations or insinuations that the school was of little spiritual value. His annual reports make constant reference to this point, occasionally telling of individual cases where he was hopeful of genuine spiritual impressions being made. The most striking of these, however, came to light six years after Renwick had left the school. A letter reached the Headmaster from a former pupil who had travelled to Japan, his parents' homeland, for business reasons. On Japan's entry into the Second World War, he was thrown into a concentration camp, and passed through a time of much suffering. But, he said: "Much of what I learned in the Anglo came back to me and in the darkness I found God." He went on to tell how he had since been led to prepare himself for the work of the ministry, and hoped to devote his life to the preaching of the Gospel to his fellow-countrymen.

The influence of Colegio San Andrés was not limited, however, to known instances of lives transformed by the Gospel. In its early years, and particularly as it gained a solid reputation for educational achievement and moral rectitude, it became one of the main forces in Peru leading to changed attitudes towards Protestantism and the Bible. When in 1929 news reached Lima that the Free Church of Scotland was considering closing down the school, Evangelical leaders of various denominations were aghast. One of these, John Ritchie, the doyen of Evangelical missions in Peru, wrote at length to the Foreign Missions Committee:

In the course of a conversation a few days ago, Mr Renwick mentioned to me that the possible discontinuance of the Colegio Anglo-Peruano as part of the activity of your Church in Peru was coming up for discussion at the Assembly this year. I wish to say that I am confident no man of God living in this land at this time and at all conversant with the present conditions would consider such discontinuance other than as a great calamity to the Church of God and to this republic.

The school is reaching a class of people who otherwise would not be reached, and is giving to the students a degree of knowledge of Christian truth and character which they could not otherwise get in Peru by any means known to me.

Did you but know Peru and perceive at close quarters the work of the Free Church of Scotland through the Colegio Anglo-Peruano, you would be, everyone of your whole Church, proud of the privilege God had given of having a share in bearing such a testimony, and proud of the men and women who represent you in carrying the battle within the gates of the enemy for the Truth and for our Lord and Saviour.

And from Ruperto Algorta, Superintendent of the central district of the Methodist Episcopal Church in Peru came similar sentiments:

The Anglo-Peruano school has acquired such a prestige as a Protestant school that to have it closed would be like giving a hard blow to the missionary work here.

During the early decades one of the most effective forms of Christian outreach was the Anglo-Peruvian Sunday School, especially in the nineteen thirties under the active leadership of Herbert Money. As many as eighty boys attended voluntarily, and while some were attracted by Dr Money's enthusiasm for excursions and Mrs Money's famous parties, some of those who attended still attribute spiritual impressions to the lessons taught them each Sunday.

One of these, retired Air Force general, Jorge Barbosa, tells of how he made his first tentative explorations in biblical knowledge at the Anglo Sunday school. He would go along each Sunday at 8.00 am and then attend mass with his family at 10.00 am. During his military career he had several brushes with death, which kept him aware of the hand of God on his life. Later friendship with Wycliffe Bible Translators brought him back to a study of the Bible and a personal faith in Christ. In 1976 a concerted effort was being made in Peru to expel Wycliffe Bible Translators (who as the Summer Institute of Linguistics worked officially with the Government on behalf of jungle tribes), accusing them of being CIA spies and agents of American imperialism. Jorge Barbosa, who had just retired from the Air Force, wrote a powerful letter to the two main Peruvian newspapers, praising the work of the linguists, and saying that if they were to leave Peru they should not be driven out as enemies, but rather decorated by the nation for their valuable work, humanitarian, educational and spiritual, on behalf of the all-too-neglected jungle Indians. As a result of his letter, a special commission was set up and a new agreement was signed with the Summer Institute of Linguistics, who have been able to complete the greater part of their work among Peru's minority linguistic groups.

Jorge Barbosa, a leader in the Community Bible Study movement, remembers with affection his pupil years in the Anglo-Peruano. He recounts how his Primary class were sometimes kept in writing lines by their teacher, Joanna Miller, usually because of continued talkativeness. On one occasion he rebelled, since he knew he was innocent of the charge, and after all the others had handed in their punishment and gone home, he sat there sullenly, refusing to write a word. When eventually he explained his reasons to the teacher, she threw her arms around him, and became from then on the weeping schoolboy's greatest friend. He tells of how Miss Miller would take groups of the children on outings or to children's films in a local cinema, and through it all showed the reality of a simple Christian faith.

A fellow classmate of his, retired army general Guillermo Schroth, also speaks appreciatively of the formative influence of the school and Sunday school on his life. While remaining a Roman Catholic, he claims that the Bible and its teachings, including passages learnt by heart at school, remained central in his thinking. In his professional life, he singles out discipline, honesty and punctuality as qualities instilled in him by the school's teaching. On one occasion he shocked civic and military dignitaries awaiting his arrival for an Independence Day parade by arriving in a bashed old Volkswagen "Beetle". The official limousine had broken down, and he refused to arrive late – an Anglo habit, he comments, if not a very Latin American one.

Transformation in Family Life

In the early nineteen sixties Eugenio and Sara Sánchez were looking for a good school for their first child. Eugenio, a young accountant from the mountains, came from a Seventh

Day Adventist background and Sara from a Catholic one. Since neither gave religion much weight, they compromised by leaving it out of their lives altogether. A relative recommended Colegio San Andrés, and their first interview was with the head of Primary. Among other things he explained that while the school respected the religious affiliation of its pupils, its own stance was Evangelical, firmly based on the Bible. He asked them if they ever read the Bible and when they answered in the negative, he suggested they reflect carefully before putting their son in a school where he would be taught the Bible, if at home he were to be taught differently. As they discussed the matter at home, they felt the teacher was right, and that they were not fulfilling their spiritual responsibilities as parents. The very next Sunday they made their way to the San Andrés church, and over the years they and their children professed faith in the Lord Jesus Christ. Now resident in Brazil, where the little boy they matriculated as a pupil in San Andrés practises as a doctor, they never cease to thank God for leading them, through Colegio San Andrés, out of their spiritual ignorance into the truth as it is in Jesus.

A dozen years before the Sánchez family made their way to Colegio San Andrés a young man from a Chinese family completed his education in the school. Humberto Lay was a good student, having been appointed head prefect in his final year. He was pleased to be receiving a good academic grounding that was to make it possible for him to become a successful Lima architect. The school's religious element made little impression on him; indeed he feels that the lifestyle and known views of at least two of the non-Evangelical teachers nullified at the time the positive impact of the actively Christian teachers whom he admired, especially Mr Sam Will. Nine years later his younger brother, Fernando, was also Head Prefect of the school. As described in Chapter 7, he was brought to faith in Christ, and immediately made clear at home that a real change had taken place in his life. Within two years, his entire family, – parents, brothers, sisters and other relatives – became Christians, last of all his architect brother. Humberto is now pastor of Emmanuel Biblical Church, one of the largest in Lima, and while his personal view is that the school should be more aggressive in its presentation of the message of salvation, acknowledges

196

unreservedly its vital role in the development of the Evangelical church in Peru.

In 1919 a Free Church minister wrote in the following terms to the Church's magazine:

> It has not been sufficiently debated whether an educational institution should have been put up in South America for missionary purposes ... I would not probably have written this letter if our Church had begun its operations with the original inhabitants of the country; but I am indeed very, very doubtful about the success of missions to the Roman Catholics. They shall take your good education, but Rome is too vigilant to permit her people to accept the Gospel.

In 1991 a young doctor, involved in missionary service in the Peruvian jungle, wrote in the following terms to the same magazine:

> I think that the most important thing in a definition of myself is that I am a Christian, and almost every time I have to give my testimony of how I became one, I begin by saying that I studied in Colegio San Andrés, because it was there that I heard of the Living God for the first time in my life ... Coming from a school run by Irish Catholics to another one run by Scottish Presbyterians was quite a change in many ways, but the most important one is that I had contact for the first time with God and his Word.

13

Just a Privileged Few?

According to the respected economic survey, *Perú en Números* by Richard Webb and Graciela Fernández Baca, in 1991 21.7% of Peruvians lived in "extreme poverty" and 53.7% in "critical poverty". In Lima alone there were 475 euphemistically termed "human settlements", which refer to the very worst shanty-town conditions, without water, sewage, electricity or roads. Millions more live in shanty-towns with varying degrees of basic amenitites. Malnutrition in children under the age of six is officially put at 62% in rural areas and 15% in urban areas, but the true figure in urban areas is undoubtedly higher. Cases of TB notified in 1990 were 41,100, and in 1991 there were 20,927 cholera victims who received some medical attention. All authorities are agreed that since 1990 there has been an alarming increase in malnutrition and tuberculosis in all age groups. The Government admit that 27% of Primary age children are not receiving education, but again it is to be feared that the true figure exceeds that percentage. Taking the average wage in 1980 as 100%, the 1990 wage in real terms was 39%. *Perú en Números* does not give statistics for the number of children whose only home is on the city streets, either because their parents have abandoned them, abused them or simply cannot feed them. They give no statistics, because these are unknown, but workers in that field consider that up to half a million children live in destitution on the streets of Peruvian cities.

Behind such cold statistics lies a shocking catalogue of human suffering and degradation. And if the church is not found ministering comfort and compassion where pain and poverty are at their worst, she is failing in her task as a witness to God's love. Against such a background, it is not surprising that voices have been raised in the home churches, accusing Colegio San Andrés of being elitist, perpetrating a continued position of privilege for the few at the expense of the millions of poor and under-privileged.

In 1980 an editorial in *The Monthly Record* claimed that any teacher offering to serve in Colegio San Andrés would be bewildered to discover that the school was "reaching only a privileged sector of Lima society."

In 1986 a correspondent wrote, in response to an editorial calling for separate Protestant schools in Scotland:

> I recently attended a talk on Free Church mission work in Peru. In a city where a large proportion of children sleep on the streets, the Colegio San Andrés provides a Christian education for the intellectually and financially endowed. In reply to my question as to whether there were any plans to extend this education to the less privileged, I was told that a bursary might soon be made available for *able* children from poorer families.
>
> Formal education, as provided by schools, should in my opinion, be free, comprehensive and independent – independent, that is, of any specific banner or battle cry, where children are free to learn.

And when in 1982 Rev and Mrs Sherwood Reisner, son-in-law and daughter of Dr John A. Mackay, lectured to Mexican students in Mexico City on Mackay's life and thought, the students expressed admiration for his spiritual vision and intellectual calibre, but questioned the rightness of his working among the more privileged sectors of society as also in education rather than direct evangelism. When poverty and injustice abound, should the church's messengers not give prior attention to the poor and oppressed who are neglected by everyone else?

How are such legitimate concerns to be addressed? Can Colegio San Andrés be absolved of the charge of elitism? Does it contribute anything to meeting the clamant social and spiritual needs of Peru?

A missionary strategy

As one traces the missionary journeys of the Apostle Paul, one finds him concentrating his efforts on strategic urban centres from which the Gospel would fan out to surrounding areas. Not that his preaching was exclusively in such places nor solely to people likely to exercise decisive influence over many others. He was as ready to devote his time to a handful of women by a riverside or to forgotten prisoners in a Roman jail, as to the intelligentsia of Athens, the merchants of Corinth or the religious leaders of Jewry. He was a debtor to all men for the sake of the Gospel, and these "all", as he tells the Christians in Rome, included "the wise".

When John A. Mackay highlighted Lima as being "the centre of Spanish culture in South America", and spoke repeatedly of moulding the minds of the educated youth of Peru, it was with one supreme aim in view. He desired these young men to bow to the lordship of Jesus Christ, and so to go out and demonstrate God's love and justice in their lives that the whole of the nation would feel the difference. His vision was nothing less than the Reformation that in the sixteenth century had been denied the Hispanic world. It was with this in view that he and his successors urged the home Church to send out men and women of the very highest calibre and preparation, and not to lose the unique opportunity they believed had been given them to influence a nation for God and for good. Mackay increasingly saw his role as an evangelist to the student and educated classes of Latin America, and his subsequent career as a "religious lecturer" with the YMCA gave him unfettered scope for such an activity. But never exclusively so. Some of the twenty or thirty youngsters looked after in the Anglo-Peruano boarding department were from poor families. Mackay's preaching nearly every Sunday was to humble believers in unpretentious churches and mission halls. Whenever the opportunity presented itself, he travelled to rural areas, some of them very remote, and preached with as equal fervour to the poorest Indians as to the leading citizens of provincial towns such as Huancayo or Cajamarca. His reports urge the establishment of medical missions and the planting of churches in the mountains and the jungle, and he worked hard to bring these about.

Mackay's successors accepted and practised the very same missionary policy. Without exception they spoke enthusiastically of the unique opportunity granted to the Free Church of Scotland through Colegio San Andrés, and saw no conflict in educating the sons of the rich while being committed to the welfare of the poor. Every single one of the Scottish head-masters either came from the Highlands or had his parental roots there. Their sympathies ran strongly with their oppressed forebears, unjustly driven from their ancestral lands during the nineteenth-century "Clearances". There was not one of them but would gladly have spent his days with other missionary colleagues alongside Peru's needy and oppressed, had God not sovereignly directed them to labour in another strategic and spiritually equally needy field.

Not all the school staff were able to travel widely and reach forgotten regions and peoples with the Gospel. But those who could, did. Vere Rochelle Browne, Alexander Renwick and Herbert Money travelled indefatigably when school duties allowed. The greater availability of air transport coincided with James Mackintosh's headmastership, and his reports tell of many journeys, especially to Cajamarca, Chachapoyas and Moyobamba. While there he delighted in meeting and ministering to local believers, some of them with very little formal education and scraping a subsistence living from the soil.

God called Peter as an apostle to the Jews and Paul as an apostle to the Gentiles. In the history of the church some have been specially gifted for witnessing to the aristocracy or the intelligentsia or the framers of a nation's laws. Others have exercised their calling among slaves or leprosy patients or refugees or drug addicts or AIDS sufferers. All should recognise and support the others' gifts and ministries, for "there are different kinds of gifts, but the same Spirit. There are different kinds of service, but the same Lord. There are different kinds of working, but the same God works all of them in all men" (1 Corinthians 12:4-5). Certainly John Ritchie was far from being the only church leader in Peru who unreservedly thanked God for the Colegio Anglo-Peruano's special entry into the educated and influential classes of Peru. They saw its role as vital in creating a much more favourable attitude towards Protestantism, and facilitating their own work, often carried out among the dispossessed and despised masses.

Colegio San Andrés is seen today in the same light, even though its prestigious standing and social composition have been modified over the years. In 1992 Dr Carlos García, the Deputy Vice-President of Peru, who has used his high office to work tirelessly on behalf of Peru's vast army of hungry, homeless and unemployed, has confirmed this view of San Andrés's place in Peruvian life. He considers it to have been a bridgehead for Evangelical truth, for training in good citizenship and for social justice, and hopes it will long maintain its special place in the country. When he was unable to accept an invitation to address the final year pupils at a service in the school chapel, due to a prior engagement in Israel, he specifically asked for another opportunity to address the whole of Secondary at a morning assembly. He urged them to hold firmly to the school's motto that "the fear of the Lord is the beginning of wisdom", and to pray and work for a truly Christian ethic to permeate every sphere of Peruvian life.

Motivating others

In the early nineteen sixties a San Andrés schoolboy responded to Christ's call to repentance, faith and discipleship. Ernesto Zavala's spiritual growth was nurtured only through school and Scripture Union camps, until he left for studies in Canada and the United States. Many years later he qualified as a specialist teacher of the deaf and as an interpreter with the United Nations. In spite of his comfortable lifestyle, he heard God's call to return with his wife and children to Peru, in order to serve the handicapped and under-privileged. As a worker with Scripture Union he brings hope to the deaf for whom little else is done, and compassion to many street children, on whose behalf he has spearheaded valuable projects in Lima and the Amazon city of Iquitos. He is in full agreement with San Andrés's policy of concentrating its main efforts on those able to pay for their own education. So little does he feel that this is neglectful of or prejudicial to his own work among the poorest and neediest, that in 1992 he offered to do voluntary English teaching in the school. This was, he said, an expression of gratitude for all that Colegio San Andrés had meant in his life, bringing him to Christ and motivating him to Christian service.

Ernest Zavala's experience illustrates a fundamental aim of Colegio San Andrés. No doubt some boys and their families

see the good education offered as a means of ensuring a prosperous future for themselves, with little concern for the many
under-privileged who may live only a few blocks away. But the
Christian staff have always striven to present Christ both as the
object of faith and as a model for action. If hundreds or even
only scores of pupils are so motivated, they will accomplish
far more on behalf of their own people than a handful of for-
eigners ever could. And so there are former pupils who have
worked in community development and in house construction
among earthquake victims. Others have initiated projects on
behalf of the widows, orphans and refugees resulting from terrorism. Still others have given freely of their time and skill in
medical programmes for those unable to pay. Some have been
involved in programmes of Christian social concern in other
Latin American countries and as far away as India. There are
also former pupils in other spheres of life who contribute
regularly to the alleviation of poverty, such as the successful
family of businessmen who anonymously provide meals regularly
for large numbers of poor children, or former pupils who offer
scholarship help for San Andrés pupils from needy families.

An important area where Colegio San Andrés has used its
prestige and experience on behalf of others is in encouraging
and guiding the formation of other Evangelical schools. These
are often small and poorly resourced, but they provide a good
basic education for thousands of under-privileged children. In
1992 San Andrés took the initiative in forming an Evangelical
Schools Association which is intended to provide mutual help
and encouragement. San Andrés, as a founding member of a
separate Association of private schools sponsored by cultural
organisations, all from the top category of Lima schools, may
well not need the help of an Evangelical Schools Association.
But it is aware of a call to service on behalf of others, and on
this basis has taken action.

A self-supporting policy

Free education has to be funded by someone, whether tax-
payer or charitable donor. Were Colegio San Andrés to provide
an equal number of destitute children with the same education
as its fee-paying children receive, it would have required in 1991

an annual donated income of £340,000. Where would the money come from? Certainly not from the Free Church of Scotland, which has for several years struggled with inadequate income for all its needs.

But even were large funds to be available to start a more modest educational venture for the under-privileged, the wisdom of such a course would have to be questioned. Several Evangelical educational institutions in Peru at present are heavily dependent on foreign funds, even for their running costs, and are anxiously looking for ways to increase their own income. Colegio San Andrés, on the other hand, has insisted from the beginning that it should be self-supporting, although this has often meant that its facilities do not match those of other schools and colleges with wealthier benefactors. Donations are always welcome for special projects or the scholarship fund, but the principle of self-support ensures that were all Free Church sponsorship and personnel to be withdrawn, Colegio San Andrés would continue its task without undue difficulty.

Self-support, of course, means fees. In an article in *The Monthly Record* of September 1986, Dr Donald MacDonald, a missionary surgeon in India, tackles this question in a series of letters to an imaginary young teacher:

> I am committed to serving the rural poor in India, but that does not stop me being a supporter of the Colegio San Andrés in Lima. It appears to me that, though we must give priority to preaching the good news to the poor, following Christ's example, we must not neglect the intellectual, powerful and influential sections of society.
>
> Some of the advantages of the school as I see it are:
>
> (a) Being fee-paying it can be self-supporting, apart from a proportion of expatriate salaries. Scholarship facilities for poor children could be expanded. Remember that we charge fees in Lakhnadon Christian Hospital, and our Charity Fund covers the fees of those who can't afford to pay. If we did not charge fees we would have to find £30,000 annually to run the hospital!
>
> (b) It can influence for good those who may occupy leadership positions in society, not only by winning some of them for Christ, but by instilling Christian ethical and moral

values, and ideals of service, which are not generally found in society.

(c) The good reputation of the school helps relationships of Evangelicals with the Government.

(d) The Christian staff can work in the local evangelical congregations as well as take part in training Peruvian Christian teachers.

One of the results of our Highland heritage and history is an ingrained anti-elitism; but is this matched by a radical concern for and involvement with the correction of injustice, inequality and oppression in society? I rather doubt it. If you choose not to go to Lima because of the elitist flavour of the school, I would expect you to teach in a really under-privileged area in Britain, or elsewhere.

Help for the Needy

In 1992 over 100 pupils received scholarship help from the school's own resources, leading to their fees being reduced by a quarter, a half, three quarters or totally. The austerity measures of President Fujimori's Government since 1990 have hugely increased unemployment and drastically reduced the income of formerly well-off families. Some of them have been unable to pay their school fees, and special short-term scholarship help from a Bursary Fund in Edinburgh, contributed to by supportive friends, has come to their aid. About forty more pupils have received help through this means. The fees themselves are kept at as reasonable a level as possible, but the temptation to reduce them to an unrealistic sum which would prejudice staff salaries or harm the quality of education is strenuously resisted.

Looking back to his schooldays in the Anglo-Peruano, a retired Army colonel tells how he and his four brothers were all educated in the school. The family was not poor, but neither was it able to pay the fees of five boys in the Anglo-Peruvian College:

> Each year Dr Renwick was approached for help, and each year his answer was the same: "Fifty per cent reduction!" Tell your readers that the Vargas family are forever grateful, and are proud to be counted among the old boys of the Anglo.

As far as direct help to the needy is concerned, the ordinary tussle to keep expenditure below income, and the demands of the scholarship fund do not leave much scope for specific aid. But attempts are made, particularly to keep parents and pupils sensitive to the needs of others. In 1990 some of the more talented members of staff gave a concert in the school assembly hall to raise funds for the work being done by two former pupils who were providing a health service for the rural poor and houses for earthquake victims. Each year the pupils are encouraged to give to collections taken on behalf of the Red Cross, the Cancer Society or children in poorer schools.

One programme of help, initiated in the mid-nineteen fifties by missionary teacher Sam Will, is still looked back to by those involved as vital to their understanding of Christian social responsibility. It began in a Bible Study when a senior pupil asked how they could in practice fulfil the words they were studying: "If anyone has material possessions and sees his brother in need but has no pity on him, how can the love of God be in him?" (1 John 3:17). This led to the group, consisting of senior pupils, young former pupils and a few friends, which met regularly in the Wills' home under the name of *Forward Christian Youth*, spending most of their Saturday afternoons in one or other of Lima's shanty-towns. In *Leader* of 1961 one of them described the group's activities:

We go with the message of faith and salvation, and to show these people that in spite of their poverty they are deserving of the love and friendship of their neighbours; and as far as we are able, we take some material aid for the neediest.

In the same issue of the magazine another pupil wrote:

Hunger walks in the slums and looks out at us from the faces of the children and the old. Let us never try to escape from the thought of their tragedy.

Thirty years later Elizabeth Mackenzie reported in *The Monthly Record* on a conversation she had with a teacher in the Diego Thomson College of Education:

You're from Scotland, aren't you? We in Comas owe so much to Mr Will. The work he began is now a big church — hundreds of families have been touched. Children have been brought up under the influence of the Gospel, who otherwise might now be involved in terrorism. People have been rescued from the gutter.

Over 800 boys, most of them neatly uniformed, well-fed and educated far beyond the national average, constitute a privileged group in Peru. Every day on their way to school they pass hundreds of abandoned children, impoverished street vendors and handicapped beggars. They learn in Colegio San Andrés of One who "went about doing good", and who left an example that they should follow in his steps. They are told of former pupils who live out their lives in the service of others. They learn of teachers involved in various areas of human need — camps for under-privileged or handicapped children, homes for old people, visits to prisons and hospitals, adult literacy programmes. They discover in 1993 that one missionary teacher, Laura Simon, has devoted herself full-time to preparing a signing manual for the deaf, as part of the Scripture Union's social service programme. They are urged to "do justly, love mercy and walk humbly with their God" when they take their places of influence in society. Perhaps through some of them the Peru of the future will experience a greater healing for its hurting millions, a greater liberty for its many victims of oppression, of disease and of sin. If not, the sooner the school's doors close for the last time the better, for Peru has no need of more bastions of privilege, insulated from the real needs of real people. And the Christian teachers who, all of them, see their work as a fulfilment of the command to love God and their neighbour with all their heart and soul and mind and strength, will no longer find a place in an institution whose glory will have departed.

But this has never been, and cannot be, the spirit of Colegio San Andrés. As far back as 1926 a Secondary schoolboy, who hailed from a remote village in the Andes, addressed a passionate plea to his schoolmates on behalf of the despised and downtrodden Indians. As a title for his article he used a phrase often heard, expressive of racial prejudice and empty paternalism: *Poor Indians!* In the first issue of *Leader* he wrote:

I have seen tears flow on the cheeks of our disinherited brothers, and I say brothers because in our veins there flows Indian blood, and even those who have none live in the land of the Incas.

Because of their miserable situation they suffer immensely, always enslaved down through the centuries, and worst of all in this twentieth century when we boast of our civilisation, they are the target of injustice, still being sold by their masters as if they were animals.

Aladino Escalante, later to become a teacher of the school and an active elder and preacher of the Evangelical Presbyterian Church, went on to urge his readers to visit the mountain regions with eyes wide open to the plight of their fellow-Peruvians, adding:

May your lips never dare to sing, "We are free" (the opening words of Peru's National Anthem) unless you are prepared to enter the fray and fight for the Indian's rights to be restored to him.

Just one school. But under God it can be a powerful catalyst for change and blessing throughout a nation.

14

Towards the Centenary

Paul Clark, General Director of Scripture Union for the Americas, has described Colegio San Andrés as:

> the focal point for Scripture Union's ministry in Peruvian schools for well over thirty years. It is a model, both in showing others how to work effectively across denominational lines, and in demonstrating how the Gospel can be presented in a clear, thoughtful and sensitive manner.

He is grateful to the school "for providing us with some of our finest leaders", citing as an example the current Chairman of Scripture Union's Advisory Board in the Amazon city of Iquitos:

> This respected citizen and outstanding businessman is grateful to his old school not only for having provided him with a solid education, but for having encouraged him to attend regularly the Scripture Union meetings in the school from the time he was a very small boy until the day of his graduation.
>
> In Iquitos he is one of those responsible for a successful and imaginative project that has brought employment, education and spiritual hope to many otherwise abandoned young people.

Other examples of such Christian service have been described throughout this book, and more could be cited. The school's success in riding out crises, and in overcoming serious obstacles has also been demonstrated. But is that all there is to say? What have been the school's shortcomings, and what are the lessons for the future?

Some drawbacks are obvious. The chronic lack of space will never be adequately solved until there are new premises; meanwhile teachers and pupils overlooking the playground or within earshot of the generator or the incessant noise of traffic will continue to suffer. An average class size of almost forty has meant that pupils with learning difficulties or withdrawn temperaments rarely receive the special attention they require, in spite of the sometimes herculean efforts of class teachers and the school's part-time psychologist. Neither the time nor the resources have been available to cater for less academic pupils, or to introduce courses of a more technical, commercial or vocational nature. While English is taught on a daily basis from first grade, and some pupils attain a high standard by the time they leave school, there are former pupils who regret that they were not immersed more in an English-speaking environment, and compare San Andrés unfavourably with some other schools which had equally few native English speakers. And in spite of attempts to eliminate it, there have always been teachers far too dependent on rote learning, for so long the bane of traditional Peruvian education, and parents have sometimes despaired at the time required by their children to copy and memorise pages of facts, instead of more creative work or the memorisation of more valuable material.

On the pastoral level, a vast area of opportunity in pupils' homes is scarcely touched. Moral breakdowns and economic pressures have created many problems in Peruvian homes, and troubled families would welcome the guidance and support of their children's Christian teachers. In 1987 the school psychologist along with a missionary teacher who was giving part of his time to counselling carried out a study of the home situation of pupils with behavioural or abnormal academic problems. They discovered that in a very high percentage of cases, the parents were separated or divorced or were involved in some extra-marital liaison. Were missionary teachers available, or were it financially possible to free gifted Peruvian Christian staff to offer parents ethical guidance and present the Gospel message of forgiveness and hope, much could be accomplished. But all too often the claims of the classroom and the office have left the deeper needs of pupils and their families unattended.

Much, however, has been accomplished. The school has been, and will continue to be an instrument for good in the hand of God. It could still produce the best male athlete in the 1992 inter-schools tournament, or pupils to win city-wide poetry or mathematics competitions, and others as champions in nation-wide television general knowledge competitions. But more importantly, it has not wavered in three quarters of a century from its commitment to the Scriptures as God's Word and its firm belief that there is power in the Gospel to transform individual lives and entire societies. This was stated emphatically in a 1964 interview in *From the Frontiers* by Dr René Padilla, General Secretary for Latin America of the International Fellowship of Evangelical Students:

> What I know of Protestant schools in Latin America has been generally very disappointing because of the little impact which they are making on society with the Gospel. I would say that, in my experience, Colegio San Andrés is the only one of which this is not true. Among the outstanding leaders of the University group are some who have been converted in San Andrés or pointed towards the Gospel through its influence. I have had several opportunities of speaking to the boys in morning assembly, though I would like to stress how good it is that no one set method is followed for bringing the Gospel to the boys. In addition to the morning assemblies, there are the smaller Scripture Union meetings, and especially the tremendous personal influence that young Christian teachers, both Peruvian and foreign, have on the boys.

In 1980 Dr Neil A. R. Mackay, with his unrivalled knowledge of education in Latin America, expressed himself in similar terms in a policy document on Colegio San Andrés prepared by the Foreign Missions Board:

> There are about thirty schools in South America that could at one time have been compared spiritually and academically with Colegio San Andrés, but none of them has produced people prominent in public life in their respective countries as the Colegio has done in Peru. It is unique. Of these thirty schools some of them started as the Colegio did, but none of them today maintains its original missionary standing.

Words such as these must, of course, be tempered by the recognition that outside Latin America there have been many outstanding Protestant missionary schools and colleges that have risen to greater heights than Colegio San Andrés has ever attained. It should also be gratefully admitted that within Latin

America there have been Protestant schools that have succeeded in areas where Colegio San Andrés has failed. In Dr Webster Browning's words of 1920, quoted in chapter 4, he emphasised the crucial need for the school to be "well equipped with buildings and grounds" and to have an adequate "faculty of men and women whose final aim in all their teaching is the bringing to the Peruvians of the pure Gospel of Jesus Christ".

These hopes were never fully realised. but something was done. Something of abiding value. And the foundation for doing much more has been truly laid.

Looking ahead

It is likely that Colegio San Andrés will soon be the responsibility of a local Board which will continue its task with the same vision and the same striving after excellence that characterised the founders. Organisational changes should not, however, sever or reduce the harmonious working relationship between the school and the Free Church of Scotland. Through the Anglo-Peruano, now San Andrés, many lives have been laid at the roots of a nation which was not their own, and there has been an entwining of destinies and a reaping of many shared harvests. The people of the Free Church of Scotland, the Presbyterian Church of Eastern Australia and the Evangelical Presbyterian Church of Ireland, of other Churches which have sent their sons and daughters to Peru, and of Churches which may yet do so, are called not to less participation, but to more. The Parents' Association, the school staff, the Old Boys' Association, church leaders of various denominations, and pupils who may have no corporate voice but whose feelings are readily gauged, all together say: "Come over and help us."

How can help be given? The ways are old, but better ones will never be found.

Pray

In 1956 the pressure to adopt a non-biblical scheme of religious education was intense. Not only were the ecclesiastical authorities determined to win the battle and pulling every available lever at Government level, but the school had fallen foul of the President's wife by not accepting a boy she had recommended for admission, a boy who would have been unable to cope with the academic demands of the Secondary class for which he was supposedly prepared. The Deputy Head, a Member of Parliament, worked tirelessly on the school's behalf, and eventually one afternoon, when the outlook seemed very bleak, phoned from the Ministry of Education. He had just received assurances from a former pupil in high office in the Ministry that no punitive action would be taken against San Andrés and that its religious stance would be respected. The school's Christian staff had been much in prayer, and when James Mackintosh and Sam Will shared the news in an upstairs corridor, they thanked God for his abundant answer. But what James Mackintosh has never forgotten about that moment is the overwhelming sense he received that their victory was a victory of the whole body of Christ, and that praying people in the homeland were sharing equally in the divine blessing on the school.

How many were praying for these two missionary teachers in Lima? Enough for God to hear and answer. How many pray today for their successors in the work?

Tell

In relation to Lima's eight million inhabitants or Peru's twenty-two million, a school with 830 boys, hemmed in on every side in downtown Lima, cannot be expected to make much impression. Nor is a Church with an overall membership of some 15,000 people in the small country of Scotland likely to have its activities known very far afield. But even the most insignificant Christian has a duty to proclaim his experience of God:

> Come and listen, all you who fear God,
> let me tell you what he has done for me (Psalm 66:16)

Centuries after David spoke in these terms, Paul and Barnabas returned from overseas missionary work to the church in Antioch that had sent them out. "On arriving there, they gathered the church together and reported all that God had done through them and how he had opened the door of faith to the Gentiles" (Acts 14:27).

Ten years after Herbert Money left full-time service in the Colegio Anglo-Peruano, he spoke about God's work there to a young New Zealander, Donald Mitchell, who was then called to serve God in the school.

In Belfast, Methodist minister Luis Baldeón and his wife, Estela, who was head of English in Primary and whose son, Toshío, was head prefect of Colegio San Andrés, have told many of the school and its work, leading one of their church members, Fiona Sheeran, to spend one summer holiday as a volunteer there, and others to be informed and prayerful.

In his many travels throughout the world in connection with the International Fellowship of Evangelical Students, the Latin American Theological Fraternity and the Peruvian Bible Society, former pupil Pedro Arana has presented the ministry and challenge of Colegio San Andrés to thousands of Christian people. From Europe, the United States, Australia and elsewhere have come messages of support and enquiries about service.

But not only former teachers and former pupils have told others of one of the works of God with which they personally were involved. Many Christian people, who have never seen the Pacific or the Andes and never will, have become ambassadors for Colegio San Andrés. Their reading and recommendation of this written record of God's faithfulness to one school community in Peru will help ensure its continued ministry and even expand its usefulness.

Give

For three quarters of a century Colegio San Andrés has maintained its financial independence. It has no desire to change that pattern, nor to direct funds to its own use that are required for other needy causes. But there have been times of crisis; there have been members of the school family: pupils, parents and staff, in need of special help; there have been repeated occasions when lack of finance has blocked the purchase of a suitable site for necessary expansion.

Again and again a timely gift from Christian friends to the Bursary Fund has alleviated the distress of families genuinely unable to pay their school fees. More than once when mega-inflation rendered the school unable to make the purchases necessary to maintain its educational standards, special donations came to the rescue. One from Australia made possible the purchase of a modern internal telephone system; another from Scotland permitted the exceptional payment of a staff bonus at a time of savage devaluation of the currency; yet another from Northern Ireland provided the school nurse with valuable medical equipment. And one of Peru's best-known Christian leaders will never forget how as a recently converted schoolboy, eager to learn more of the ways of God, he had an account opened in his name in a Christian bookshop by a missionary teacher, and every month was able to buy another book to aid the growth of his spiritual understanding. Such gifts are, in Paul's words, "a fragrant offering, an acceptable sacrifice, pleasing to God" (Philippians 4:18).

Go

If one overriding impression is left by the hundreds of reports and articles sent over the years from Lima to the home Church, it is surely summed up in Neil Mackay's words written in 1945: "the magnitude of our opportunity and the paucity of our means". By "means" he was not referring to finance but to people, for he went on to say: "Perhaps never before in the history of the School has it been granted so much liberty by the authorities, or enjoyed so much favour with the public ... that this should also be the moment at which our missionary staff is reduced to the lowest possible level is a source of constant sorrow to me, and I am sure it will be so to the home Church."

Today there are more Peruvian Evangelical Christians on the staff than ever before, and indeed others who, though not in membership with any Protestant church, identify wholeheartedly with the school's spiritual aims and openly confess that it is their contact with God's Word through the school that has brought this about. This means that spiritual opportunities do not go by default to the extent they did half a century ago.

215

But, as has been constantly stressed, there is still a specially warm welcome reserved for Christian teachers from abroad, able to devote all their energies to their work in the school, and enabling San Andrés to keep abreast with educational advances in other countries. If they are native English speakers they are doubly welcome, whether they are trained teachers willing to spend as many years as God might ask them to in the school, or volunteers from varied backgrounds able to devote what time they can to stimulating, if demanding, short-term service. The writer of these chapters heard God's call to the ministry of the Word while teaching in Colegio San Andrés. There was no disenchantment with the classroom nor any lessened sense of the high privilege of sharing in the moulding of young lives for the service of the best of all masters. God in his wisdom chose other places and other tasks, but even then surprisingly reopened the door of Colegio San Andrés. The honour was as great, the fellowship with colleagues as warm, the opportunity to serve the Lord Christ as extensive as ever. As Christ's words come home with sovereign authority to a new generation, "Go and make disciples of all nations", there are undoubtedly some for whom the nation will be Peru, and the task in view will centre on Colegio San Andrés.

Two evocative scenes bring the book, but not the story, to an end. The first focuses on a man in a wheelchair, paralysed from the neck down. Jorge Gadea made a fighting recovery from four experiences of paralysis due to an inherited spinal disorder, but the fifth, in 1979, left him quadriplegic. His active service with the YMCA in Peru, Uruguay, Australia and the Dominican Republic merely took a different direction, as he turned to writing leadership training manuals and then to heading up a Canadian-based programme to provide housing, education and medical care for abandoned street children in Santo Domingo. In 1988, to celebrate the fortieth anniversary of his class's graduation from Colegio San Andrés, he published at his own expense a fresh edition of *The Meaning of Life* by John A. Mackay.

In a personal prologue he expresses his thanks to "those teachers who came to Peru from far-off Scotland as also to our Peruvian teachers". He commends the school for the

216

academic preparation it gave its pupils, and for "its emphasis on honesty, sincerity, integrity, punctuality and love for work." Referring to his grave handicap, he says that it is "the pure waters from the spring of Colegio San Andrés that slake my thirst in the dark nights of discouragement, and I feel that the sun of hope arises to renew my convictions every morning."

In describing himself in 1992 in a letter to the Headmaster as *un sanandresino hasta los huesos* (a San Andrés man to the backbone), he goes on to quote "the comforting promise of the written Word" in Isaiah 40:30-31:

Even youths grow tired and weary, and young men stumble and fall;
But those who hope in the Lord will renew their strength.
They will soar on wings like eagles; they will run and not grow weary,
they will walk and not faint.

San Andrés can do nothing greater than point young men to such a Saviour.

The second scene focuses on a boy in fourth year of Secondary. He goes up to Mrs Ann Dunlop, his English teacher, and asks to speak to her. The reason is to confess that he had forged his father's signature on his recently failed English test. "I've become a Christian, so I know I did wrong and that I've to put it right with you and my father."

Each new Government in Peru promises to root out the corruption practised or tolerated by its predecessors. A San Andrés schoolboy can show them where to begin:

My son, if you accept my words and store up my commands within you, turning your ear to wisdom and applying your heart to understanding ...
Then you will understand the fear of the Lord, and find the knowledge of God.

(Proverbs 2:1-2,5).

Appendix 1

Chronological Summary

1532	Fall of Inca Empire. Spanish colonisation begins
1535	Founding of city of Lima
1570	Establishment of the Holy Office of the Inquisition in Lima
1780	Rebellion of José Gabriel Condorcanqui "Tupac Amaru II" crushed by Spaniards
1814	Abolition of the Holy Office of the Inquisition
1821	Declaration of Peruvian Independence
1822	Arrival of James Thomson in Peru
1824	Departure of James Thomson from Peru
	Final defeat of Spanish forces at Battle of Ayacucho
1843	Disruption of Church of Scotland and formation of Free Church of Scotland
1845	Ramón Castilla elected President of Peru
	Permission granted British community in Lima to hold Protestant services in English
1854	Abolition of slavery in Peru
1879-83	Chile defeats Peru and Bolivia in War of the Pacific
1888	Arrival of Francisco Penzotti in Peru
1890-91	Imprisonment and Release of Francisco Penzotti
1891	Arrival in Peru of Methodist missionary Thomas Wood
1893	Arrival from England of Harley College graduates, later to become RBMU missionaries
1900	Majority of Free Church of Scotland enter union with United Presbyterians
	Minority continue as Free Church of Scotland
1906	Arrival in Peru of RBMU missionary John Ritchie
1910	World Missionary Congress in Edinburgh
1911	Founding of Evangelical Union of South America

1914-18 First World War
1915   Peruvian constitution amended to permit public non-Roman Catholic worship
         John A. Mackay makes exploratory tour of South America
         Opening of Panama Canal
1916   Arrival of John and Jane Mackay as first Free Church of Scotland missionaries in Peru
1917   Founding of Colegio Anglo-Peruano (Colegio San Andrés)
1923   Víctor Raúl Haya de la Torre deported from Peru. Founds *Alianza Popular Revolucionaria Americana* (APRA) in Mexico
1924   School limited to boys only
1926   Founding of *Leader*, magazine of Colegio Anglo-Peruano
1929   Free Church General Assembly rejects proposals to close Colegio Anglo-Peruano or transfer to some other body
1930   Inauguration of new school building
         Overthrow of President Augusto Leguía
1933   Founding of Peruvian Bible Institute. Dr Alexander Renwick represents Free Church on governing body
1939-45 Second World War
1942   School name changed to Colegio San Andrés
1954   First Scripture Union camp held in Peru
1957   Construction of block of flats for foreign teachers, chapel and gymnasium
1961   Rev James Mackintosh receives MBE for services to education
1962   Former pupil General Nicolás Lindley assumes Peruvian Presidency
         Founding of Evangelical Seminary of Lima (from Peruvian Bible Institute) with Rev James Mackintosh as first Chairman of Board
1963   Evangelical Presbyterian Church of Peru receives legal recognition as an independent body
1964   Last visit to Peru of Dr John A. Mackay. Receives *Palmas Magisteriales* from Peruvian government
1967   School's fiftieth anniversary. Free Church Missions Board represented by Secretary, Rev Clement Graham
         Dr and Mrs Herbert Money retire after 41 and 48 years missionary service in Peru. Dr Money receives *Palmas Magisteriales* from Peruvian Government
1968   General Juan Velasco deposes President Fernando Belaúnde. Institutes wide-ranging programme of reforms

1979   Constituent Assembly frames new constitution with former
        pupil Pedro Arana as member. Complete religious lib-
        erty granted

1980   Election of Fernando Belaúnde as President for second
        term. Former pupil Sandro Mariátegui Prime Minister for
        part of the time
        Sendero Luminoso (Shining Path) begins its terrorist cam-
        paign

1985   Block of flats remodelled for school use

1986   Founding of Diego Thomson College of Education

1991   Dr José Vidal retires as Director after 36 years service in
        the school

1992   President Alberto Fujimori dissolves Congress, suspends
        constitution and calls elections for new Constituent
        Assembly
        Capture of Abimael Guzmán and other Shining Path
        leaders
        School's seventy-fifth anniversary. Free Church Missions
        Board represented by Chairman, Rev Innes MacRae and
        Secretary, Rev Finlay Mackenzie

1993   Programme of remodelling school premises begun with facil-
        ities for co-education to recommence in 1994. Ultimate aim
        is new school on new site.
        150th Anniversary of Disruption and formation of Free
        Church of Scotland

Appendix 2

Full time missionary teachers of Colegio San Andres, contracted either by the Foreign Missions Committee/Board, or by agreement between the Headmaster and the Foreign Missions Committee/Board or locally by the Headmaster.

	NAME	COUNTRY	POSITION	DATES
	Bailey, Clive	Scotland	English teacher	1977-79
	Brand, Janis	Scotland	English teacher	1981-88
*	Brewster, C.W.	U.S.A.	Secondary teacher	1926
	Browne,VereRochelle	New Zealand	Science teacher	1918-22
	Clear,Valorous	U.S.A.	English teacher	1943
*	Coombe, Malcolm	England	Science teacher	1964-68
	Cutbill,Leslie	England	Science teacher	1922-24
*	Donaldson, Florence	Northern Ireland	Administrator	1963-85
	Florit,Marcos	Spain	Headmaster	1989-
	Fraser, Alan	Scotland	Headmaster	1973-88
*	French, Joan	England	Primary teacher	1954-56
	Hutchison,Mary	Scotland	Primary teacher	1922-27
	Jonkers,Pieter	Holland	Science teacher	1982-86
*	Kemp, Janet (later Money)	Scotland	Primary teacher	1920-39
*	McDonald, Isabelle (later Bell)	Scotland	Primary teacher	1949-53
*	Mackay, Christina	Scotland	Primary Head	1922-24,33-64
*	Mackay, J. Calvin	Scotland	Acting Headmaster	1945-47
*	Mackay, Jane	Scotland	Primary teacher	1917-18
	Mackay,JohnA.	Scotland	Headmaster	1917-25
	Mackay,Neil	Scotland	Headmaster	1935-45
	Mackay,William	Scotland	Headmaster	1961-77
	Mackenzie,Elizabeth	Scotland	Primary Head	1963-
	Mackinnon,	Scotland	Primary teacher	1957-66
	Mackintosh,	Scotland	Headmaster	1947-65
*	MacLullich, Flora (later Graham)	Scotland	Primary teacher	1927-31
*	MacPherson, John	Scotland	Headmaster	1959-73,88-91
	Marshman,Robert	U.S.A.	Secondary teacher	1946
*	Miller, Joanna	Scotland	Primary teacher	1932-41
	Mitchell,Donald	New Zealand	English teacher	1952-59
*	Money, Herbert	New Zealand	Secondary teacher	1927-39

221

	More, Isabella	Scotland	Primary teacher	1928-32
*	Nicolson, Murdo	Scotland	R.E. teacher	1942-44
	Rennie, Ruby	Scotland	English teacher	1988-
	Renwick, Alexander	Scotland	Headmaster	1926-42
	Rycroft, W.S	England	Deputy Headmaster	1922-40
*	Simon, Laura	U.S.A.	English teacher	1990-91
*	Stanger, Frank	U.S.A.	Secondary teacher	1924-25
*	Varnes, Hugh	Australia	Primary teacher	1965-67
	Will, Samuel	Scotland	Secondary Head	1947-63
*	Wolters, Joop	Holland	Science teacher	1983-90
*	Yeats, Elsie	Scotland	Primary teacher	1918-20

Notes

(1) Several of those referred to exercised a variety of functions in the school, either simultaneously or consecutively. The position indicated is normally the one that occupied most of their time, or the one carried out most recently.

(2) Those marked with an asterisk spent additional time in Peru, either with the Free Church Mission or in other activities.

Sources Consulted

In order not to weigh down the text with footnotes, various background works on Peruvian history, religion and politics and on educational missions have not been specifically named, nor are they listed here. The following are the sources consulted for the main details of the story of Colegio San Andrés.

Minutes of the Foreign Missions Commitee/Board of the Free Church of Scotland, 1900-87

Reports to the General Assembly of the Free Church of Scotland, 1900-92

The Monthly Record of the Free Church of Scotland, 1900-92

The Instructor, youth magazine of the Free Church of Scotland, 1900-92

From the Frontiers, quarterly missionary magazine of the Free Church of Scotland, 1949-79 (incorporated into *The Monthly Record* from 1980)

Leader, magazine of Colegio San Andrés, 1926-91

Testimonio Político by Pedro Arana, Ediciones Presencia, Lima 1987

Compendio de Historia del Perú by José Antonio del Busto, Librería Studium, Lima 1983

Precursores Evangélicos by Samuel Escobar, Ediciones Presencia, Lima 1984

Has the Free Church Mission in Peru been a success? by David Ford, unpublished manuscript

A study of the Older Protestant Missions and Churches in Peru and Chile by J.B.A. Kessler Jr, Osterbaan & LeCointre N.V, Goes 1967

La Iglesia en el Perú by Jeffrey Klaiber, Universidad Católica, Lima 1988

The Other Spanish Christ by John A. Mackay, Third Spanish edition, Colegio San Andrés, Lima 1991

The Money Memoirs by Herbert Money, Mac Research, Tayport 1989

La Libertad Religiosa en el Perú by Herbert Money, Concilio Nacional Evangelico, Lima 1965

British Missionary Activity in South America by Alonzo Ramírez, Free Church College Essay

Juan A. Mackay: un Escocés con Alma Latina by John H. Sinclair, Ediciones CUPSA, Mexico 1990

Memoirs of Life in Three Worlds by W. Stanley Rycroft, privately printed

Addresses

Colegio San Andrés
Apartado 930
Lima 100
Peru
Fax: (010 51 14) 332771

Foreign Missions Board
Free Church of Scotland
The Mound
Edinburgh EH1 2LS
Scotland
Fax: 031 220 0597

Index of People

Index of People

Index of Places and Topics

228